Journey Through
TRAUMA

A TRAIL GUIDE TO THE
FIVE-PHASE CYCLE OF HEALING
REPEATED TRAUMA

Gretchen L. Schmelzer, PhD

AVERY
an imprint of Penguin Random House
New York

AVERY

an imprint of Penguin Random House LLC
375 Hudson Street
New York, New York 10014

Most Avery books are available at special quantity discounts for bulk purchase
for sales promotions, premiums, fund-raising, and educational needs.
Special books or book excerpts also can be created to fit specific needs.
For details, write SpecialMarkets@penguinrandomhouse.com.

ISBN 9780735216839
ebook ISBN 9780735216846

Printed in the United States of America
1   3   5   7   9   10   8   6   4   2

Book design by Meighan Cavanaugh

for Gail

~ with gratitude for holding the other end of the rope

Author's Note

This book is meant to complement, not substitute for, the advice and recommendations of a treatment provider or support network. It should not be used as an alternative to appropriate medical or psychological care. *Journey Through Trauma* is considered a support and adjunct to ongoing treatment. You should always consult your own treatment providers about your health, diagnosis, and symptoms.

The names and identifying features of patients in this book have been changed to protect their privacy. In some cases, the patients are composites. The focus of clinical examples is on clarification of the issue being discussed.

A Note on Trauma

While this book is written specifically for people who have experienced repeated trauma, trauma that happens more than once, and often over months and years, I make no claim to define for you what trauma is or to diagnose your current state. My goal is to help you heal from the hurt that you experienced, dismantle the protections from trauma that are no longer serving you, and experience the growth and development you may have missed. In my work there have been plenty of people who would not have identified themselves as "trauma survivors" who have found this process of healing helpful: people who have endured physical illness or loss of a family member—or people who have lived under difficult stress for long stretches of time. If you identify as a trauma survivor and find this work helpful, that is fine. And if you don't identify as a trauma survivor and find this work helpful, that is fine too. The aim of this book is not to categorize or label how you were hurt. The goal of this book is to support your journey of healing toward health.

Contents

Invitation

Dear Reader,

There are so many things I want you to know. I want you to know that healing from trauma is possible. I want you to understand how being hurt, how living through trauma, how the difficult act of survival has affected you. I want you to know how all the things you did to survive and protect yourself have saved your life and how they may also now be robbing you of the life you could live. How they could be robbing you of your ability to do the work you want to do in the way you want to do it. How they could be robbing you of your important relationships with the people you love and who love you. And most especially robbing you of a relationship with yourself: of any kindness or compassion toward yourself. I want you to understand this because understanding how trauma has impacted you helps you know why the hard work of healing is worth it.

I want you to know that healing is possible regardless of how long it has taken you to get here. No matter when you come to healing, it is possible. I know that many of you think that it isn't. I know you believe that it is too late. But actually, it's never too late. However old or young you are, healing is possible. Our brains are malleable and they continue to grow throughout our lives. The brain's ability to grow is what allowed for our survival, and that same plasticity allows for our healing. It will take work. It will take help. It will take practice and persistence. It may involve tears, sadness, anger, and frustration. But it is possible.

I want you to understand how trauma works—how it impacts brains and bodies. I want you to understand the genius of our brains and bodies for survival. For getting us through. I want you to understand the mechanisms of trauma because understanding them will help you understand yourself, and will help you know what to expect in the process of healing. I want you to understand how trauma works so that when you catch yourself doing certain things, your attitude isn't mean or judgmental—but instead you think to yourself: *Of course, this is what I do.* And then you have the ability to say: What else can I do? Understanding how it all works gives you a solid platform from which to grow and leap and try new things.

I want you to understand that all that turmoil that can happen inside you makes sense. You aren't crazy. This is just what happens when you survive trauma. That doesn't mean that what you are feeling feels good, or how you are behaving is necessarily the best thing for you or is supporting your relationships. It means that what you are feeling and how you are acting makes sense in the context of surviving trauma.

I want you to understand that all trauma is not the same. It can look like it if you are trying to find information on the Internet. If you look up post-traumatic stress disorder (PTSD) you will find a list of symptoms and a set of recommendations. But it is not all the same. Just as physical trauma is not all the same. If you were run over by a car, there couldn't possibly be a standard protocol for your healing. It would entirely depend on how the car hit you—did it break your arm or leg? Cause a head injury? Internal bleeding? And psychological trauma is no different. Trauma is the very definition of something being utterly shattered. And what gets shattered differs for each person.

And I especially want you to understand what I call *repeated trauma*. This is the trauma that happens more than once. There is a big difference between the trauma that happens one time, like a car accident, and the trauma that gets repeated. If you are in a car accident, a whole host of responses are expected from any onetime trauma. When a traumatic event happens once, humans are generally spurred into action by their biology—a huge release of adrenaline that makes you ready to fight, ready to act, and that sharpens your memory of the event so you can remember it clearly to protect yourself from it in the future.

But what if instead you were in a car accident every day for years? It sounds crazy—a car accident every day for years—but this is exactly what it is like when traumatic acts are continually repeated, as they are for people who live through war, or child abuse, or sexual abuse, or domestic violence, or gang violence. When trauma gets repeated we have a different set of reactions. Our human physiology is built for efficiency. Traumatic events require a lot of energy. Our brains and bodies tell us that we can't afford that much energy and attention. So if trauma gets repeated, instead of gearing up, we go numb. When a smoke alarm goes off in your house once, you pay attention; if it goes off every day, then you cut the wires or pull the battery so you don't have to hear it anymore. Going numb is the trauma equivalent of pulling the battery on the smoke alarm. Going numb serves the important purpose of allowing us to go on with our lives. It is what allows soldiers to keep fighting, and survivors in war zones to keep living. It is what allows abused children to keep going to school. It keeps you from taking in each new act of violence. It protects you from the extremes of emotion that could affect your memory, your health, and your safety. It is the emergency response system that your body automatically employs when trauma gets repeated—hunkering down so you can conserve energy.

So, repeated trauma isn't just about what happened to you. It is also about how you survived it. It is about how you protected yourself from the years of it. In order to understand why it is so hard to heal from trauma, it is important to understand that repeated trauma is really three aspects of trauma that combine to make up what we call repeated trauma. The first aspect of repeated trauma is *what did happen*—the experiences of terror and helplessness that you remember. The second aspect of repeated trauma is *what aided survival*—the protections you created to survive the trauma, the ways that you shut down or geared up or escaped. And the third aspect of repeated trauma is *what didn't happen*—the growth and development you missed because you were surviving being hurt, the help you didn't get, the conversations you didn't learn to have, the skills of everyday life that you missed learning. Healing from trauma requires you to work with and repair all three.

I also want you to know that no one heals alone. You will need to find help in order to heal. This book is a way to understand the impact of trauma that you lived through, how you protected yourself, and what you missed in your growth. It is a way to understand the impact of what happened to you and how you may be still living as if the trauma could still get you, as if it were still happening. But this is not a self-help book. This is a how-to-understand-and-use-help book. It is a what-to-expect-from-trauma-treatment book. This book demands that you get help, but it also provides the information you need to feel empowered and secure in your helping relationship.

Understanding trauma is not enough to heal it. Healing from trauma requires leaning your weight on the support of a therapeutic relationship in order to let the traumatized parts of yourself heal. If you broke your leg and didn't use crutches to take your weight off the broken leg, you couldn't properly heal the break. It is the same with trauma. Some of you may choose a therapist: a psychiatrist, psychologist, social worker, counselor, or member of the clergy. Some of you may choose some form of group therapy. But I am telling you up front, at the beginning: in order to heal, you will need to get help. I know you will try to look for the loophole in this argument—try to find a way that you can do this on your own—but you need to trust me on this. If there were a way to do it on your own I would have found it. No one looked harder for that loophole than I did.

The problem isn't that you or I aren't self-sufficient enough. Or strong-willed or brave or tough or hardworking enough. The problem is that the trauma most people experience happens between people. I'm not talking about the traumas that are natural disasters—tornadoes or hurricanes. I'm not talking about car accidents or medical illnesses, even though all of these things can be traumatic. I am talking about relational disasters—the nightmares of people perpetrating violence and terror on other people: war, child abuse, domestic violence. That is what most psychological traumas are—they are *repeated relational traumas.*

And herein lies one of the most difficult paradoxes of trying to get help when your problem is trauma: you have to get help in order to heal, and because the trauma happened in a relationship, it is very hard to believe in and trust help. It's the moral equivalent of surviving a plane crash and being told that the only way to get help is by getting therapy on a plane every week. I want you to understand that the things you did to survive being hurt repeatedly are the very things that can get in the way of asking for and trusting help. This is a normal and expected response to repeated trauma. This doesn't mean there is something wrong with you. It means that you did a good job surviving and now you have the difficult task of healing.

And even though you can't heal alone, and you will need help, healing from trauma is still your job. The trauma that happened to you wasn't your fault, but healing from your trauma is your responsibility. Only you can do the hard work of healing your trauma—no one else can do it for you. Your therapist or group can help guide you and be there with you along the way. And your family and loved ones can support you and cheer you from the sidelines. But no one can fix it for you. This is your journey. Your healing belongs to you. You are creating your life, and your healing is your accomplishment—the gift you give to yourself and the people in your life.

Healing takes a lot of hard work, and you will likely feel worse before you feel better. Healing from trauma doesn't mean that in the end you will feel great all the time in the same way that a "happy childhood" doesn't mean that kids are happy all the time. Happy childhoods are filled with lots of struggles and difficult moments. Complete and utter meltdowns occur for all the good reasons that children need to have them. Happy childhoods aren't happy because the kids are always smiling. They are happy because the kids are free to grow up—to focus on their own growth and development—in a safe enough environment that supports that growth. Growth can be hard. And a healthy adulthood, or an adulthood where you have healed your trauma, doesn't mean you are never sad or angry or frustrated. It doesn't mean never getting triggered by your trauma again. Healthy means whole; it means you get to have a self, with all of its complexities. It means you get to have a whole life made up of all your experiences: the traumatic ones and the nontraumatic ones. It means that you have the right to have all the ups and downs of normal growth and development for your developmental age. It means that you are living in the present with a sense of a future—not just surviving or living in an ever-present past, protecting yourself from what has already happened.

I am writing about trauma because I believe it is possible to heal. I believe it because I have seen it. I have worked as a therapist for over two decades in large clinics, clinics in housing projects, in residential treatment facilities, on psychiatric units and medical hospital units, and in private practice. I have worked with survivors of World War II, the Khmer Rouge, Vietnam, and 9/11. I have worked with survivors of childhood physical and sexual abuse, domestic violence, and community violence. I have seen people struggle through their trauma and come out on the other side.

But my motivation for writing this particular book—about *what the healing process is actually like*—is also that I have watched many people who experience trauma give up. I have watched them give up on treatment, give up on themselves, on relationships or jobs that were important to them. I have watched them despair and lose hope. I have watched them start the healing process and not know ahead of time that the road to healing is difficult; it is steep. They hit hard spots. They think they are going to "feel better" and instead find that working with trauma is challenging, and that it brings up lots of painful feelings and memories. I have watched as their old protections or defenses begin to crack, or they know they need to give them up and they hit the inevitable long and difficult stretches of healing, the relapses, the setbacks, the slowness of the healing process—and they think, *This is impossible. I can't do it anymore.* And they quit.

And I understand why they quit. I have wanted to quit many times myself. I am not only a psychologist who has helped others with their trauma, I have lived through it myself. I grew up with the stories of trauma that my parents lived in their childhood, and the terror and fear that they created in our household—to watch my mother taken away in an ambulance, unconscious after being hit, or to stand for hours while she screamed in a rage, not knowing who she was talking to. I know what it is to watch my brother get slammed against the wall because he didn't put his napkin in his lap, or to watch as furniture got broken. I know what it feels like to feel terror, and I know what it feels like to live with the consequences of that terror. I understand and believe in healing from trauma because I have guided others, but I believe it in my bones because I have traveled these difficult miles of healing myself.

Healing from trauma is not an event or a linear process. It is a series of cycles that spiral through recognizable phases. These are stages you will cycle through again and again as you move toward health and wholeness. This new method of healing allows you to know where you are, what the work is, what the challenges are, and what you can do to move through the stages gaining the healing and learning you need. So I have written this book as a trail guide, as a way to know and recognize the terrain of the work that you are doing, of the healing you are seeking. This is not a book about other people's stories, and it is not even entirely my story, though I will speak to some of my experiences and the experiences of others to deepen your understanding where I can. This book is intended to be as accurate a description of the trail and the territory as I can give you so that you can make your own journey, create your own maps, tell your story, and heal from trauma.

PART 1

The Trail Guide

Exploration is still the epic journey—to dream, to prepare yourself, to assemble your team of argonauts, to go forth to be tested mentally and physically by the gods. To pass the test, to be given the truth, and then come back and share the new wisdom.

ROBERT BALLARD, National Geographic[1]

Understanding Trauma

I spent my senior year of high school as an exchange student in Germany. I lived for a month in the far north with a very kind woman named Karla. Whenever she heard the sound of an airplane, she jumped to the window to look up to the sky to find it. Even though World War II had ended long ago, she told me that she wanted to make sure that the plane was not going to drop bombs. Although the bombing had stopped thirty-six years earlier, her startle response continued relentlessly. This response is like having your own personal fire department in your brain. At the slightest trigger, the alarm goes off so that the body literally prepares itself for the emergency it knows best, even if that emergency is decades old.

When we use the word *trauma*, we are talking about an experience or event that overwhelms your capacity to depend on or protect yourself. The hallmarks of trauma are feelings of terror, horror, and helplessness. Your body and mind have created a specific set of responses to the trauma to help you survive. When a traumatic event happens once, as in a car accident or a gunshot wound, the normal system of psychological defenses is temporarily overwhelmed. Like water breaking through a levee during a great flood, your body is flooded with adrenaline in such large amounts that the system actually builds new receptors to take in the overflow.

When the adrenaline levels recede, the extra receptors create an ultrasensitive environment in which the smallest amount of adrenaline is immediately picked up by the brain and nervous system—producing what is known as the *startle response*. Jeff, a veteran from the Iraq war, still jumps out of the way whenever he hears a car backfire. It is as if the brain receptors have been waiting and scanning for that sound, and they are on emergency alert to respond. And this startle response, once activated, can last a long time.

First, the body and brain identify a danger and become hypersensitive to it, causing the trauma to become etched in the mind. The flooding of adrenaline during a trauma can create an intense memory of the event, which can lead to *flashbacks*—a vivid recall of the trauma that can interfere with daily life and perpetuate the traumatic experience as if it were recurring daily. My colleague's niece was in a car accident. She says, "Every time I see an SUV, I see the car I was in rolling over in my mind. I see it as if it is happening to me again."

With short-term trauma, the body is overwhelmed, and the effect is an oversensitized system. It is as if your body becomes allergic to anything that might remind itself of the trauma—any loud noise, any fast motion. The psychological and physical aftereffects of a onetime trauma, if they persist for at least a month, are diagnostically called post-traumatic stress disorder (PTSD), a term you probably know. PTSD is defined by a set of symptoms:[1] startle responses, flashbacks, nightmares, hypervigilance, difficulty eating, difficulty sleeping, difficulty concentrating, or persistent avoidance of anything that reminds the person of the traumatic event. PTSD sometimes describes the after-effects of short-term trauma, but it never seems to capture the full picture of repeated trauma.

A single terrifying event can be traumatic. How then can we understand the experience of multiple terrifying events? A car accident that lasts only forty-five seconds can trigger all the symptoms of PTSD and require significant psychological treatment. But what happens when trauma gets repeated relentlessly? What happens when it is not one frightening event, but a frightening event every night for years? When there is a onetime trauma, the system gets "caught off-guard" and overwhelmed. But imagine how exhausting it would be to get "caught off-guard" and overwhelmed every night for most of a childhood, or ten years of war? For better or worse, the human body and brain are designed for efficiency and survival. And survival means finding the least demanding and most protective way to cope.

When trauma is repeated, as it is in child abuse, domestic violence, community violence, or war, we don't wait to get caught off-guard. Instead, we unconsciously, yet wisely, build a system of defenses against being overwhelmed and getting caught off-guard again, because building defenses to withstand repeated trauma conserves our energy for survival. Instead of getting flooded with emotion—with terror, fear, and all the responses to it—we build walls, moats, and methods of escape. We go numb, we feel nothing, and we do whatever we have to in order to maintain our distance from ourselves and others.

There are really three separate aspects to the experience of repeated trauma. The first is the traumatic experiences that actually happened— the exposure to repeated experiences of terror and helplessness. These are the events that one may have a clear memory of, the actions or words of abuse or neglect or violence. The second aspect of repeated trauma is what we do to survive the trauma—the system of psychological defense or protection that we construct to survive the trauma. People change themselves to survive. Responses to trauma become protective responses that get incorporated into your personality—into the very way you function.

The language of psychology distinguishes between a *state* (a short-term experience, like anxiety about a big exam) and a *trait* (something that is an enduring part of your personality, like being generally anxious, even when there is no event to trigger the anxiety). With short-term trauma, the symptoms that one uses to cope can be temporary. These short-term solutions could actually be described as a *defensive state*. For example, during a hurricane, you might put plywood sheets over your windows to protect against the wind and water. The plywood is a temporary fix that you can put up and take down at will. In situations of repeated trauma, the coping strategy is better described as a *defensive trait*; the protective response becomes a core aspect of your personality. Instead of choosing how to respond, you have one fixed, protective response. This is the body and brain's genius of efficiency at work. Your body and brain can't manage the repeated high-energy responses to each particular trauma; the need to respond just becomes too tiring. Rather, they find a way to use their energy and resources more efficiently.

When repeated trauma occurs, rather than rely on something temporary like plywood to protect yourself from the hurricane, you might instead cover the front of your house with brick and cement up to the roofline. True, you'd effectively protect yourself from the hurricane, and water wouldn't get in. But neither would air or sunlight. Your wall has no flexibility, nor can it be easily removed. In protecting yourself from repeated trauma your defenses protect you from the things that are most frightening, but they also cut you off from the things you need most.

The third important aspect of trauma can be the most difficult to see initially, yet it can have the greatest impact. It is *what didn't happen.* Repeated trauma is about both *what did happen* and *what didn't happen.* What didn't happen is the normal developmental growth that would have taken place during the years that the trauma was occurring. The effect of repeated trauma can be confusing because it's not just the trauma per se—the time your father grabbed you and held you up by your throat against the wall, or the time you watched your mother get hit—but the repeated patterns of the relationship that maintained that violence. Similarly, it's not just time spent at war, but the time not spent doing other things related to growth and relationships; it's not just the remembered violence, but also the necessary and healthy developmental aspects of the relationship that weren't provided while the violence was occurring. While you were being terrorized, you were not negotiating aspects of your healthy development: you weren't getting help on your homework, talking about your day, relaxing with friends. Because all of the arguments you may have witnessed as a child were violent, you never got to learn that there is such a thing as a healthy argument—that disagreements can be a normal and healthy part of relationships.

Let's look at an example of what these three aspects of repeated trauma look like in real life. Lacey is a woman who is now in her late twenties. When she was ten, she was referred to a clinic because she was getting into trouble at school. When she was eleven, she was hit by a car and survived with a head injury. Six months later she was removed from her family by social services and placed in foster care. Over the next five years she was moved at least eight different times to different foster homes and then to group homes. The attachment to each foster parent and then loss of each relationship was wrenching. Lacey, in her own words, began to wall herself off, saying, "I didn't want to get hurt so I stopped letting people matter. Now years later I don't know how to let those walls down. I don't know how to let love in, even when I know it's there." Lacey's example perfectly describes these three aspects of repeated trauma. Being hit by the car, removed from her foster families, and experiencing repeated losses were some of the trauma that *did happen*. Her emotional numbing and her disengagement from relationships were *her protection* from her trauma that has become an everyday part of her personality. And learning to experience and manage her feelings and trust in relationships is *what didn't happen*: the developmental learning about relationships that she is working on now to heal.

Lacey created high walls to protect herself from the vulnerability of abandonment and rejection. She learned not to get attached; she learned not to let anything in. This did protect her from the feelings of sadness and rage that would have come along with having to leave people she cared about repeatedly. But the temporary fix has become permanent, habitual. Even when she wants to feel her feelings, or take in or understand the love around her, she can't seem to. Her protection from past loss is keeping her from the benefit of her current relationships.

When I say things like *learn* as in "she learned not to let anything in," I mean the way we "learn" to walk with a limp when we have an injury, rather than conscious, intentional learning. We find a way to move that hurts the least and we begin to move in that way. If we do this a long time, it simply becomes the way we walk. So the second aspect of trauma is the long-term protective response to trauma, in the way we form ourselves around the trauma for self-protection.

Let's look at a country after it has experienced a war. It is not only the war atrocities and physical destruction of a country that affect how the country recovers and functions. It is also, and maybe more importantly, the aspects of development of the country and growth of its people and economy that can't happen during a war. Examples include when the country can't build roads, schools, and businesses or maintain the country's water supply; when there is no safe governance or rule of law; when infrastructure is not built or maintained; and when no one in the country is training for new jobs other than in the defense business. When the war is over, these missing parts must be attended to first so that the country is strong enough to take on the devastation. A country can't support its people if there are no roads, if there is no safe water or food. The year 2010 marked the first war crimes tribunal of the Khmer Rouge, a regime that lost power in 1979 but whose chaos continued for another two decades. It took thirty-one years to develop enough of the infrastructure, to build *what didn't happen* during the war and the years that followed, in order to have the strength and resilience to confront *what did happen*.

Another example of this "postwar reconstruction" phenomenon can be seen in a family I saw during my internship year. Lena, the mom, had finally gotten the strength to leave her husband and their violent marriage. She had a few difficult years, going through various state agencies for help, living in a homeless shelter, and eventually getting housing for herself and her two children. During this time she completed a certificate as a medical technician and found employment. Two years later, when she finally had a safe home and a good job to support her children, she was shocked to watch her oldest child, Nelson, deteriorate at school and at home. He failed classes at school, argued and cried at home, and seemed to regress in age. Lena couldn't understand why Nelson, who had been such a rock during the difficult years in her marriage and during the rough transition, was suddenly having a hard time when everything was finally good.

What was difficult for Lena to see at first was that Nelson had indeed been a rock during those years, but that being a rock came at a cost of his normal growth. Nelson, recognizing that the "war" was now over, was going about the business of doing some of the work of growing he had put off when his mother was too fragile or busy to support him. Nelson could now let his walls down and let go, and let his mother help him learn how to express and manage his emotions and talk about difficult things. By acting out, Nelson was attending to the emotional growth he missed when he was four, or six, or eight.

These three aspects of trauma are why treatment of trauma is not a one-size-fits-all event. Short-term trauma and repeated trauma share some important characteristics, such as the physiological responses to stress. But they differ in significant ways that affect how to understand and approach the healing.

The Hero Journey

There is what I would call the hero journey, the night sea journey, the hero quest, where the individual is going to bring forth in his life something that was never beheld before.

JOSEPH CAMPBELL, *The Hero with a Thousand Faces*[1]

Once you decide to get help for your trauma, you open the door and the journey begins. There is so much at this point that feels unknown—so you sort through the things you do know and the things you don't know. You don't know where you are headed, but you *do* know that you don't want to keep feeling the way you are feeling. You know you need a break from the constant anxiety, anger, or edginess. Or your family or the people at work have let you know that they are aware that you are having a problem. You want something new, but you may also be anxious or frightened about making a change.

The apprehension and energy you feel about beginning this journey is not misplaced. This journey requires a lot of work and attention, and you will be leaving the safety of what has felt familiar, even if it doesn't always feel good. In every country and in every culture, the journey of the hero begins with this step into the unknown. For reasons that the hero can't know, yet cannot ignore, the journey begins. Whether the hero falls into it, gets called into it, or gets pushed into it, this adventure will change his or her life.

The hero journey is an archetype of a quest for a new self,[2] a new life, a chance at something bigger. I am not the first person nor will I be the last to describe the process of healing from trauma as a *hero journey*. Probably no other metaphor does a better job at creating understanding of and respect for a process that can take a long time and a lot of hard work. This process of healing involves leaving what feels familiar, even if unpleasant, and venturing into an experience that feels foreign, awkward, and frightening.

"Okay," I can hear you saying, "*journey* I understand." But I can see you shaking your head at the word *hero*. Most people who have experienced trauma do not feel *heroic*. Words that describe heroes— *courageous, brave, fearless*—these are not words that describe the felt experience of being traumatized or working with a trauma history. I have to admit that I sneered at the metaphor myself. Every time my therapist used the term *courageous* I would roll my eyes and look away. *Yeah, I would think, it's really courageous to stand there terrified and frozen and do nothing while someone is getting hit.*

Trauma involves repeated experiences of helplessness and terror. These experiences usually result in *shame*, not courage; in *fear*, not bravery; in *hopelessness*, not resilience. But I misunderstood my therapist when she was using the term *courageous*. I heard the word *courage* and thought she implied that I had acted courageously as a child. But I had done what all people who come through trauma hope to do: I survived it. Some people might say that survival takes courage, but mostly it takes perseverance—the perseverance of feeling hopeless and going forward anyway, of doing whatever needs to be done. It takes the ability to put your head down and keep going. It takes some kind of hope.

Surviving trauma isn't the hero journey. That is your history. The hero journey is deciding to go back and witness what you lived through, retrieve the parts of yourself that you left behind, the parts of yourself that splintered off, and to bring that knowledge and experience into the present, where all of you can be woven back into an integrated whole. What I didn't understand was that the journey of healing would be heroic—that it would require courage, bravery, and connecting with my strength and resilience.

The hero journey is a cycle, which was another reason I really liked it as a metaphor for my own journey of healing. It helped me appreciate that the work was done in a circle—not on some linear path. The hero doesn't typically just walk out the door, meet his or her obstacles, and solve his or her problems. It's not like finding out there is a problem with your car, taking it to a mechanic, having a part replaced, and driving away. In the famous hero story of Beowulf, he kills the monster Grendel, and he believes he is done with the journey he set out on. But the next morning Grendel's mother appears—an even bigger and more dangerous monster—and Beowulf must gather new strength, gather new tools for the fight, and begin his struggle again.[3] The importance of cycles is crucial because growth and healing are not linear. Much of the patience and tolerance needed for healing come from accepting the cyclical nature of the journey.

Let's look at the example of Jim, an Iraq War veteran who lived with his wife and son. When he came back from the war, even though he knew he should be happy to see them, he felt incredibly distant. He worked as an auto mechanic and over time he spent more and more time after work drinking with the guys, or coming home and drinking with his wife. When his wife began to get concerned about her own drinking, she urged him to get help too. He didn't listen to her at first, but he did notice after a while that his wife seemed happier and he wanted to feel the way she did—so he began to attend Alcoholics Anonymous (AA) meetings to get sober. By starting the journey of sobriety, Jim had started on his journey. He stepped into a new possibility, he had guides (his wife, his twelve-step group, and eventually a counselor) and he was well on his way to his goal of sobriety. Jim had conquered the first monster. What he didn't know was that there would be another trial to test him. Once sober, he began to experience the feelings he had from the war and from his history of childhood trauma. Now he had another cycle of healing to do.

The Trail Guide

It is my contention—my superstition if you like—that who is faithful to his map, and consults it, and draws from it his inspiration, daily and hourly, gains positive support, and not merely negative immunity from accident.

ROBERT LOUIS STEVENSON, *Essays in the Art of Writing*[1]

The hero journey is a powerful metaphor for heading into a path that has both difficulties and possibilities. But most hero journeys are fairy tales or fiction—which makes them perfect metaphors but imperfect guidebooks. The hero in a hero journey must rely on internal strengths—courage, persistence, loyalty, honor, passion—which is what makes it such a great metaphor, but his external world is the stuff of legends: magic, spells, enchantment, and prophecies.

In fairy tales and myths, your guide just appears: Merlin for King Arthur, or Obi-Wan Kenobi for Luke Skywalker. The guides show up, they have the perfect knowledge for your journey, and they offer you magical powers. But let's face it, King Arthur did not have to look on his health plan's list of "approved providers" to help him find Merlin.

In healing from trauma, you will need to seek out a guide: a therapist or some supportive person or structure who will guide you and support you in your healing.

My healing journey was not fiction. Your healing journey is not fiction. It is very real. We certainly will use the universal inner strengths exemplified by the heroes in the tales, but as I went through my own healing process I began to look for stories and guides that were more grounding. I found myself reading adventure books: stories of Arctic exploration, Everest climbs, and harrowing nature expeditions. I began to believe that if a description of healing from trauma could be accurately written, it would look a lot more like Shackleton's voyage to the South Pole than the average self-help book.

You need to know that in many ways, healing from trauma is actually more difficult than many of those dangerous expeditions. A mountain climber can actually see the mountains he or she is climbing or the distance he or she is covering. But for you on your healing journey, those miles can feel just as steep and arduous, but they are less visible because they are internal. Mountain climbers and explorers also get to do one thing at a time. You won't. You will have to take on your healing journey—a very difficult climb—while simultaneously living your life. Shackleton didn't explore the Antarctic *and* go into the office every day. He didn't survive the trip *and* take his kids to school. He got to do one thing at a time. You won't.

The other thing I came to appreciate and rely on in the old adventure writing is that their journeys were true descriptions of *exploration*. For all of the early explorers, at some point in their journey they were completely off their map. Their maps simply no longer worked—the maps were too vague, the maps were wrong, or no one had ever actually been there to create an accurate map. On Shackleton's voyage[2] to the

Antarctic he suddenly found himself in uncharted territory—no one had been there to make an accurate map—and he and his explorers had to find their way and create the new map. When Maurice Herzog's team[3] was doing its initial ascent of Annapurna, the climbers hiked into what they thought to be the mountain's base camp. But once they got there they looked at all of the surrounding peaks and realized that they weren't sure *which* of the mountains Annapurna was. They had to spend weeks doing reconnaissance hikes to figure out which mountain they were there to climb—*they had to map the journey* before they could even begin the journey they had planned. They were *by definition* explorers because they were in territory that was not yet named, had not yet been crossed, had to be found.

The territory of your healing and your trauma is equally untamed and unexplored. Like the explorers who were going up Annapurna, you have an idea of the mountain you need to climb. Your paths and obstacles may be similar to those of other people who have healed from trauma, but your territory is your own. No one has been there—in some ways, even you. You must respect the wildness, the danger, the beauty of the terrain. You must respect the need for care and the need not to travel alone.

The other similarity between these old explorers and your work of exploration is the need for motivation that is all *yours*. I don't think you would embark on a two-year Antarctic journey in a wooden boat just because someone else thought it was a good idea. And you aren't going to take on your trauma history to make someone else happy. This is not a matter of taking a pill or taking a six-week class. This is an expedition to uncharted territory. You will be walking these long miles mostly alone, though the people you love may be cheering from afar. Other people may figure into your motivation, certainly at the start, but in order to complete the journey it is important to be able to tap into and rely on your own motivation, not theirs.

This expedition is nothing less than your search-and-rescue mission to reclaim those parts of yourself you left behind. You are going back to retrieve your self. For you, unlike the traditional hero, it is *not* a journey to the unknown. This mission requires crossing dangerous terrain—for you must both cross the terrain of the original trauma and explore the new territory of your self. This book is a trail guide for that expedition.

The inspiration for this book is *The Appalachian Mountain Club Guide to the White Mountains in New Hampshire*. It's a comprehensive guide to all of the trails in the White Mountains. It comes with maps of each of the mountain ranges, and every trail is described with some suggestions from experienced hikers who know the trails. The summer after my freshman year in college, my friend Jane and I loaded up our backpacks and headed to the White Mountains. We planned a five-day trip. We picked a stretch of trail that seemed interesting, had good views, and had good places to spend the night.

At that time I was nineteen years old and had competed in Nationals for rowing, so I was in really good shape. So good that on the second morning I was unprepared for and a bit disappointed at how difficult the climb was. It was very steep from the start. We climbed relentlessly up, and then relentlessly down, losing all the ground we worked so hard to get. This loss of ground was more painful for my morale than the ascent had been for my legs. When we hit the bottom, we started straight up again.

After the second round of up and down, I demanded a water break. Really, I wanted to look at my map and prove that we were on the wrong trail. *How long will this last?* I wondered. *Will I make it? Who thought this was a good idea? There has got to be another way—please let us be on the wrong trail.*

I found my water and my bag of gorp and sat down on a rock to look at my map. I found the hut we left that morning, confirmed the name of the trail, and looked it up in the White Mountains guide, which described this seven-mile trail perfectly as "a seemingly endless series of ups and downs."

Yes, there it was in black and white (and plain English). Seeing someone so accurately describe this trail in print made me feel better. Even the guidebook writer (whom I imagined to be the uber-hiker) described the trail as "seemingly endless." I didn't want to keep going on that trail, but after I had an idea of what to expect, the trail felt tolerable.

In the White Mountains I needed the trail guide to help me know where I was and that my struggle with the hike was to be expected. The trail guide helped me tolerate my frustration and gave me some idea of what to look forward to. It made an unknown journey more predictable. The purpose of the maps and the trail guide for the White Mountains is not only enjoyment but safety. You can use them to figure out where you are and what you need to do—how you might prepare or gauge yourself for the next leg of your trip.

When I began my own process of healing from trauma twenty years ago, I searched for an equivalent to my White Mountains guide. I wanted to know: Am I on the right trail? Is it supposed to feel this steep, or take this long? How come it often feels like I am losing ground? I wanted a book that would describe the trail in a meaningful and hopeful way. Something that would explain why some parts of the journey were so hard, and what I might look forward to. Something that would explain the need for so much repetition and so much frustration. I wanted a book that might suggest what to consider for safety, what I needed to have in my pack, and what other maps or guides to consult. I wanted a trail guide to tell me not only about the terrain, but also about why it was so hard to trust and lean on my therapist—the person who was guiding me. I wanted some help with getting help, and I wanted to understand the help I was getting.

As a psychologist whose job it is now to guide others on this trail, I often wish I had had such a book to give my clients or their parents, spouses, or friends. Though I never did find the equivalent guide for myself, I was fortunate that as a psychologist-in-training I had access to many books, articles, and texts that most people do not. I found encouraging and helpful words in many books that I wouldn't generally give my clients: old psychoanalytic texts, neuroscience research, Buddhist psychology, attachment research, child development, and quantum physics. And in an instructive but somewhat metaphorical way I also found help in books on writing, art, poetry, fairy tales, house construction, gardening, and high-adventure expeditions. While some of the information was enormously helpful, the useful parts of these books were often buried in large, complicated, and seemingly unrelated contexts. It would be the equivalent of having to find the trail descriptions of my hike of the White Mountains spread throughout massive old volumes of *Mountain Ranges of North America* or *Great Trails of the Appalachians*. Imagine having to carry old, heavy books on your hike to find the trail you were on. I wanted something more tangible, more helpful to hand to those who needed it.

Most books on trauma fall into one of two categories. One is the study or *narrative* of trauma: what trauma is, how it affects you, how to understand it. These books help you understand the larger context of trauma: the symptoms of trauma and its impact. Most books in this genre tend to end with a short chapter or two on getting help, which mostly amounts to this: Find a good therapist.

The other category is the self-help book. These books have a series of questions and exercises designed to help you acknowledge your trauma, remember and tell the trauma story, and then reconnect with your life. These books tend to make the process look like a simple linear here-to-there experience. These books also usually end with some sort of statement such as this: If it is too hard to do alone—find a good therapist.

As I mentioned earlier, this book is not a self-help book in the do-it-yourself sense of the word. This trail guide starts where most other books end. This book assumes, encourages, *demands* at the outset that you have some type of healing relationship: a therapist, a counselor, a group, a guide. Healing from trauma is not a solitary activity. It requires support and guidance. I would no more recommend that you use this book to heal from trauma yourself than I would recommend using a medical guide to perform do-it-yourself open-heart surgery.

If you are an individual, your guide may take the form of a therapist, or it may take the form of a therapeutic group, or a twelve-step group, or a member of the clergy. If it is a group, an organization, or a community that has experienced trauma, the helper might be a consultant, an intervention team, a nongovernmental organization (NGO), or a government agency.

Every successful hero journey in legend has something in common: a guide who provides the information and tools to conquer the challenges. And this will be the difference between your original trauma and your expedition back to it: you will have a professional guide who can provide the support, direction, and instruction you will need as you integrate what was lost. Healing relationships provide the support, the guidance, and the secure and supportive environment to mend what has been broken apart, as well as providing the environment that is necessary for the needed and missing growth to take place.

While it is simple for me to say, "Get help," this is not easy to do for anyone who has lived through trauma. Healing relationships are a required element for healing from trauma. But if you have been hurt by someone, the idea of trusting someone, even someone who is there solely to *help* you, can seem impossible. I know that you want to believe that there is an easier way to do this, *alone.* And chances are, you have already tried to do this alone. I am guessing you have tried almost anything and everything to avoid the journey you are now on.

In the past you may not have been supported in getting help. You may have heard, "Can't you just get over it?" or "It's all in your head." There is a strong ethic in America and in Western culture in general that psychological problems need to be handled alone. You should be able to fix the problem, fix yourself on your own, or just plain "suck it up." It may be that with the more modern Prozac-type medication, this pressure has become even more pronounced. If you can't fix the problem yourself, then take medication and "make it go away." At any rate, don't talk about it or rely on someone else.

But think about it. If your body is sick or injured, you don't have the illusion you can do the job yourself. You understand the need for doctors, splints, casts, and crutches for broken bones. You understand the need for surgery, recovery, and medicine. If you broke your leg, refused medical care and a cast, and opted, instead, to hop around and walk on the broken leg anyway—you would be considered crazy. Your ability to make sound judgments would be questioned. You would, ironically, get hauled in for psychological help. Yet when you are psychologically run over by a car—breaking multiple psychic bones and walking on them anyway—you will get a pat on the back and be told that you have "a strong character." In most cases, this is exactly what happens. In situations of trauma, you were hurt badly and not taken care of. You had to let everything knit together as it was and work around it, trying to hide your limp. Now it's time to go back and do the work of healing.

The Whole Trauma Story

So this book is a guide for your own hero journey, for your own quest to retrieve parts of yourself, parts of your history so that you can be whole, so that you can have access to your whole story. When you experience trauma as a child, the trauma interferes with your ability to create a self, or to see yourself as the narrator of your story. When you experience trauma as a teenager or adult, the trauma shatters your identity and robs you of the story you knew about yourself and your world. The goal of healing from trauma is to put all the shattered pieces together and make yourself whole again—really, to create a *new whole self*. This is a crucial point. You are not creating a whole from new whole cloth; you are creating a whole from shattered pieces, from what you lived through, from the experience of healing, and from the new experiences you get through the process. You are not creating an oil painting, you are creating a mosaic. And the process of integration—the process of creating your *whole* life story, the process of becoming whole—is the process of creating your mosaic. It will be a *new* whole.

The visual world offers more opportunity to understand this dynamic of creating a whole out of what is broken—mosaics and patchwork quilts offer a way for us to see beauty and wholeness where there were once pieces. We get to see the pieces transformed from fragments into parts of a beautiful whole. But language is different. We are verbal beings, and our life stories are both visual and verbal. It's hard to see our words reborn and our stories created anew as a new whole made up of old fragments. John Lederach, an expert who works in the field of peace building in postconflict communities, talks about *restorying*,[1] and this may be the most accurate description of what we are trying to do with our narratives and life stories in the healing from trauma—we are taking all the pieces of our story and imagining them into something bigger, the way a mosaic takes fragments and imagines them into a coherent, beautiful whole. Terry Tempest Williams said that "a mosaic is a conversation between what is broken."[2] This is the process of restorying. It is a conversation between yourself and each of the fragments that will make up the *whole* mosaic of a story that you create for yourself through this healing journey. These conversations with and between the fragments of your self and your story will happen in different ways across the journey of healing from trauma—within each phase of the cycle.

The act of *restorying* is an act of integration—that is to say, the goal is to bring together all the pieces of yourself, your life, and your story so that you can become whole. It means having a *whole* story. And it means having a self—a self who is whole, who is integrated, and who is the main narrator of that story. It means having a story of your life that includes your past and your present. It means having a story of your life that includes the trauma that you lived through and how you healed from that trauma. And it means having a story of your life that includes the meaning you make from your various life experiences, including the trauma, and how all those experiences connect to and create your future. Integration allows you to be open and flexible to learn and grow—to meet your life and future with possibility and not with the rigid assumptions and protections of trauma.

Both the world of psychology and Webster's dictionary use the words *story* and *narrative* interchangeably, and in this book, I will too. Neither of these words will fit the entirety of your life or capture the complexity of your life with trauma, but they are the best words I can find for describing the various threads and experiences that run through our lives. There is a difference between a healthy life story or narrative and a trauma story. Healthy life stories have a past, a present, and a future. Healthy life stories have coherence. The simplest definition of coherence is "a story, placed in time with a beginning, middle and an end."[3] A coherent narrative has *thematic coherence*, which means that the story hangs together; it makes sense. And a coherent narrative also has *causal coherence*, which is an understanding of how one event led to another. In fact, psychology researchers can identify adults who have had healthy, secure attachments or who have healed their trauma by the coherence of their narratives of their lives.[4] And this coherence isn't just something that's nice to have—it is one of the biggest predictors of whether parents can pass on secure attachments to their children. Even in a life without major trauma, a life we would call "normal" (whatever that is) creating a life story—having a coherent narrative—is an accomplishment. It requires thought and some effort to link the various aspects of self and experience into an integrated whole.

But trauma shatters your story. Trauma shatters the self you knew. Trauma is processed in your brain differently,[5] and this processing interferes with your memory and language.[6] Trauma doesn't just change your story. It changes who you are, the way you see the world and rela-tionships, and the way you can talk about your stories. And this is why the primary goal of becoming whole is so challenging. All the pieces that have been broken have to be brought together, and the means to do so—relationship, emotion, language, and story, which all have been affected by trauma—must be mended along the way in order for the integration to happen. If a country was bombed during a war and had its roads and bridges destroyed, it would need to repair them in order to function again. But moving the materials around the country to repair the roads and bridges without the ability to use the roads and bridges would be the great challenge.

Each aspect of the three forms of trauma has or needs its own story, and in each section I will talk about how the work of the phase of heal-ing is connected to telling your story. There's the story about what did happen—the trauma that we lived through. There are the protections we created to survive the trauma—and these protections have their own story. And then there's what didn't happen—the stories about our experience and the future that couldn't happen while we were still hurt—and these are the moments where you get to experience the possibility of a new story. Over the course of your journey of healing through trauma, you will have the opportunity and the challenge to tell what Richard Mollica, a trauma expert who has worked a lot with refu-gees, calls the *full trauma story:*[7] not just the story of the event of the trauma but also your life before the trauma, during the trauma, and after the trauma. The story of trauma needs to not just come in contact with your other stories, it needs to be *connected* to them—woven into the fabric of your whole story.

Understanding how stories work can help you understand why, with a history of trauma, telling your story is both part of the process of healing and an outcome. Here's the thing: It is the act of bringing the pieces together and the work of repair that this requires that creates the possibility of a whole self and a whole story. Dan McAdams, a psychologist who studies life stories, discussed important principles that are common across disciplines in understanding and working the narrative aspects of our lives.[8] By looking at these principles, you can come to understand how trauma impacts your story and how you will need to approach healing.

The first principle is that life is storied.[9] Stories are the best way we humans know to explain to ourselves and others—what happened, why it happened, and what we want to happen next. The self is the sum total of both our stories and the storyteller. We rely on a continuity of self to know who we are, and we use this self to create continuity in our stories. But trauma breaks this continuity—either in our sense of self, or in the experience of our stories. Trauma survivors often state that they feel like they are not the same person they were before the trauma happened. As a veteran who did three tours in Vietnam states, "Why I became like that? It was all evil. . . . Where before I wasn't. I look back. I look back today, and I am horrified at what I turned into. What I was. What I did. I just look at it like it was somebody else. I really do. Somebody had control of me."[10] The veteran has lost the continuity of himself and therefore the continuity of his story. In order to hold the story, he removed himself from it.

The second principle is that stories integrate lives.[11] Our life stories are there to help us integrate pieces of our lives that feel disparate or disconnected. We weave together the experiences we have over many years into a meaningful whole. But with trauma the gap between disparate parts can feel too wide, and it can feel impossible to bridge the different realms of existence. Because of the way traumatic memory

36

works, either we may have intrusive memories of the trauma that interfere with our day-to-day life, or we may have whole stretches of our experience and memory that are dissociated—pieces we are so detached from that they can't be integrated into our experience or our story.

The third principle is that stories are told in social relationships.[12] Stories always imagine a listener—and healing from trauma, healing your story, *restorying* your story requires a listener, a witness, someone to hold you and your story as you bring forward the fragments. If *a mosaic is a conversation between what is broken*, then the healing from trauma happens because the first conversations are between the broken fragments and a caring listener. This process of listening gives each of the fragments the possibility of being integrated into the whole story. Sharing the trauma is what makes it narratable.[13] We need people to listen[14] to our stories in order to heal—remember, no one heals alone. But as I have stated earlier, because trauma shatters our belief in relationships, trusting relationships enough to tell our stories will take time, practice, and effort.

The fourth principle is that stories are located in time and change over time.[15] And time is one of the greatest casualties of trauma. Causal coherence—the notion that this happened and then this happened—and this happened because of this—depends on time. Trauma destroys time—and stories depend on time. They depend on time to locate when they happened. Our stories depend on time so that we can understand cause and effect. And stories and our sense of our selves depend on time because time is what gives us the experience of continuity—of having a past, present, and future. Trauma shatters time. Trauma often razes the past—it gets obliterated through memory, or silence, or the need to distance yourself from what you lived through. But it's not just the past that you lose; you also lose the future. People who experience trauma stop believing in a future; they stop believing that they will live long lives. Any thoughts of the future are imagined to be as dangerous as the trauma that was experienced, so any planning for a future is not about what you want or hope for, but rather to protect yourself from what already happened. In the experience of surviving trauma, Jonathan Shay observes in his study of combat trauma in Vietnam veterans that "the destruction of time is an inner survival skill."[16]

Cause and effect, one of the main elements of coherence, is also damaged because of time. First, because one of the biggest impacts of trauma is helplessness, trauma survivors construct false stories about trauma that aren't necessarily true. We construct coherent but false stories because they make us feel better. People who experience trauma often misremember the order of events so that there was some sort of omen or something they "should have known" was going to happen. They will perceive a bigger portion of responsibility of the traumatic event so that it didn't just happen to them, it was something they caused; that way, if they just do it differently next time, then it will never happen again. These false stories about time make us feel less vulnerable about the situation we were in, and they give us a sense of control over the future. The fact that time gets altered with trauma is one of the biggest invisible wounds of trauma—and it interferes with a lot of well-meaning interventions. Many children and teens can't make use of the programs designed to help them plan their future because they fundamentally don't believe in their future; they need to heal before they can believe in a future. And many adults believe that the stories that they first told themselves about their trauma are what is true, and not a story that helped them cope with the trauma. Both trauma survivors and therapists must understand and work with this issue of time.

The Five-Phase Cycle of Healing Repeated Trauma

I am a pilgrim, but my pilgrimage has been wandering and unmarked. Often what has looked like a straight line to me has been a circle or a doubling back . . .

WENDELL BERRY, Jayber Crow[1]

My method of healing from trauma—the Cycle of Healing Repeated Trauma—is made up of five distinct phases. These five phases of the cycle of healing are *preparation* (getting ready), *unintegration* (a controlled coming apart), *identification* (sorting, identifying, and experimenting), *integration* (weaving the pieces back together), and *consolidation* (solidifying and stabilizing). From an emotional, cognitive, spiritual, physical, and relational perspective, each phase has its own focus and purpose, as well as its own set of needs to attend to. Each phase will require a different set of skills and capacities from you and your guides or support system. What works well in one phase doesn't necessarily work well in another phase, which is why one-size-fits-all treatment plans usually don't work.

This cycle shares elements with elite athletic training. In athletic training there is something called *periodization*, which is based on the stress response system. In athletics if you continually stress the body through training, it won't recover. With too much training and not enough rest, the body will break down, and performance will decrease, not improve. Instead, periodization requires that you prepare your body for the work, go through the training, and then plan time for recovery. The discovery of periodization radically changed sports training and has become the standard for how athletes train. In sports there are different cycles of training—macrocycles, which encompass the training program for a year, and within them are microcycles, periods of training that contribute to the whole of training but are made up of the same elements of preparation, training, and recovery.

Similarly, the Cycle of Healing Repeated Trauma is also made up of a macrocycle that is the trajectory of your healing or treatment over time, as well as smaller phases of microcycles. So you will be in a phase of the Cycle of Healing Repeated Trauma that aligns with the larger macrocycle, but you will also be in one of the phases in a microcycle as well. In this guide, each stage is in its own part so that there is no pressure to move to the next part until you are ready. And there is no pressure to see your healing as a linear project. It is fine to go back and forth between parts, or reread sections before moving on. This book is meant to be useful to you wherever you are in your healing; when some piece of what you are reading resonates with you, stay in that section. You will serve your healing the most if you stay connected to where you are and focus on what will help you both be with and move through the phase you are in.

The first phase of the Cycle of Healing Repeated Trauma is the Preparation phase, or *getting ready*. The Preparation phase prepares you for the strenuous task of trauma treatment. In this first phase, most people are in a rush to get to the "hard part" of healing, and you may find that you are overwhelmed. You may not have the emotional regulation skills to manage your feelings or the relational skills yet to lean on the therapeutic relationship when you do get to the hard part. The task of the Preparation phase is to strengthen all of your resources, both internally and externally, and build the healing relationship with the therapist. In this phase you will strengthen your self-awareness and emotional management skills. You will work on your communication skills and relationship skills. You will make sure that you have a safe place to live, free from violence, and that you have meaningful work (whether paid or unpaid). Trauma work takes people to very difficult places, and both you and the therapeutic relationship must be strong enough for the challenges you will face. This phase mirrors preparation for a safe high-altitude climb. A climber must be physically healthy and strong, must be knowledgeable about the climb and how to use the right equipment, must acclimate to the altitude, and must be part of a well-functioning team in order to manage a trek safely. It is not possible to skip the Preparation phase of a high-altitude climb without risking failure or injury, and it isn't possible to skip the Preparation phase in trauma treatment either.

In the Preparation phase, you will attend to your health—in basic and important ways. You will attend to your sleep, making sure you are getting enough rest. You will attend to your eating, making sure you are getting nourishing food. In other words, you will begin your healing journey by making sure that your body is nourished and cared for.

The Preparation phase is not only the foundation of the whole healing journey you will take; it is also the beginning of each new piece of work as you complete the smaller cycles and begin again. The Preparation phase is a chance to check in and make sure that all systems and supports are solid before heading into difficult territory. It is a chance to adapt or repair as necessary before moving on. It can be the "base camp" to come back to if the climbing proves too difficult given a new set of circumstances.

The middle phase of treatment is divided into three distinct phases: Unintegration, Identification, and Integration. In the simplest terms, Unintegration is a *controlled coming apart*. It is where you slowly dismantle the protections and behaviors that made it possible to survive, and you untangle beliefs that you have about the world from living through trauma. What comes out are feelings, images, experiences, and pieces of your trauma story.

In Unintegration you wrestle with dismantling the protections you used and the old story of how you understand yourself and your world. These defenses, beliefs, and behaviors can keep you from being able to live the life that you want to, and they can get in the way of you talking about your trauma. I know that *Unintegration* is a weird word to use— but I like the planful part about the word. It is not *Disintegration*— which would mean falling apart in an uncontrolled way, where the parts are no longer usable. Rather, Unintegration is more akin to slowly taking a jigsaw puzzle apart, attending to the pieces. Earlier I used the example of how a temporary fix to your house during a hurricane would be plywood over the windows, but the metaphorical equivalent of repeated trauma was to put bricks and cement up to the roofline. In the Unintegration phase, we slowly take down the brick wall. We don't hit the wall with a wrecking ball or even a sledgehammer; instead we work to take each brick down and set it aside. If any of the bricks were supporting the weight of the house, we build or restore the supporting beams and structures so that the house remains solid while we are restoring it.

But the Unintegration phase is uncomfortable. It starts because you feel safe enough to let the pieces of your trauma story come out, and your emotional experience can quickly shift from feeling safe to feeling like you are in a crisis. The crisis you feel is old—it is the trauma that is coming back to be healed. Understanding this dynamic doesn't make it necessarily feel easier, but it does give you more patience with it, and yourself.

Let's look at what the Unintegration phase looks like in real life. Jennifer grew up in a household rife with domestic violence and child abuse. She had survived by overfunctioning and doing everything herself; this self-reliance looked mature when she was a child, but as she became an adult it got in the way of her relationships at home and her ability to collaborate as a team member at work. While in therapy, she has recognized that while she wanted to tell her therapist more about the abuse she experienced and witnessed, whenever she tried to talk about it she went numb—she couldn't feel what she was feeling when she started the conversation, and she felt disconnected from her therapist—as if this person weren't really there to help her.

The Unintegration phase begins when you feel safe enough to lean on the helping relationship, when you are able to inhabit a calmer self in order to slowly dismantle defenses so the story can come out in words, feelings, and experiences. Then you can begin to see either the trauma that you experienced or the protections you used to survive the trauma— and often both at the same time. In Jennifer's case, in trying to talk about the abuse, Jennifer experienced the same feelings in therapy that she had as a child when the abuse was happening—she went numb and felt like there was no help available to her.

The Identification phase is where you bring words to all of the aspects of your experience and your story. Traumatic memory and experience is fragmented, and trauma affects the way we tell our stories. Trauma stories aren't one story. They are the story of what happened, of who you were before it happened, of how you protected yourself from what happened, of how the trauma has woven itself into your life—and, at some point, of what you are hoping for in the future. It's not just about getting out the facts of the case. The facts are important, but they aren't a whole trauma story. I worked many years ago with a teenage girl who could recount her child abuse history in detail, but she would tell it in an almost robotic tone. She had most of the facts, but it wasn't her story. Missing from her story were her emotions, the impact of these experiences on her belief about the world and relationships, and how they connected to her as she was now. In the Identification phase you are trying out different ways of telling your story or describing your feelings. You are trying to get to a place where the feelings, images, experiences and the meaning you make of those experiences all come together in one place. And when all of these pieces do come together— you are in the Integration phase. This is the phase where you can bring all the pieces of your story together—to mourn the losses of what you lived through, to begin to experience what you might have missed, and to open yourself to the possibilities of a different future—a future that can hold your past, but not be determined by it.

The Identification phase—*sorting, identifying, and experimenting*— involves bringing language to each of the fragments that come up in the Unintegration phase. This allows you to sort through the information to learn what was necessary and may have helped you then, what may be helping now or may be getting in the way, and what you want to keep or let go of. As you take each brick down, you will discover its properties, sort it, name it, and decide where it came from and where it needs to go. As you tell your story, you will sort through what was important, what worked for you, what didn't work for you, and what no longer works for you.

In the Identification phase things come to have names—feelings, experiences, thoughts. As you put words to your feelings and experiences, you can sort more easily what has happened and how you want things to happen in the present and the future. The nature of trauma is that it can defy language—many experiences feel *unspeakable.* A big part of the healing in Identification is trying out words, sentences, even metaphors—anything that helps you try to describe how you feel and what you lived through in the past, and what your experience is in the present. For Jennifer, Identification involved sorting through the words and feelings in the story of the abuse and differentiating them from the experiences and feelings she was having in the session with her therapist. Identification meant learning about her difficulties in talking and trusting. When she said that "it is hard to talk," she experimented with different aspects of the experience, trying on different conversations over the course of months: "Is it hard to talk because it is hard to trust someone to listen?" "Is it hard to talk because I don't really know how I am feeling?" "Is it hard to talk because I can't find the words?" "Is it hard to talk because I never got to talk to anyone about what was hard for me?" The feeling that came up in Unintegration, "It is hard to talk," gets elaborated on in Integration. Identification is slowing down enough to match the experience with words and feelings.

The fragments of traumatic memory are the different pieces—the feelings that you had and also the feelings that you couldn't have; they are the images and smells, the sounds and words you heard, the words you weren't able to speak. These fragments come out in the Unintegration phase and get elaborated on and clarified in the Identification phase, and then when they finally come together, you enter the Integration phase.

The Integration phase—*weaving the pieces back together*—takes place when all aspects of the trauma come together to allow you to create a coherent narrative of your experience. Think of the Integration phase as the place where all three aspects of repeated trauma come together: *what did happen*, what you did to survive, and *what didn't happen*. It is also where the fragmented parts of traumatic memory—the story, the feelings, the experience—all come together in one place. For example, Jennifer was gradually able to bring what did happen (the physical abuse she remembered) and her protections (her ability to go numb and not have any emotions, her feeling that "there is no help") into one place and begin to tell the story of her abuse with all of the feelings that went with it. In being able to tell the story and get help with the conversation—and have someone patiently listen as she sorted her story out—Jennifer was able to experience what didn't happen as well. She got to feel distress but also to experience being helped and cared for. Integration is made up of two distinct parts: *mourning* (facing the impact of what actually happened and feeling the grief and anger associated with that) and *new beginning* (coming to understand the learning and growth experiences that you missed). It is important to recognize both aspects of Integration, as they touch different aspects of what needs repair. The moments of new beginning allow for new skills and healthier protections to be learned and practiced, but they also offer a window into what didn't happen—an often painful opportunity to witness what was missed. Some of what needs to be mourned must be found, not just through our story of the past trauma but also through new experience. Sometimes we can feel what was missed only when we have finally felt it in the present. The Integration phase slows the process and creates enough opportunities for repetition that you can absorb, digest, and process your experience. In the Integration phase, through mourning the past truly becomes the past, and through new beginnings, the possibility of a future begins to emerge.

The last phase is Consolidation—*solidifying and stabilizing.* Consolidation allows the healing to solidify and become part of your history. Early in therapy, Consolidation often happens because there is a break— maybe your therapist goes on vacation, or perhaps there is an agreement to focus the treatment more on the present, such as current work issues, for example. An opportunity for Consolidation came up for Jennifer, who was working on her history of physical abuse and allowing herself to be helped when her therapist went on vacation. They discussed ways for Jennifer to consolidate the work she had been doing in therapy, while also giving her a chance to take a break from the hard work while her therapist wasn't there for support. Jennifer decided that since they had been working on her asking for help more, she would get some friends and family to help her with a project clearing out space in her house for a home office. She got to consolidate some new learning, and she got to slow down and enjoy the work of cleaning and painting the new space.

The book is set up so that each phase of the Cycle of Healing Repeated Trauma is in its own part, so you can learn about and develop the skills and strategies for navigating within the phase. You will cycle through the phases, and when you come back around to a previous phase there is some familiarity, saying, for example, "Oh, I am back in the Preparation phase; what needs attention or strengthening?" So there can be familiarity but also the experience of facing new challenges and new pieces of work.

A great strength of working through this cycle is that it provides a common language of healing for both you and your therapist. You can more easily name where you are in the healing process, which honors the work of each phase of healing and helps you know what to focus on at any given point.

The Treatment of Trauma

In the United States, there is an irony with trauma treatment. Much of it is focused on interpersonal trauma (child abuse and domestic violence), while much of the research on trauma is focused on the trauma experienced by war veterans—a trauma that is often not generally interpersonal in nature, but instead group on group. In addition, war veterans in the United States have a dual-culture issue affecting their processing of the trauma. The culture of the military is group based, meaning that allegiance to the group and their country is primary and the individual has no particular power or rights; then when they return, veterans are often isolated as individuals again, and the treatment happens in the context of the individual.

The problem with viewing trauma treatment only in these terms is that important interventions get ignored or lose funding, while others get lots of support and don't deliver results—not for a lack of good intention but for a lack of understanding where the broken places are.

A crucial element in the treatment of trauma is the basic premise that *trauma shatters*, and this means different things in different contexts. For each person who goes through repeated trauma, something different is shattered. Take, for example, a child who was abused young and often has to use very immature defenses. What is shattered is a belief in the safety of relationship and the world, and any chance at using more flexible defenses.

If a soldier goes to war and is repeatedly traumatized, what is shattered is the soldier's identity and often, his or her values or worldview. The soldier experiences trauma with a more fully formed brain, identity, and set of coping strategies than the child in the previous example. His or her loss in the face of trauma will be different from that of the child. But the soldier will not have gone through the trauma alone—he or she will have been in a group. So the work of healing that the soldier may need to do will be about gaining back a view of a self that can integrate who he or she was at war with who he or she was and who he or she wants to be. And this integration may need to be done in the context of a group.

We heal best in the configuration in which we were hurt. This is another reason why the treatment of trauma is not one-size-fits-all. Some people heal better in groups; some people heal better in individual therapy. One form of treatment is not objectively better than another—there is only the consideration of whether it is allowing the person to heal.

In different cultural contexts, the notion of *self* is different. In the United States or the West, the notion of self is one of *agency*—the self is the primary unit of accountability and action. In other cultures, the self is not the primary unit. The primary unit of agency might be the family, or it might be the village or a larger community. In order for the trauma to be understood, one needs to understand if and how the primary unit was shattered. For example, a man who lives through war in his country in Africa has watched his village be destroyed by rebels. Writers criticize the Western view of trauma treatment, saying that people in African villages are healing themselves without therapy, but they all point to the NGOs in the area that are engaging the country and the village in the act of healing: rebuilding the infrastructure, providing food and security, and providing a connection to the outside world. The heart and identity of the villagers is connected not to an individual self but to a community-as-self. When the community is cared for and healed, so are the villagers. We need to understand that trauma treatment works—but we also need to be aware of what was shattered, in what context, and at what developmental level, and apply this information to the right level of system: individual, family, group, community, country.

I had the wonderful fortune to work on a project helping leaders in Cambodia strengthen their response to HIV/AIDS within their country. This project was aimed at leadership development and was not intended to be a trauma intervention. However, we recognized quickly that in Cambodia, while the individuals each endured and witnessed unspeakable atrocities during the genocide of the Khmer Rouge, one of the greatest casualties of that traumatic era was the social fabric of Cambodia itself. The citizens were forced out of their communities, forced into new communities and new marriages. Each night they were forced to betray other community members, usually with false accusations, in order to prove their loyalty to the Khmer Rouge leaders. The next day, those betrayed community members would be gone. The Cambodians learned not to talk to their fellow community members; no one could be trusted.

Our project brought together 150 Cambodian leaders and community members at a time: government ministers, NGO leaders, community leaders—groups that had to work with each other and speak to each other, in which the personal and the communal came into contact with each other. Given the nature of AIDS, gender and personal norms and taboos needed to be discussed, which both strengthened the communities' capacity to talk and allowed personal histories to be revealed. The structure of the program required small-group work in multiple and repeated configurations. They had to meet within small groups, talk, and tolerate the experience of sharing their thoughts. The configuration of the group discussions mirrored their negative experiences during the Khmer Rouge. The new experience of having people listen and give positive feedback with leaders to support them began to break the association they had of group contact equaling danger.

Our presence as outside consultants and the structure we created for the work provided the safety net that helped the Cambodians work through their fears of speaking in a group. Healing or mending relationships—regardless of whether the healing is done at the individual, family, group, community, or even country level—are the primary antidote to sustained trauma.

How to Get Help

A mountain this size doesn't get climbed by one person. It gets climbed by people who pool their talents and spirits.

ALEX LOWE, *On the Edge of Antarctica: Queen Maud Land*[1]

One of the biggest roadblocks in healing from trauma is this idea: "I don't need help, I can do it myself." Here is the common refrain: "I don't need a therapist or a group—I have my friend (wife, husband, partner, children . . .)."

Why? Seems like they could help, right? They love us. We feel good with them, safe with them. In fact, it feels like they *should* be the ones to heal us. They can listen to our problems, and often do. They often listen nonjudgmentally as we recount our stories. They often have advice for us, and they certainly tell us they love us. They can hold us tightly and kiss us good night. Why isn't it enough?

Before tackling the issue of trauma, let's consider the differences in healthy relationships in our lives—the difference between a mother and an aunt, for example. The mother has a specific role for the child—to help the child navigate through the many cycles of growth with love, support, and necessary limits and protection. This often means that a mother isn't always popular—at bedtime, for example. The mother doesn't base her behavior on whether she is liked or popular, but on what the child needs for optimal growth. So she takes the hit on her popularity and survives the "mean mom" tirade at bedtime.

An aunt has a decidedly easier task: she can often say "yes" (ice cream for dinner!) when a mother must say "no" (eat your vegetables or no dessert). It's not that the aunt would feed the child ice cream every night for dinner, but she knows that she is not responsible for all of the limit setting, or for the trajectory of growth, and therefore, she can be "fun."

Healing relationships (therapists, groups, coaches, consultants) are more like parents in the sense that their primary task is to help us heal and grow—not to be liked, and not to be part of our lives forever. Therapy at its best is a developmental process. The job of therapy is to help us shed the behaviors or defenses that we no longer need or are no longer helpful, and to help us build new skills, negotiating the developmental or healing shifts that we need to make.

We expect our friends and our spouses to be on our side. When we feel bad, we want them to help us feel better, not hold us accountable to change. We want them to say the right thing, not the growth-promoting thing, or worst of all, *nothing*, and let us sit there with our thoughts. When we complain about how our lives are going, we expect that our loved ones will sympathize and see the world from our perspective; when we complain about our boss—then they should blame the boss too, not ask us what *we* did to cause the problem.

It's funny, people automatically understand the need for a couples therapist when a couple is having a problem. Friends know that they can't say what they need to say to both parties and still be loyal to their friend, or not be seen as taking sides. They know that there are truths to both sides and that they are in over their heads to try to help. Most often you hear, "I'm not going to get in the middle of that."

A healing relationship is like a couples therapist for both sides of the self: the self that wants to change, grow, or heal—and the part of the self that wants to stay the same, the part that is afraid of or unable to change. A therapist's role is to hold both of these realities—not to take sides, but rather to support both sides by creating an environment in which both sides can grow and integrate.

Healing from trauma is perhaps the most complicated form of therapy. As I mentioned earlier, most trauma is really three interrelated traumas: the experience of repeated trauma, the defensive structure built to survive the trauma, and the loss of healthy growth and development during the period of trauma. While your friends and loved ones may be able to listen and help you with your experiences of trauma, often it feels impossible to talk with them about it; often these experiences are described as *unspeakable*. And often we don't want anyone to see us at our worst moments of helplessness. There is simply too much shame. Even if you could share this with your loved ones, and you could tell them how much you are hurting, in some fundamental way they really can't hear or take in how broken you feel. Not because they aren't listening, or they are bad, or they don't love you—but because either they can't truly understand, their experience is too far away from yours, or it would simply be too hard for them if they did. They need you. They need the relationship with you. You are important to them and they know on some level they can't fix it, and they don't know how to hold this piece of information with all of the other aspects of you.

So how do you find help? What kind of help is best? These are important questions with a lot of answers. There is no perfect guide or therapist. When friends and family ask me what to look for, I give a pretty basic answer—what you want in a good therapist or guide or consultant is what you would look for in a good parent. You want someone who can be consistent, patient, and hopeful, and who knows that this journey is about you and your growth, not their needs or success. You want someone who knows about trauma or is willing to learn. You want someone who can laugh at himself and who can tolerate his emotions and coach and support you with your emotions. You want someone who is willing to let both of you make mistakes and who can have a conversation about it when it happens. You want someone you can respect. You want someone whose basic premise is: whatever it is, we can talk about it. And, you want someone who is a good match for you—where you feel safe, and where you feel like you will be understood, challenged, and heard.

Finding the right person or group is mostly a matter of trial and error. You have to "try them on for size." You have to see if they are a good match for you, and the only real way to know that is to meet with them and talk with them. That being said, sometimes you don't get a lot of choice. Depending on your healthcare coverage, and where you can obtain help, sometimes there are limited options. But limited options doesn't mean poor care. Almost all of the therapists I know have spent part of their careers in systems where they were the only option for people getting help. And this situation is not much different than other aspects of your healthcare. If you go to the emergency room, you don't get to choose your doctor.

All therapists are trained to work with a wide range of clients and a wide range of issues. The most important thing you can do is have a conversation about what you want and need—to the best of your ability.

You need to see if the person or group you seek out will be a good match for your healing journey. Can I work with this person? If I have differences of opinion or have doubts about their capacity—can I ask about them?

Here are some questions for you to consider and perhaps journal about:

- What do you hope to get out of treatment?
- What symptoms are bothering you the most right now?
- What is the most difficult thing about going to see a therapist or being in a group?
- What would help you talk?
- What gets in the way of talking?
- What gets in the way of taking care of yourself?

And here are some questions for you to ask your potential therapist, guide, or consultant:

- How long have you been working in this field?
- What do you enjoy about it?
- How do you typically work with clients?
- What happens if we disagree?
- What are your expectations of clients?
- Have you worked with clients who have a trauma history before?

These questions are just a start, and you are free to ask a helper anything that would help you feel more comfortable working with them. Some people find help on the first try and some on the second. I found it on the sixth. Remember that it is the combination of you and your therapist or your group that is the healing relationship. You each hold an end of the rope. Contrary to rumors, your therapist cannot read your mind. The healing relationship relies on both of you—so you need to trust yourself and your experience, and you need to communicate what you want and need so that the relationship can support your work.

How to Use This Book

Lather, rinse, repeat.

INSTRUCTIONS ON EVERY SHAMPOO BOTTLE

E ach of you will use this book differently depending on where you are starting your journey, what your experience of trauma is, and how much support you need. Some of you have been on this journey for some time—and you are now going to use this guide to understand it and work with it differently. Others are still pondering whether to begin, how to begin, or where to begin. Maybe some of you are part of the support team of someone who is healing from repeated trauma and want to use this guide to understand them better and maybe understand yourself or your relationship with them better. There are many treatments for trauma—some body-based, some talking-based, some group-based, some individual-based. There are many books on healing from trauma. All the healing work you do can fit inside this framework—it provides support for the work you are doing and in no way replaces it or negates it. I encourage you to use whatever support, information, or practices help you stay engaged in your treatment and support your path to a whole self and a healthy life.

Because this model of healing from trauma is set up in phases, there will be a natural desire for a quantified length of time for each phase. For example, you may wonder how long the Preparation phase lasts. There isn't a specified time—but for some it may be weeks, if your resources are solid, and for others it may be months or even years. This model is about what it takes to work toward health and wholeness—and there is no prize for speed. You will be living your life as you go through healing, so I would caution you to work at a pace that allows you to live a healthy life and to heal. Each of the other phases will move as they are ready—sometimes you move through them quickly and sometimes, depending on what you are working on, you spend a chunk of time in a particular phase. There is no right way—there is only what is supporting your healing. And you and your therapist or group should stay in conversation about what is and isn't serving your healing.

Some of you may want to read through the whole book first and get a sense of the whole journey, and some of you may read until you get to a place where the discussion resonates with where you are and decide to stay in that part for a while. You may finish the book, put it down for a while, and pick it back up again when something shifts in the work you are doing with your healing—or if you find yourself feeling stuck or needing support. In the spirit of a trail guide it is meant to support you on whatever trail you find yourself. Or, you can read ahead if you want to prepare yourself.

I encourage you to bring whatever is helpful in this book into your work in therapy or share this book with loved ones who are struggling to understand what you are experiencing on your journey of healing.

Having language and some mental scaffolding for where you are and what you are going through can be immensely helpful, and being able to share the language will help you feel less alone and more supported—and it will allow those who are doing their best to support you to be as effective as possible.

PART 2

Preparation

Our bodies need time to adjust to thin air of extreme altitude, an acclimatization process that takes weeks. We heed unwritten rules, taking necessary time and moving slowly up the mountain, learning the route, anchoring ropes to facilitate going up and, more important, to provide for quick escape in the face of bad weather. After each foray, we return to base camp to recover. When the next good weather occurs, we go back to the mountain and attempt to climb high.

JIM HABERL, *Risking Adventure*[1]

Preparation

When we're guiding here on Everest as in any guiding situation, we're always assessing our clients every single day. Just because they got here and paid their money does not mean that they get a chance to go to the summit. They have to prove to us from camp to camp that they're capable of going to the next higher camp. The whole process is an evaluation. That's the only safe way we can do this.

ED VIESTURS[1]

When I was in high school, my father got his pilot's license. Before each flight, on the tarmac at the airport, he took out his flight manual and went through a prepared series of steps. He checked the plane over in a sequence. He checked all of the rivets holding the plane together, he checked the fuel mixture, checked the tires, the wings, the latches on the doors. Then he got in the plane and the flight preparation continued. He checked the instruments and checked the communication systems. The rule was that if everything wasn't in order, the plane didn't fly. If he found something awry on his checklist, the plane went to the garage to get fixed immediately. Sometimes this meant a delay in flight. Oh well. Safety was the highest priority. This is true for the preflight of an airplane, and it is equally and just as importantly true as the prework to the treatment of trauma. The Preparation phase is the first phase of the treatment of trauma, and it is also the beginning of any new piece of work while going through the process of healing. Whenever you begin, or begin again, you start in the Preparation phase.

In the case of the preflight check my father did on his plane, I have to say that initially the flight check didn't make me feel safer. Instead, at first, it made me overly conscious and nervous: You are really checking every rivet? Are they that likely to come apart? Like most people, taking a hard look at things made me feel uneasy—looking deeply at things makes you take in how much is there.

But the preparation a pilot does is also a chance for the pilot to get to know his plane, as pilots often switch aircraft. It is a chance for the pilot to shift gears and get his mind into pilot mode and away from the other concerns of his day. Going through the preparatory checklist is orienting for a pilot. Preparation is about getting physically grounded and getting mentally connected.

The Preparation phase is echoed in your daily life thousands of times without your notice unless you ignore it. It is the minute or two in the car in the morning when you scan that you have enough gas to get to work and you have your wallet and your briefcase with you. It is the extra ten minutes you add to staff meetings at work to check in with all of the team members to see that everyone is okay and on board with the project. It is the checking and rechecking your surgical team does to make sure that they have the instruments necessary and that they know and understand your medical condition. And in flight, as in medicine, having a structured way to prepare significantly improves safety.[2]

Typically, you ignore the Preparation phase completely or you don't pay attention to it. There are two main reasons that this happens. The first reason is that you often come to the process of healing or growth in the midst of a crisis. You are frantic—you have lost your job, your marriage, your health. You are in severe emotional or physical distress. You want help and answers *right now*. This state of crisis often jettisons you into the second phase of healing: Unintegration, ahead of any preparatory work. Most often this means that the Preparation phase is skipped over or rushed through. You believe that since you are already in the deep end of the water, you might as well swim. This idea is tempting, and from the outside it can look logical, but it is a mistake. The Preparation phase builds the foundation on which the rest of the work will find secure footing. If you rush through or skip over the Preparation phase, when the going gets rough, there will be little solid ground on which to work.

If you are starting trauma work in the middle of a crisis, you may be frustrated by your therapist or guide, who will ask you to slow down, talk about your health, your life, your family, or your sobriety. It may feel illogical or crazy in the middle of a crisis to head away from what you see as the big issues and not head toward them, but this is absolutely necessary. You must pull yourself back toward shore, down from the mountain, off the train—whatever your metaphor—and work through the Preparation phase.

The second reason that the Preparation phase is often ignored is that it can feel slow and can take a long time. This makes this phase seem like it's not the real work. Conversations in the Preparation phase aren't what you think of when you think of drama or movie catharsis. These conversations are much more basic—although they can still feel incredibly difficult. You may feel like you should be talking about the trauma, and instead you are talking about how to talk about feelings—and it doesn't fit your idea of what trauma therapy is. In addition, your partner or spouse can often be judgmental about this phase of work. You have to remember that they have often waited so long for you to get help that they want you to do real work and not beat around the bush. They want the work to get done. They can't believe that you aren't talking about the problem.

The task of the Preparation phase is the assessment and strengthening of all of your resources—internal and external. Internal resources are the resources that you have within you: your ability to understand, know, and manage emotions; your ability to cope with stress and have hope; the way you think; your feelings of self-efficacy; your physical health and ability; your ability to engage and keep relationships; and your spiritual resources. External resources are the resources that exist around you: your work and financial life, your family life, your relationships, your recreational life, and the resources in your community and the larger system that you live in.

Probably the best question to ask yourself to assess whether you have completed the Preparation phase is this: "What needs to be in place to safely and effectively work with my history of trauma?" You need to be free from any dangerous addiction (alcohol, drugs, eating disorders, gambling, sex), you need to attend to your physical health and safety, you need to be engaged in meaningful activity/work whether paid or unpaid, you need to have some supportive relationships, and you need to have ways of managing stress that serve you well and don't hurt you or anyone else. If these things are in place, you are ready to have more difficult conversations. You are ready to work with your trauma history.

But the Preparation phase isn't only about strengthening yourself. It is also about strengthening the relationship with your therapist or guide or group. As you work through the Preparation phase you get to know yourself, but you also get to know your therapist, and they get to learn about you. They get to learn how to help you have difficult conversations and how to keep your stress level in a manageable zone. And together you create language and strategies for working with each other—through areas of challenge, through stress, through crisis, and the various stages of learning.

Base Camp

Despite the many trappings of civilization at Base Camp, there was no forgetting that we were more than three miles above sea level. Walking to the mess tent at mealtime left me wheezing for several minutes. If I sat up too quickly, my head reeled and vertigo set in.

JON KRAKAUER, *Into Thin Air*[1]

Many years ago a college student came to see me at the clinic because she had experienced a date rape. She had stopped attending class, she wasn't eating or showering, and she had isolated herself from her friends. She was brought to counseling by her mom and they both thought that she had to come in and talk about what happened to her. They were right that she would eventually need to talk about the date rape, but they were wrong that she needed to talk about it *now*. She couldn't talk about the rape yet. She needed to slow down and do the work of getting to Base Camp. She needed to be able to take care of her physical self. She needed to be able to eat and shower and sleep. She needed to reconnect with people. She needed to get her anxiety in control enough to attend class. She needed to get reconnected to her more solid self before she could take on her trauma work. I had her begin managing her day and her anxiety by creating a schedule for each day. She would take a notebook and write out the entire day in thirty-minute increments—and then she (and her mom in the beginning) wrote down what she would be doing in each time block. This helped her know what to do and not have to make decisions when she was feeling overwhelmed. She and her mom met with the school administrators and created a plan for her to attend school for a half day each day for the first week, and then gradually increase her attendance. She received support from her guidance counselor, who worked with her teachers to get the work she would miss. She also worked with the guidance counselor and the school psychologist on a plan to go to the nurse's office if she felt overwhelmed and needed a time-out. She and her mom also identified two friends who she agreed could come to the house and help her with homework. By having her friends focus on schoolwork, she felt less overwhelmed that she would have to talk about or be confronted with the trauma of the date rape. By the end of four weeks she was attending school full time and had resumed most of her normal routines. This preparation allowed her to be in a much more solid place to begin talking about what had happened to her.

For every expedition in which an explorer has to cross dangerous terrain that requires physical stamina, mental toughness, specialized equipment, and skill expertise, the most crucial part of the trip is the preparation. It's the part of the adventure movie that you never see. Shackleton planned for nearly *five* years for his famed Antarctic journey. In preparation for their expedition to explore the West, Lewis and Clark spent months not only gathering supplies but also educating themselves.[2]

Keep in mind that the adventures of these old explorers were to places that were still, in many ways, terra incognita—they were lands yet to be fully mapped. There is something about the experience of healing from repeated trauma that echoes these old explorers. The world of repeated trauma is its own world—it is not an event, it is the fabric of a life survived, it is its own country—with its own borders, rules, language, and rituals.

Perhaps in the modern era, a relevant metaphor for this type of journey is high-altitude climbing. On expeditions such as Everest or K2 there is the need, the *requirement* for preparation. In fact, a climb up Everest has not one but *multiple* preparation phases. For a mountaineering expedition, the first phase of preparation begins while you are still at home, before you even encounter the mountain you wish to climb. If you wanted to go up Everest, you would first need to get yourself in solid physical condition, and this physical conditioning usually takes about a year. You would need to know or learn mountaineering skills. You would need to learn about and acquire the right equipment. You would make your travel arrangements and arrange for your equipment and gear to get there. You would train by practicing on other high-altitude climbs closer to wherever your current home base is. You might tackle other tough climbs that require some of the same preparation and skills, such as hiking up Mt. Kilimanjaro. As Everest is a six-to-eight-month journey, you would also need to prepare your work and your relationships for your absence. Minimally, preparation for Everest lasts at least a year to a year and a half before you even leave home.

And then in country there is another stage of preparation. You would land in Kathmandu, gather your provisions and equipment, and meet up with your guides. Your goal from here is Base Camp. If you were taking the southern route through Nepal you would likely fly from Kathmandu to Lukla—and then hike for about two days to Namche Bazaar (11,290 feet) following the Dudh Kosi river. You would spend two days in Namche Bazaar resting and acclimatizing and then walk for another two days to Dingbuche (13,980 feet), where you would rest another day. Then you would hike two more days to Everest Base Camp (18,192 feet) at the foot of the Khumbu Icefall. It is more than a week since you left home, and you are now just arriving to Base Camp.

Base Camp is the key to preparation. Yes, Base Camp is an actual location and a set of structures and resources to rely on. But Base Camp is also all of the activities associated with the time spent there. Base Camp creates a literal home base from which to launch climbs and return to recover from them. On an Everest climb there is time spent at Base Camp, setting up and putting together gear, practicing skills, getting to know the team, and getting your body acclimated to the altitude. And there are daily trips by different teams to move gear from Base Camp to Camp 1. These repetitive trips provide important physical training at altitude and a chance for the guide and team to work together without the stress of the more difficult aspects of the climb. The team members can learn how to communicate with each other and what motivates (or doesn't motivate) each other.

In Base Camp you assess your resources: your food, gear, fitness, and mental stamina. You make sure that your body is acclimating and that your gear is holding up in its first trials. If your backpack, your boots, your stove, or your sleeping bag is problematic, you certainly want to know that when you are closer to Base Camp rather than at 26,000 feet, because at 26,000 feet problematic gear becomes life-threatening. The time in Base Camp is not a luxury. It is not a waste of time. The time in Base Camp is a necessity. It is what makes the climb possible. You can't skip this phase and hope to make the summit.

And you can't skip the Preparation phase or your time in the Base Camp of trauma treatment. It is what makes healing possible. It is harder to see and understand than the more tangible metaphor of Everest. The Preparation phase for the beginning of trauma treatment is no more a luxury than for an Everest climb. How can we understand Base Camp and the Preparation phase of trauma treatment and why do we bother?

And I can hear you saying, "What?! This is going to take forever! I'm outta here!"

Listen! You could no more fly to Kathmandu and just start climbing than you can just walk in and begin to hammer at the most difficult parts of your history and your life. It's not safe. In Kathmandu you would get altitude sickness and would be required to return to sea level. In therapy you would trigger whatever protective response you usually employ in danger: drinking, violence, recklessness, escape.

In healing from trauma, the first element of the Preparation phase is the same as it is for mountaineering: physical health and safety. Trauma is both an emotional and physical experience—the aftereffects of trauma reside in our mind and our body. One of the first elements of treatment is to attend to the physical aspects of our lives—the health and safety of our bodies and the concrete aspects of our well-being. This is not a "nice to have"; this is a *must have*.

The journey to Base Camp begins as soon as you get started. And it takes a lot of courage just to walk to Base Camp. Keep in mind that Base Camp on Everest is still at 18,000 feet, higher than most people ever climb. When I was working at my postdoctoral placement, a woman in her fifties came in for her first meeting and told me that the day that she called our health center for an appointment she was so nervous that she took the whole day off work to get herself ready to make the call. She said that she sat all day struggling with her anxiety about calling the health center, and at four o'clock she made the call. It had taken an entire day of work and bravery to call for help. And then, because of the scheduling in a clinic, she had to wait for two weeks to be seen by someone. By the time she came to me, she was exhausted. We needed to spend a good deal of time at Base Camp helping her recover from her climb there, and helping her gather the support she would need for the work ahead.

When I was in my twenties I had a similar experience as a client. I called my local HMO for an appointment for severe anxiety and then had to wait for four weeks for an appointment. By the time I went in, I was frantic. The clinician who met with me was clearly seasoned but mostly bored. She took notes on what I was saying without ever looking up. I remember feeling really scared and frustrated that I had waited so long to talk, and she didn't even look like she was listening. She was concerned about getting through her paperwork. I was running for my life. As clients we all need to understand that Base Camp is our first destination and that the work at Base Camp can be nothing but slow and deliberate. We can't run headlong up the mountain, and for the mountains we need to climb, there is no chairlift or auto road. We need to remember that the trail to Base Camp is actually difficult, and to give ourselves credit as we make our way there.

As treatment providers and guides we need to hold in our hearts the bravery and terror it takes to show up for treatment of long-term trauma. We may have done hundreds of intakes and first sessions in our career. We may think we have heard everything. We may be having a bad day. But for the person sitting in the chair talking with us, this may be their bravest moment. This may be the one time they have risked asking for help, risked speaking even the smallest of their truths.

The Base Camp of trauma treatment typically begins with some sort of conversation or interview, which clinics often call an *intake*. Sometimes this intake happens over the phone, and it usually continues with a series of questions and forms once in the office. The most typical question in an intake is "What brings you in today?" And "Why now?" As a client, all you can do is be as honest as you can be at the time. If you can't share something or don't want to yet, it's okay to do it when you feel more comfortable. The world of psychology and psychiatry hitched its wagon to the world of medicine. The result is a huge emphasis on the "presenting problem." Insurance benefits for treatment are parceled out by diagnosis, and your diagnosis is made by your description of your symptoms—and your description of your presenting problem. As a professor I always warned my students about being too sure about the presenting problem early on. Symptoms like anxiety, sleeplessness, depression, and social withdrawal have many possible causes and different treatments. And many people, myself included, present not with the symptom that is most difficult for them or most important medically, but instead with the one that is easiest for them to talk about. They talk about the symptoms that elicit the least amount of shame or anxiety to talk about. For me it was anxiety, and for other clients I have had it was insomnia, family issues, or binge eating. Base Camp provides the safety and time for you and your therapist to explore your symptoms and get a sense of what you have lived through and what you are grappling with so you can get a sense of where you need to go.

After the intake, Base Camp should also include a medical physical. Not only is it proper self-care, but many medical issues affect mood and anxiety—and you want to make sure that anything that can help your physical state is attended to. Your physical state has a huge impact on your mental state. As a therapist I have had far too many experiences of sending my clients to get a physical only to find that they had thyroid conditions, allergies, or blood sugar conditions that had been affecting their mood or sleep for years. You will also talk with your primary care doctor about any mental health symptoms that may be alleviated by medication (such as anxiety, depression, panic, or sleeplessness). In your conversations with your doctor or your therapist, they may have you consult a psychiatrist to discuss medication.

Medication can help you manage symptoms, which can make healing more effective—for example, if your anxiety is lower, you will be better able to talk about your issues, and you will be better able to take care of yourself. But medication won't cure trauma, and it is not a substitute for the work of healing. The most important thing is to work with your medical doctor and your therapist to make sure that your body is healthy and supporting your mood and your work in healing— and certainly not getting in your way. You will also want to get medical clearance for moderate exercise, because light exercise, like walking, is one of the best activities to improve mood and well-being that there is.

While you are at Base Camp, it is also important for you to look at any behaviors that are affecting your physical health and safety. These issues could include alcohol abuse, drug abuse, eating disorders, cutting, or sexual addiction. You might think that these are issues that most people would come in to treatment for, and sometimes they do, but as a therapist, I can tell you that many people live with addictions for a long time. They often come to treatment for other reasons—such as relationship problems or work issues. This is why it is important to assess for yourself as you begin this work of healing: Are there behaviors that are getting in my way, that are unsafe or unhealthy? If you are battling addiction, this will be the first part of treatment. This will be *the work*. It is a very important part of treatment—which will all happen at or close to Base Camp. Addictions are old solutions to old problems that continue to get used in the present. But they are solutions that come at great cost. Almost all addictions had some power at one time to help you manage your anxiety in one way or another—but as time goes on, this solution stops helping you manage your anxiety and instead starts creating more of it in your life. The initial solution now becomes the problem.

You also need to be in a safe living arrangement, so it's important to assess whether you are in an abusive or dangerous relationship. It wouldn't be possible to climb Everest with any of these serious issues, and similarly, you can't engage in trauma treatment until any of these issues are substantially managed. This part of the work of healing is going to require some honesty on your part—to look at your behaviors and then discuss them with your therapist or guide. Your therapist can't read your mind and can only know about some of these issues if you tell them directly. I know it's not easy, and I know that your willingness to disclose issues often hinges on your willingness to give them up. But I can reassure you that you are entirely in control of what behaviors you give up and when. Your therapist can help you move toward these important changes and will do it at your pace.

For people who have experienced long-term trauma, the Preparation phase lasts sometimes weeks, often months, and sometimes years. It's not that your life isn't changing or growing during this time; in fact, sometimes it can be the change you notice the most from treatment. You become sober, you get a job, your anxiety is lower, or your relationships are stronger. The Preparation phase *is* work: It's just not trauma work, per se. It's not what you will think of as work, and the work ahead of you will be difficult. The year spent getting physically ready for an Everest climb *is* work, but it is not the same as the long climb. For some people with histories of repeated trauma, the work at Base Camp is all they will want to do—it may be enough to alleviate the symptoms or stop the addiction. It may be enough for now, until there is more desire to heal, or more resources to heal. You get to choose the pace at which you walk this path.

Awareness

One of the first skills to work on in the Preparation phase, here at Base Camp, is awareness. What do I mean by awareness? Awareness is the ability to pay attention in the moment and to know what you are thinking and feeling at the moment in which it is happening. It is the ability to observe, to feel, and to notice. Awareness is the first requirement for learning and change of any kind because you need to know where you are starting from. You need to know what you are feeling, what you are thinking, and how you feel in your body.[1]

It may sound simple to be self-aware, but it is not—especially not for people who have been deeply hurt by trauma for a long time. Remember that a single terrifying event will create a fire-alarm system in the body, making it hypersensitive to any trigger for a time. If you have ever had a faulty alarm system in your house or car, one that beeps or flashes past its usefulness, like most people you will have found a way to dismantle it—take out the batteries, cut the wire, pull the fuse. When it stops beeping or flashing there is tremendous relief. Ahhhhh. Peace.

Essentially, with repeated trauma your brain does this to your body. It pulls the fuse on awareness. It says, "You don't have to feel this pain anymore. I'm cutting the connections to your feelings so you have some rest from the alarm, so you can have the energy to pay attention and get through your day." Surviving trauma requires numbing. And healing from trauma requires waking the numb parts back up. And in order to wake up what has become numb, you need to practice self-awareness.

A crucial element that makes self-awareness truly useful, often left out of the discussion, is being nonjudgmental. I have found in my work and in my experience of healing that it is one thing to be self-aware: to be able to feel, experience, see what is there. It is another thing entirely to be able to just stay with it, observe it, sit with it, and explore it. You may start with the intention to be mindful and self-aware, and then you may get a big wave of remembered trauma—emotions that are difficult, thoughts that race—and you start to judge. You decide that these feelings, thoughts, sensations are wrong, bad, immature, yucky. "Wasn't this supposed to make me feel better?" you ask. And then you may be tempted to quit practicing awareness because it's too hard or scary.

Lucky for us, some cultures have been practicing awareness for centuries and have created simple practices that have served people over time. My favorite way to teach self-awareness is through the practice of mindfulness. Mindfulness is the practice of paying attention to this moment, observing it, and not judging it.[2] Mindfulness is the building block of any meditation practice, and it begins with the simple instruction to breathe.

Yes, breathe. Just take an easy deep breath in and an easy breath out. Pay attention to the breath coming in and the breath moving out. What do you notice, even in this small act? What do you observe? I notice that when I try to pay attention to my breathing, it often feels awkward. As if it weren't something that I do all the time, like I was trying some really complicated dance step. With each breath I can stay present with the breath, or expand my awareness. What do I notice about my body? Where is it tight? Where is it relaxed? What are the sensations? What are my feelings? What are the sounds around me? What are the thoughts traveling through my brain?

This act of mindfulness allows you to build self-awareness muscles. It helps you recognize what you are feeling and thinking as it is happening—in real time. It allows you to begin to know certain things for yourself, which only you could know. No one else knows the thoughts running through your mind. No one else knows the sensations you feel in your body, or the emotions you feel in your heart. Mindfulness and self-awareness are the smallest and most manageable steps toward taking back this country called yourself.

Repeated trauma is the experience of being colonized; for a long time someone else may have controlled your safety (or lack of it), your boundaries, your speech—it may have felt like they even controlled your thoughts. This colonizer might have been a person, or a group, or in some of the communities and countries I have worked in, it was literally colonization. Survival meant staying quiet, staying unaware. When you experience repeated trauma, not-knowing, not-seeing, not-feeling is what protects you. The mandate is to stay numb, stay quiet, stay under the radar screen. Mindfulness and self-awareness are the behavioral equivalent of an antidote to this numbness and state of not-knowing. But make no mistake. This is powerful medicine.

Given how strong a medicine awareness is, mindfulness practice can be difficult for people with histories of trauma. Mindfulness brings you in direct contact with yourself. You come to really sit inside and observe all of what is going on inside you. It is a chance to visit and explore the country that is yourself. Now, if your country has been at peace for most of your life, and the weather is pretty good, then sitting and visiting that country won't be too stressful, and being aware of all the aspects won't require too much help. You can just relax and enjoy the scenery and the sidewalk cafés. But if your country has been at war the last ten years, if you are going back to sit in reconciliation meetings, if you are walking through inner villages that have been decimated, then awareness is going to require shorter trips and more support because it is much more stressful to visit a war zone. Thus, it is important to be aware of the dosage, the way you would think about it with any powerful medication, like chemotherapy.

When I was a psychology intern, I ran a mindfulness group on an adolescent inpatient unit. I created the group through trial and error, building on some established mindfulness protocols and eventually creating a script that fit the needs of the kids on the unit. There was only one rule: You couldn't distract anyone else. In addition to the script, I made a tape of mellow music that would play in the background. Kids were allowed to bring pillows to group and were given the instruction to get into any position that was comfortable to them. It was a forty-five-minute session split into three sections: a five-minute practice and a twenty-minute practice that was repeated. This gave the kids a chance to "come to the surface" and check in. In my role of mindfulness lifeguard, I could make eye contact with each kid and make sure they weren't "drowning."

Some kids could lie down and relax into the experience, while others, on the first day, sat stiffly in a chair and stared at me for the entire forty-five minutes. But as difficult as it was for them, mindfulness is a powerful medicine: In a safe and caring environment, self-awareness and self-control muscles actually mend and repair fairly quickly. I had a kid on the unit who had been kidnapped and put in the trunk of a car. She couldn't manage a minute of quietness when she started, but two weeks later, she could sit and experience the entire forty-five minutes, even saying she felt relaxed. Relaxation isn't necessarily the goal of a mindfulness practice, although many people report this feeling state as an outcome. Mindfulness is the capacity to rest in one's own awareness, and resting of any sort has healing properties. From my vantage point the goal of mindfulness is to be able to observe whatever is there and stay: to be aware and not abandon yourself. Mindfulness is perhaps the best way to mend the fabric of a self.

When it came time to do my dissertation,[3] I decided to study the group I had created. I couldn't do this at the hospital because the length of stay on an inpatient unit was often too short, and certainly too variable, so I chose to study a group that had just as much difficulty with self-control and managing emotions: juvenile delinquent boys. I ran my group in four different juvenile detention centers and, similar to my experience in the unit, found that the boys built mindfulness muscles over time. They started off fidgety, but at the end of the eight weeks they could easily settle into the experience. The group had an effect on the aspects I was studying: self-control and aggression. The boys in my group were less aggressive than boys who didn't participate. It appeared that my meditation group offered a buffer from the stress of being in a locked setting.

But even more interesting to me were the anecdotal comments of the boys. Many of them started reporting that they could fall asleep more easily. One said, "I couldn't fall asleep last night and then I just started hearing your voice talking about paying attention to the feelings at the top of my head. And then I just did as much of your talking as I could but then I was asleep." The boys could find within the country of themselves a place to experience calmness, to rest. Another boy, who had gotten into trouble on the unit and put into a chair for a time-out, said that he was staring at the sheet he was supposed to fill out and was just about to start a fight with a staff member when he decided to just take three breaths instead. And then he said, "I figured I'd take three more." He got through his time-out in three-breath increments and didn't lose his temper or his privileges. You can build self-control muscles three breaths at a time.

Mindfulness isn't magic and can be too hard in certain situations. I had kids who came to group and had to leave. At the beginning of group, they would sit and as it began to get quiet they would look around with the eyes of someone who was caught in a fire. They were panic-stricken and typically would try to get others to start talking—to stop the quiet, to stop any chance of sitting in their own awareness. They couldn't sit in awareness yet, and not in that setting. On my good days as a group leader I caught those kids early—and either asked them if they were up to it or set a limit on them, giving them the chance to push their behavior or require them to leave. Sometimes I didn't, though. Especially in the beginning, when I was still learning to run this group, I wanted to believe that mindfulness itself would just work. But instead that kid would fall apart or pick a fight and this would disrupt the group for everyone. It took me a while to respect what each of these kids was experiencing, to respect the war-torn countries they were visiting when I asked them to be quiet, to breathe, to be aware.

What can starting mindfulness do for you? Just the simple practice of awareness can give you so much data about where you are and what you may need. Awareness, in and of itself, is an act of preparation. Taking three minutes to breathe and scan your body, your feelings, and your thoughts is a complete parallel to a pilot doing a preflight check on her plane—checking it over piece by piece, rivet by rivet, to make sure the plane is safe for flight. In engaging mindfulness and doing a scan, you are checking to see if there are physical or emotional rivets that need attending to.

Mindfulness and awareness is something you should only practice initially with a group leader or therapist, but only you can do it for yourself. No one else can do it for you. Only you are capable of scanning your internal states and your thoughts. People may have information or feedback for you by observing your outsides: your behavior and expressions. But only you have access to all of the information—if you choose to slow down, stay still, and pay attention to it.

Trust and Ropes

When I was fifteen and a Girl Scout camper, I learned to rock-climb in the mountains of the Western Catskills. Before we began, our instructor taught us about the concept of belaying. Belaying is the act of being connected by rope to a person whose job it is to hold the rope, anchoring the climber to safety, while also letting out the right amount of rope to allow the climber to keep climbing. The belayer is the person who makes it possible for someone to climb up a very difficult mountain by continually adjusting the rope, making sure that it's not too tight and not too slack. The belay rope allows you to climb up difficult terrain knowing that if you slip or fall, you will be held by the rope. The first thing we had to learn was how to get connected—how to connect our ropes to the belayer before we could start climbing.

So what does the initial connection look like? What supports trust and connection? One of the first things is just the rules and expectations of treatment: for both you and your therapist or your group. When I first started therapy I asked my therapist what her expectations were—and she said that she had just two expectations of her clients. These expectations were that I needed to (1) show up and (2) be as honest as I could be. In twenty-five years of doing clinical work and reading about clinical work, I haven't found a better set of expectations that holds the work of healing. Showing up is your willingness to hold on to or hook into your end of the rope: to literally show up physically. To be present and to be in someone's presence. As a therapist, I pictured that each time someone came for help and stayed, we passed a thread back and forth, as if our first goal together was to weave the rope that would connect us. The weaving we did was a combination of the constancy of the relationship and the conversations that we had: Was I there when they expected me to be? Were they there? Did I start on time? Was I able to listen and respond well enough? Were they able to talk?

I learned that weaving this rope happens on the client's time frame and not mine. For three years I worked at an outpatient mental health clinic in a housing project in a city near Boston, and for my first six months at the clinic none of my clients showed up. Nor did they quit. One young man, named Jim, would make an appointment, and when his appointment time came, the waiting room was always empty. I would then call Jim about his missed appointment and he would apologize for not showing up and then would immediately schedule for another time the following week. He did this for five months. This was how he created connection. It was his way of testing the rope. He wanted to make sure I would stay and I would stick with him. He wanted to see if I could maintain a connection. And finally after five months I went out into the waiting room at his appointment time and he was there.

In its most basic form, *showing up* means being there for your appointments. Sometimes my clients have needed something that helps them feel comfortable being present when being present feels too hard. I have talked to kids who would only meet with me if they could talk from underneath their Tigger blanket, or talk from behind a chair in my office. I have met with adults who brought their spouses or significant others to the first meeting so that they would feel safer and more reassured. What is important, especially during this precious time at Base Camp, is to explore, articulate, and experiment with what helps you be able to *show up*. What helps the connection feel solid, comfortable, and safe?

My therapist's second request to be honest is a showing up of a different kind; it is asking not just the physical self but also the emotional self, the relational self—all possible aspects of self—to allow themselves to be seen and heard. So it means not only showing up for your appointment but, once you are there, bringing as much of your full self in as you can. And once again, here at Base Camp it is important to explore: What is hard about letting yourself be seen? What is hard about speaking? What gets in the way of being present and what helps you do it more? How will your guide know when your rope is secure and when it needs tightening? How can you tell your guide when it is too steep, or you are too tired and can't go on? How can you tell your guide that you are ready to move forward, that you need more slack in your rope to try something new?

In rock climbing there is a structured communication process between the climber and her belayer because often the climber and belayer can't see each other—the climber is far below the belayer and out of view. Both the belayer and the climber need to know when the other person is ready, whether he can begin to climb, and what each person needs so that both are safe and the climbing can be successful. They need to have a communication strategy for starting, for stopping, and for emergencies.

For trauma survivors the most basic acts of trust and honest communication can feel like radical acts—they are often big steps of new learning or relearning. Some people equate the request for honesty with an expectation or pressure to share all their secrets. This is not the intention, though there is no taboo in saying whatever is important and on your mind. But what is probably most helpful at this point in your healing journey is your ability to talk about what your experience is, and how you are feeling in the here and now—to be able to say to your guide or your group, "I don't know what I am feeling." Or, "I feel numb." Or, "I can't talk today, it's too hard." Or, "When you asked me about my work, I felt like you were judging me. Is that true?" It's important to check out assumptions and find out if you are accurately hearing the tone of their voice or accurately reading their facial expressions—and this is important for both client and guide. Something as simple as "You looked surprised by what I just said" can help both of you understand each other better.

Once you have connection and communication, then you can start climbing. When I was learning to rock-climb, the next steps of the instruction after learning to belay were a bit surprising for me. Our instructor got us into our harnesses and had us hook up our belay ropes and climb about three feet off the ground, and then we had to *fall* on purpose. He wanted us to *practice falling*. The purpose of this falling practice was twofold. First, the instructor wanted us to learn to feel and trust the rope in a safe situation so that we would feel secure as we climbed higher. He wanted us to trust the rope and trust our ability to fall and be able to get back to climbing from however we had landed. And second, the fall wasn't just for the climber, it was also for the belayer. It helped each of us, as we learned to belay, to practice catching the weight of someone and get the skill of holding them safely with the rope when the stakes weren't as high—when it wasn't as dangerous. We learned to communicate with each other and feel what it felt like to *depend on* and *be depended on* all at a height of three feet.

Remember that while you are learning to trust your guide, your guide is also learning to trust you. It is important at this stage of the journey to find out how to communicate with each other and how to call for help when you are still only three feet off the ground. This can be really concrete: "Call this number if you are in trouble," or "Only call me in an emergency—don't use email." In some groups it's permitted to use other group members for support, and in some groups you are expected to use the group leader as support. In some clinics there is an on-call person who may not be your guide but is there as the belayer in off-hours, or there might be an emergency service number that screens calls. Talking about all of this while you are only three feet off the ground is really important. And it may seem silly or awkward. You may think, *I'm never going to call for help anyway, why are we having this conversation?* And, as a climber, you may never fall, but you don't want to risk testing that where a mistake would be dangerous.

Keep in mind that even in rock climbing you want some resistance on the rope—you want to feel the other person on the other end. If the rope is too slack and there is no resistance at all, then there may be too much rope to keep you safe if you fall. But if the rope is too tight, if the resistance is too great, then you can't move. It's okay for your therapist to push you or ask you things that you may feel are too hard. And it's okay for you to push back and say, "Not yet." *Resistance* is another term for the ways we protect ourselves, the ways we keep ourselves safe. Sometimes we overprotect ourselves and we aren't able to stretch and grow, and sometimes we underprotect ourselves and we become over-whelmed. Becoming aware of these edges in ourselves helps us under-stand what we want and need; it helps us understand what has been hurt and what needs mending.

"Fine, I made it to Base Camp, but I'm not sure I can go any farther. I caught a glimpse of the mountains, they're huge, and I quit. I'm heading back down."

In my life I have heard many people quit treatment at this point. I heard them say things such as, "The therapist didn't understand me." "The therapist wasn't smart enough to work with me." "The therapist didn't live through my trauma, so how could he understand?" "Talking about this stuff isn't helping me." As always, I first want to encourage you to really listen to yourself, to that voice within you, about your experience of your helping situation. Do I feel safe here? Can I *in every real and important way*[1] trust this person? And then I want you to look at your statements about the process and ask yourself what it would be like if the opposite were true and see if that would actually be worse. What would it feel like if the therapist actually really understood you? What if the therapist were smart enough to really stay with you and hear what you had to say? What would it feel like to be truly under-stood? For many of you who have experienced trauma, the answers to these questions would probably be equally terrifying. To be witnessed and understood is to take in the truth of what you lived through.

It can be helpful to talk about other times in your life when you have gone for help. These could be stories about parents, teachers, bosses, clergy, fellow soldiers. Who has been helpful to you? Talk about times you reached out. When did it feel helpful? When did someone have the other end of the rope? And when did it feel like they let go and let you fall? Conversations about past experiences of help and your experiences of disappointment with help strengthen both your and your therapist's understanding of what it means for you to get help and allows both of you to have compassion for the process of building trust. As a therapist, I found it helpful to hear someone say, "Yeah, my last therapist was silent all the time and just stared at me; I hated it." Okay, I'll be more active, then. Or, I could just as easily hear the opposite: "My counselor talked all the time, just lecturing me." Okay, I'll hold the lectures. As a client I can remember the first session when my therapist asked me what my expectations were, and I answered, "I don't want to be fixed." This was in response to my previous experiences of help where I felt like everyone had an answer or an exercise or a protocol for my problems before they ever talked to me long enough to find out what my problems were. Your previous experience of helping can give you a lot of information about what works best for you and what doesn't.

All of these conversations at Base Camp are a chance for you and your therapist or your fellow group members to get to know one another. No single conversation is the answer to anything, but instead each conversation allows each of you to know yourselves and each other better. Each conversation gives each of you a chance to be real, authentic—not for some higher idea, but in the service of your growth, in the service of your healing from trauma.

This hard work at lower altitudes is important because there are difficult stretches ahead. I remember one conversation a few years into our work together when I was having a really hard time and my therapist looked at me and said, "We have to figure this out. It is just you and me here." And the weight of that statement, "It is just you and me here," hit me. I could feel the conversations we had had and the trust we were building. I could feel the responsibility, not unlike the belayer and climber, that we had for each other. I could feel the responsibility she felt for me in that moment, and could feel that she wasn't letting go of the rope. And I could feel, maybe for the first time, my responsibility in the relationship. That I needed to find my handholds and footholds and be responsible for the climb. That's what your bravery in these early conversations will do for you. It will help you learn about yourself, and it will help you build the important relationship skills that you need to make this long, important, and difficult journey.

Resources—The Things We Need and the Things We Carry

They carried all the emotional baggage of men who might die. Grief, terror, love, longing—these were intangibles, but the intangibles had their own mass and specific gravity, they had tangible weight. They carried shameful memories. They carried the common secret of the cowardice barely restrained, the instinct to run or freeze or hide, and in many respects this was the heaviest burden of all, for it could never be put down, it required perfect balance and perfect posture.

TIM O'BRIEN, *The Things They Carried*[1]

In one of my early clinical placements I worked in an elementary school in Boston. I had to pick up each of my child clients at their classroom and walk them back to the office. And from the beginning, each time I picked up one little seven-year-old boy, Brian, he would reach into his pocket and pull out something to show me. It might be a marble, a paper clip, or a miniature Buzz Lightyear doll. Each week he had carried something from home to share with me. Part offering, part talisman, and perhaps a representation of some aspect of himself that needed strengthening or support. Of course he carried more into the office than that, but the things he pulled from his pocket helped us know where to start.

One way to think about resources is *what do you bring with you?* And another way to think about it is *what do you have to support you?* And maybe the bigger question is what do you as the explorer need to bring to the work of your healing from long-term trauma in order to safely make the journey and successfully become whole?

You need to consider some important resources as you spend time here in the Preparation phase. The first things to consider are the resources that are outside you that can support you. You need to be living in relative safety; you can't be experiencing trauma and also heal from it simultaneously. If you are still living in trauma, then you still need the protections that help you survive. You need your protections—the plywood or bricks that you put over your windows to protect you from hurricane-force winds. It is not helpful or safe to take those protections down if the hurricane is going to continue. If you are still in an unsafe situation, the work you need to do is not yet about healing from trauma; the work you need to do is about getting to safety. A country can't heal from a war that is still raging.

If you are not living in a safe situation, the first priority of your work of healing is to get into a safe living situation—and this should be the discussion that you have with your therapist, guide, or group. These support people can work with you to connect you to the proper resources in your community so you can move toward safety. It takes a lot of courage to leave a familiar bad situation and move to an unknown situation. It also takes a lot of work and a lot of persistence.

If you have established a safe living situation, then the next aspects to focus on are food, shelter, supportive relationships, and meaningful activity. Healing from trauma can be disorienting and destabilizing, and you need your own personal version of Base Camp to return to as you do this work. You need to be taking care of yourself—eating nutritious food to keep you healthy and give you energy. You need shelter, a place to live, and you need to know where you are staying. But shelter also means "a place giving temporary protection from bad weather or danger"—and you need this kind of shelter too. A place where you know that you can take a time-out if you need to—your bedroom, the bathroom, a walk around the block, your favorite park. You need to identify some places you can go where you can feel safe and soothed, where you can recharge your batteries if you need to.

In addition to identifying safe places to take a time-out, it's also important to identify the people in your world who can support your healing process. Some of these people may be actively supporting you right now—they may be your therapist or your primary care doctor. They may be your spouse or your partner. Some of these people you may choose to talk to about the trauma work you are doing, and some people may be part of your supportive relationships because their presence in your life helps you and they may never know about the trauma work you are doing. Trauma work is difficult and can stir up difficult emotions, making you want to isolate yourself. Having a supportive network of relationships is one important way to keep you connected to the present and strengthen your ability to manage stress with support. One way I like to think of this support network is the same way that elite cyclists think of their support network for the Tour de France. The cyclists each identify a team of people who make it possible for them to complete the race: coaches and trainers and physical therapists and bicycle mechanics and drivers. So who needs to be on your healing team? Your team—Team [Your Name Here]—is just like the cyclist's team. Let them know, if you can, that they are on your team—update them on your progress if you feel comfortable, ask them for support when you feel like your energy is low or the despair creeps in, and hey, make T-shirts if it will make the whole thing more fun.

The last major outside resource to have in place is meaningful activity. Trauma can deeply challenge your belief system. Healing from trauma can bring you in contact with difficult feelings of hopelessness and despair. Meaningful activity is the ballast that can hold you up as you encounter these feelings; it reminds you that you survived the storm and have made it to dry land. Meaningful activity can throw you a rope when you feel yourself being pulled back under by the past.

Many years ago, while working at a counseling clinic in the city, I had two clients who were similar in terms of age and struggles, but they differed significantly in terms of having meaningful activity. One of the women, Vivian, was depressed and had a chronic illness, but she still worked every day as a cook at a nursing facility, and she was the primary caregiver for her daughter's three children. She struggled with poverty and keeping the lights and heat on, but she worked hard to figure out how she could cope to help her grandkids and keep her job. The other woman, Wanda, was also depressed and had a chronic illness. She lived alone and her grown kids lived on the other side of the country. She spent most of her time at medical appointments. Unlike Vivian, Wanda didn't have any real meaningful activity in her life. She didn't have any contact with people that wasn't connected to treatment in some way. An important part of her healing was reconnecting with hobbies and volunteering so that she could experience not just her illness but also her strengths and her impact on others.

The only person who can tell you whether the activity you are engaged in is meaningful is you. This isn't about someone else's notion of meaningful. It's not about money. It's not about success. The activity can be work or it can be family responsibilities. The work can be paid or unpaid. The meaningful activity helps you connect to the current world and allows you to learn about and appreciate your capacities, both strengths and challenges. It brings you into contact with yourself and your values and passions. In my experience, the more your meaningful activity allows you to connect with your purpose, values, and passion, the more it will serve you as ballast in your work of healing. This means that sometimes it is not your job but your volunteer work that supports you the most. Or your role as grandparent, dog walker, community service worker, or crossing guard that supports you. You can be the owner of the company or the receptionist, the salesperson or the janitor. Meaningful activity is a requirement for healing because it gives you a solid anchor in the present, which allows you to explore the past without getting stuck there. It allows you to explore the past and maintain your hope and optimism, which can give you a connection to and hope for the future.

Those are the resources outside you, but what about the resources that you carry inside you? These important internal resources act like a power source to keep you going on your journey—especially when the going gets tough. These internal resources are willingness, hope, gratitude, and perseverance.

Willingness is the desire to show up and try. It is the energy that keeps you showing up. Showing up for treatment, showing up on your own behalf, showing up in your life using new skills and behaviors. Willingness is an energy force. You don't have to be good at anything or know how to do something; you just have to be willing. Willingness is a habit that is fueled by hope—and amazingly, willingness can carry you through periods when your hope is low. In times of more hope, you fuel your willingness batteries through practice and habit. In more difficult times, willingness gets you to the next vista of hope.

Hope is the opposite of despair; it is the expected outcome that is positive, a vision of a different state, a different positive experience, an achieved goal. It is the ability to hold the picture of something that is not yet there, to hold the feeling that it is possible. Hope doesn't have to be realistic. These are the dreams and visions of childhood that help us practice and learn, the way we want to be an astronaut or a firefighter. It doesn't matter if you will never actually be an astronaut, because the hope of becoming one is what gets you to learn math and apply to college. It helps you explore the limits of your desires. Hopes work until they don't. Sometimes reality makes a hope impossible. At five feet ten inches, I can no longer hope to be a gymnast, for example.

I have found ways to grow hope. The best place to find hope for the future is in the present. The two practices that can best rebuild hope are mindfulness and gratitude. Mindfulness, as I mentioned earlier, is the practice of just being with wherever you are—paying attention in this moment to whatever is going on. The easiest practice of mindfulness is just paying attention to your breathing. I know it can sound remarkably simple, but one breath at a time, you can see that a future exists. In your worst moments, life can just seem unbearable. Like you can't get through another minute. You can't imagine that things will be different. But the practice of breathing and being with the breath can build a bridge from a hopeless place to a hopeful place. By breathing in this moment, and then this one, and then this one, you get to the next minute. And then the next. You get to the future that was impossible minutes ago and you realize that maybe the next minute might be possible too. Your hope horizon may only be a minute or two, but that's okay. Sometimes breathing simply gets you to a place where something else distracts you from your despair: You notice the play of light on the table, you can hear a bird sing, you can feel that you are hungry and wonder what you will eat for dinner. Your thoughts for a moment are not of despair and you can take in, just for a moment, that pain is intermittent, and that you can get a break from it. Mindfulness slows you down enough to take in what is around you.

When you can't imagine a future or generate positive hopeful emotions about it, it can be helpful to focus on gratitude for the things you have in the present. *Gratitude* is an old practice but has gained traction recently thanks to new research. It turns out that the practice of gratitude, like the practice of mindfulness, is serious medicine for our hearts and our outlook on life. As the researchers of gratitude, Robert Emmons and Michael McCullough, remind us, gratitude comes from the Latin word *gratia*, meaning "grace." At a yoga retreat I went to once, the instructor defined grace as "an unmerited divine benediction." Grace is the experience of getting a gift that is unconditional—something for nothing, something just because you exist.

Emmons and McCullough studied gratitude in two different scenarios.[2] First, they studied a group of collegiate participants in one of three conditions: a gratitude cohort, a hassles cohort, and a neutral cohort. For ten weeks participants filled out a weekly report. All groups filled out an assessment of well-being consisting of mood, emotional coping, physical symptoms, time spent exercising, and two overarching questions about how they felt about their life over the past week. At the end of the assessment, each cohort had a different question to answer. The gratitude cohort wrote down up to five things that they were grateful for over the past week; the hassles cohort wrote down five hassles they experienced over the past week; and the neutral cohort wrote down five events that impacted them that week. The results of this study showed that the participants in the gratitude group felt better about their lives and had more optimism about their upcoming week. Gratitude increased hope.

Emmons and McCullough's second study shifted the time frame. Instead of weekly diaries about gratitude, the study was two weeks long with daily diaries. Similar to the first experiment, the gratitude cohort and the hassles cohort listed five items each. The third cohort in this study was a downward social comparison—listing ways that you are better off than someone else. In this more intensive time frame, the results showed that the gratitude cohort experienced significant benefits: they had more positive moods and were more likely to help others. When the researchers replicated the study, extending the time frame from two weeks to three weeks, they found these results as well as improved sleep. All of these positive results were derived from simply listing what the participants were grateful for.

My gratitude practice is what I call "gratitude beads." Actually they are Buddhist prayer beads that I bought a few years ago in Bouddanath, near Kathmandu, Nepal. My whole experience there was one of grace—of unmerited divine benediction. On the flight to Kathmandu I was befriended by a Buddhist monk who appointed himself my tour guide of Bouddanath and his monastery—and even joined me, with his young attendant monk, for a spaghetti dinner at my hotel. I started the gratitude bead practice because I had the beads but didn't know any particular prayers—Buddhist or otherwise. I was raised without formal religion. My neighborhood was Catholic, and I did memorize the Lord's Prayer from a school book so that I could join in when I was whisked into five o'clock mass with my neighbors—who gathered any nearby children into their station wagon at four thirty on Saturday. But the

Lord's Prayer didn't seem to match the many beads on the string, so instead I started a practice of sitting with the beads and saying something I am grateful for at each of the 108 beads. In the traditional Buddhist prayer—you say your mantra at each bead, saying it 100 times, with the extra 8 added to cover any mistakes. I have no rules about it other than to say something at each bead. I have been grateful for weather, flowers, watermelon, and often the people in my life. Being grateful for 108 things each morning reminds me of my life riches—and the coolest thing is that I feel the abundance of the world. I am grateful for daffodils, even if I only have one, but in the act of gratitude I feel the riches of all daffodils.

As a therapist I often assigned gratitude practice as homework. I didn't make my clients do 108, only 3. I asked them to write down three things each evening that they were grateful for or that made them happy. The results were astounding. Their reports were consistent. As they went through the process they noticed at first that it was easy, and then it got more difficult, and then they noticed a tremendous shift: they noticed that they were aware during the day of attending to the things that they were grateful for and that made them happy. They wondered as things occurred: Could this be one of my grateful items? Their eyes, ears, and hearts were now on the lookout for gratitude, not disappointment. Their brains were rewiring themselves for the good things in their lives. It's much easier to find or resurrect hope in the feeling of abundance that gratitude provides.

Gratitude can support your work in healing and your work in daily life. As a consultant I do leadership development work that helps communities tackle trauma and social issues like domestic violence and sexual assault. Recently one group in Alaska embraced the gratitude practice as a whole group—each person made a commitment to send a group email out each week to share the three things that they were grateful for so the group got a chance to hear gratitude from all their members. And as a consulting team we start each work day with a "round of gratitude," which gets our hearts and minds together as a team.

Perseverance is defined as "the continued effort to do something despite difficulty, failure, or opposition." And in healing from repeated trauma you often run into all three at one time or another: difficulty, failure, and opposition (and on your bad days, maybe all three). Aside from living through the trauma, healing from it can be some of the most difficult work you will do. Remember, you are voluntarily heading back to the war zone of your experience. You are the one who does all of the work. Yes, your guides, loved ones, or fellow journeyers support your healing, but only you can do the work, the heavy lifting. But this isn't different from healing in the physical realm. Those of you who have experienced a physical injury, especially a serious physical injury, know that the healing process is difficult. You know that there are long periods of physical therapy. That often this physical therapy increases soreness and pain as it works to restore full functioning. That while you are healing and mending, you are not functioning at your best; you need more rest, more care, more help. It is difficult to remember that healing wounds of the heart, the soul, the self is as at least as painful as healing from a serious physical wound, if not more so. This may be one of the most difficult parts of all. And what is difficult for one survivor of long-term trauma will not be the same for others. For people who were badly hurt for a long time in childhood, there is a good chance you will be relearning attachment—learning basic trust in adulthood. This is a difficult enough thing to learn in childhood—watch any eighteen-month-old separated from her caregiver. And then imagine learning it in adulthood when you can't be picked up, rocked, and carried around. You will find that my description of *difficult* doesn't cut it at all. Those of you who have been badly hurt in adulthood will be challenged to find your identity and try to hold on to who you were before the trauma and who you wanted to be—all that you ever knew about yourself and what you value. You may feel like a part of you died. You may wonder if you can ever regain a sense of self.

Failure is guaranteed at some point. Going back to the metaphor of physical healing, you will always try something that is simply out of your range of ability at that time. You will push yourself too far. You will slide back. You will have to start again. I am not sure healing or even growth is possible without failure. I guarantee that you will slide back. You will do that stupid thing again. You will say that thing to that person again. But you will do it with a different awareness. You will catch yourself sooner. Doing that thing again will feel uncomfortable rather than familiar. When you are on a journey to heal, failures that come from persevering serve a function of learning. It's no different from trying to learn anything. I am relearning to play the guitar at age fifty-one. I make mistakes all the time. They are built into the experience. I make a mistake and try it again. And again. Healing is no different. There is no way to try a new way of being in the world without making mistakes. The antidote here is compassion and kindness. If a child is learning to play the piano, you don't scream at them for every mistake. You just let them play through. Keep going. Persevere.

When you hear friends and family talk about having to go to physical therapy after an injury or a surgery, they talk about it in groans and laughs. They talk about how tough their particular physical therapist is—how hard they made them work, how sore they are—in a way that sounds macho or badass.

This is not the conversation that people typically have about psychological therapy. There is some mistaken notion, especially the worse someone feels, that after a session of psychological therapy you will not be sore, but instead will feel better. As if you were sitting down to talk with an old kindly grandmother or a Hallmark card—and not someone trained to help you heal and stretch and grow.

Psychological therapy is exactly like physical therapy—except it is done though words instead of those colored rubber bands. Old tight habitual muscles are forced to stretch and find new ways of moving. Psychological bones that were broken and healed over are rebroken and reset and then slowly put into use for you to use again. All of this work makes you sore. All of this work requires stretching.

This is where the platitudes from other people become especially annoying because they ask you, "Are you feeling better?" and you want to shout, "No!—I am sore, I feel raw, I'm anxious, I'm trying new things!" The problem is that just like physical therapy, terms like *feeling good* and *feeling bad* don't really tell you anything: you will always feel more sore on your way to feeling functional. We judge physical health by flexibility, strength, and range of motion. Shouldn't we assess psychological health the same way? Someday we may view psychological strengthening as just as badass as we view physical training. When you hear of someone working hard on their issues, say, "Man, that's amazing work—healing is badass!" Watch them smile. You can help change the conversation about psychological healing.

In the definition of perseverance, the idea of opposition is likely imagined as an outside force, to persevere in the face of an "other" pushing against you. And you may find this. As you grow and change, there will be pushback from people in your world; this is true of any change, not just healing from trauma. There may be pushback because change is happening too fast, or not fast enough. The key to this opposition is conversation. You won't have an answer for everything, and whoever loves you will need perseverance as well, but whatever the issue, you can commit to staying in the conversation about it long enough to feel connected about the issue, even if the issue can't yet be resolved or even understood. You can tell each other why this issue is important, and what you hope for by resolving it. Some people or groups or systems may push back on your healing process, and you may decide to take a break from them. You may recognize that their pushback is not out of caring or love or support, and they don't respond to conversation. You may realize that some opposition is really just opposition and take a break from them so that you can get to your own work.

Yes, sometimes the opposition is outside, but from my experience of healing, most often the opposition is within. As Pogo wisely stated, "I have seen the enemy, and it is us." Most of the opposition you face may likely be your own—fear of changing, fear of confronting a past, fear of holding it all in your head at once. Repeated trauma requires you to create a system of defenses that protects you. And these protections were so important. They saved your life. They protected your real self. And now as you try to undo them and try to create a different set of healthy protections that match the present and not the past, you will encounter some of the strongest opposition you have ever met. You will wish the opposition were outside, where you can see it, yell at it, walk away from it. For now, know that perseverance is a crucial ally.

Safe Places

I lived ninety minutes from the college where I was getting my master's, and most of the time I just made the commute from Natick to Springfield each day. But one evening I was leaving later in the afternoon and I knew I had to be back to school very early the next morning, so I asked to stay with the parents of a friend who lived in Amherst, not too far away from Springfield. These parents, Jean and John, didn't know me well, but they happily said yes. Jean offered me something cool to drink when I arrived as a houseguest for the evening, and she made a simple but wonderful dinner of fishcakes made out of potatoes and cod. Their house was comfortable and sprawling, and conversation at dinner was friendly. The guest room was cozy, and as I lay in bed that night I realized that I was in a house where it was not my responsibility to pay attention to anything. At the time I was working as a single staff person on charge all weekend at a residential group home for five emotionally disturbed teenagers. At this job I was not only in charge of safety, I was outnumbered and I rarely slept. Here in this house, there were two caring adults who would answer the door or the phone or take care of any emergency. I knew that Jean and John got along and they weren't in danger from each other—there would be no fighting between them, unlike the house I grew up in. As I lay there in bed I was completely struck by how safe I felt that night. The feeling of safety washed over me with a heaviness that had me sinking deep into the covers. I felt safe. I fell into one of the deepest sleeps I ever recall— even at this writing.

Surviving repeated trauma does not give you the feeling of safety. It gives you the feeling of survival: an ever-present readiness to jump and run. A wariness about everything and everybody. Fear as your constant companion. I'm not knocking survival: it beats the alternative. Survival can give you confidence. But survival is constant vigilance. Survival is exhausting.

Safety is the ability to rest, to settle in, to breathe easily. Safety is the ability to focus on something else besides danger or death. As Judith Herman states in *Trauma and Recovery*, "the central task of the first stage [of recovery] is the establishment of safety."[1] As I have been discussing, the Preparation phase is entirely about attending to safety— attending to it in the present and building the necessary skills, resources, and foundations for safety during the work of healing from trauma and building your foundation to take into the future.

Base Camp is a safe place. A safe place is where you can breathe more easily and repair or mend your needed resources. What is difficult to describe in healing a deep wound, in healing from long-term sustained trauma, is that this place is sometimes a physical place, like the space where you meet with your therapist or your group. It can be a room, an office, or a meeting hall. It can be a real place that nourishes you and brings you peace: a favorite room, a favorite place in nature, a front porch. Sometimes this place is the relationship between you and your therapist in the here and now. It's the feeling that someone has the other end of the rope. Sometimes this place is the experience of the relationship that you carry with you—the comforting relationship you can conjure in your mind, where there is always a comforting voice to remind you that things are okay.

As shown by the way I described my experience at Jean and John's house, of sinking deep into the covers, safety is as much a physiological feeling as a psychological feeling. And I have found that in order to really experience safety, the two need to be linked together. Over the course of my healing journey I used my cognitive skills to practice visualizing safe places, and I used self-talk to say soothing things to myself—but these rarely had the physiological effect that would have me physically experience safety. My brain was ready to believe in safety, but my wounded animal body had no plans in letting go of its vigilance.

That doesn't mean that the practice of safety—using psychological skills of visualization, self-talk, or mindfulness—wasn't helpful. In fact, I think that over the course of time these practices helped me immensely and got me ready to feel safe in incremental amounts. It's just important to recognize that these practices didn't *feel* safe at first; they were practices I did and could use to help me self-regulate a bit. The practices were all part of the Preparation phase. The feeling of safety is an outcome, not an input, in trauma work. You create a safe environment—in mind, body, spirit, emotions, and relationships—and then you practice taking the safety in.

Why is this place so hard to describe? Because human beings are hardwired for connection, and we are hardwired from infancy to find safety in relationships. We are hardwired to seek protection from our caregivers when we are afraid. In fact, seeking connection when we are afraid is the mark of secure attachment in infancy.

Trauma breaks this connection. Trauma interferes with the feelings of safety associated with connection. Reconstruction of trust is the first task of treatment.[2] Most trauma involves an act where one human being turns on another—where the experience of relationship isn't safety but power used for harm. For people hurt badly as children, trusting a caring relationship designed to help them actually feels unsafe. I have seen a similar dilemma in treating Vietnam veterans who felt betrayed by the military and yet had to trust them to provide their treatment through Veterans Affairs.

All I want you to know at this point is that while you are working at Base Camp—while you are learning to lean into the ropes of trust—that *working on safety* and *feeling safe* may not go together. Learning to trust again, or for the first time, is part of the work—it is both a requirement and an outcome of treatment. It's okay to feel scared learning to feel safe.

We started this conversation about the Preparation phase with describing Base Camp as a place to come back to, a place where you can rest and recover. Safety is the state from which we can create health and growth. Safe places need to be plentiful as you do this work: you need multiple touchpoints of safety as you heal. The roots of the word *safety* come from the Latin for "safe" (*salvus*) and "healthy" (*salus*). One of the first places to attend to safety is in your physical body. What would that look like? Feel like? What do you have to do to feel more comfortable in your body? When was the last time you saw your primary care doctor or had a physical? Are you eating nourishing food? Are you getting sleep? Are you taking care of yourself the way you would take care of someone you love? Safety is the environment we need to heal our bodies, minds, and spirits.

By definition, trauma is about feeling helpless and powerless. In healing from trauma it is important that you feel that you can keep yourself safe and feeling safe. Sometimes you have to overcompensate to feel safe (even if logically you *are* safe). For example, there were times in my own healing when it was easier for me to talk when I was covered in a blanket—with my body hidden from view. It was a way for me to feel protected and in control of how exposed I was. I have had clients who had to sit near the door, had to have the door open, and preferred meeting while walking outside, rather than in the office. I have had teenagers who would only talk to me if they could wear sunglasses. None of these acts of self-protection and safety lasted forever. Some lasted weeks; some were used on and off for years, functioning as a way to decrease anxiety enough to get through a difficult piece of work. All were let go, like training wheels, when they were getting in the way of connection or the work, rather than facilitating it.

You will need to work at a pace that you feel is comfortable, and you will need to have a voice about what gets discussed and how much. Your guide doesn't get to move you any faster than you feel comfortable, but they do get to slow you down if they think you will not be safe.

Helpful Practices
for Preparation

Let's review and clarify some helpful practices that can support your work in the Preparation phase. In some ways, the practices that support you best in the Preparation phase are what I call "the work before the work," a phrase a long-ago colleague used to describe the important phase of work or change that had to happen before the work everyone saw or knew about. My first job after college was at Germaine Lawrence, a residential treatment facility for adolescent girls. Germaine Lawrence was a place where "the work before the work" was honored, where they taught me the value and importance of the quiet, small act.

Germaine Lawrence put a lot of time into its staff. That meant that this required something of us: we had to attend four hours of training every two weeks, whether it was our day to work or our day off. This was "the work before the work." They not only trained us in what to do but helped us make the connections about how what we did affected the girls—why it mattered. They explained that when the girls asked for something small, like a glass of water, and we provided it, we were helping the girls reestablish trust by learning that they could ask for something and have it happen. When we brought them a cool washcloth, we were helping them feel cared for. It was our job to help the girls, who often came from violent and chaotic households, relearn their ability to trust in consistency, one small act at a time. At Germaine Lawrence our small acts as child care workers weren't seen as less than; they were seen as one of the primary movers of the treatment. Our work in the dorms provided the foundation of creating a trusting safe place for the work that the therapists could do. The safer that the girls felt with us and in their daily experience, the more likely it was that they could heal their trauma. And it wasn't just theory: it worked. I watched the girls shift in their capacity to lean on adults and begin growing again. They would come into our program wearing the armor of the "tough girl"—they didn't need anyone, they didn't need any help. And then slowly they would let themselves ask, roughly at first: "Get me milk!" And then gradually they would get softer. Without the understanding that all the interactions I was having with them was therapy, I might have misunderstood the many requests of the girls—might have seen them as rude, or pushy, or needy, not as the necessary way to soften their defenses. I learned to really feel good about the small acts of my job and feel like I was contributing to the work of healing these girls. I learned that there is a lot more to healing than what most people imagine. I learned to appreciate the work before the work. And in some deep way I learned that the rest of the day[1] was as important to their healing as the one hour of therapy that was provided. I learned that healing was about creating an environment of healing: not just what a therapist said, or what medication they prescribed. It may seem confusing that my premise is that you can't heal alone, and now I am emphasizing the fact that while you do have treatment, the other time in the week is just as important to your healing. Healing from repeated trauma is a bit like taking music lessons for your heart and mind. You need to meet with a teacher to teach you how to play your instrument, but once you learn the new scales or notes, you need to practice so you can build on them every day to strengthen your skills. In the Preparation phase, anything that helps you build self-awareness, strengthen your resources, or practice leaning into the therapeutic relationship—and your own experience of safety—will support your work in preparation.

One of the first practices that I recommend for your work is to practice sitting quietly. This is the step even before meditation—before mindfulness. This is a practice of learning to simply sit and not do anything in particular, and to do so in such a way that you feel comfortable and soothed. I call it *the quiet place*. The quiet place is not a new concept. Almost every organized religion has some concept of this stillness. Prayer and meditation are common examples. These have existed for thousands of years because stillness was useful to the practice of the religion. But how is stillness useful to us? Why be still? From my perspective, stillness, regardless of how you choose to use it, is like letting the water settle in a tidal pool. Suddenly all of the life that lives below the surface, which feeds the health of the whole sea, can be seen clearly. When the water is churned up, the life below the surface can't be seen in it. It doesn't mean it isn't there, it just means that you can't see it. When the water is still, you can see it, and appreciate it, and get a better sense of what lives beneath. And we all know that the water will get choppy again. No sea on earth remains at the same level all of the time. Tides rise and fall; winds pick up. It is all part of it. But learning to create stillness is an important balance to the choppiness we have all learned to create. All of our addictions and busyness keep us away from the rich life below the surface.

In this spirit, perhaps you need to find a comfy chair and wrap your-self in a blanket. Or maybe you will choose to sit on the porch or patio. There is no right place. If you need music to keep yourself soothed and comfortable, that is okay too. (Wordless music would probably be best so that you can be more aware of your own words, but remember that the "music police" will not show up at your door—do what works for you.) I advise the adolescents in my meditation groups to "get into any position that is comfortable to you." For now you are just going to prac-tice the experience of quiet and stillness. Later on you can experiment with more formalized sitting/meditation practices. But right now the goal is not the posture. The goal is the state you are creating for yourself with this practice of sitting quietly: letting yourself just *be* with what-ever comes up.

Okay. You have your comfortable position. "What do I do?" you ask. Just sit. Just notice what it is like to sit. What happens for you? Does your mind wander? What does it wander to? No judgments. Just explorations. It is like looking into a tidal pool. What is below the sur-face? What do you see? Starfish? Seaweed? Nothing? What if you get distracted? Just notice it and go back and look into the tidal pool. What if you get bored? Be bored and look at the tidal pool. How long should you stay in this quiet place? And here I go back to the swimming meta-phor. Stay in the water long enough to stretch your new skills, but not so long that you get overwhelmed or your lips turn blue.

I have found in my work with adolescents and adults who have had either trauma in their childhood or grief work of any kind that learning to sit still is a difficult task and should be broken up into smaller steps. I like to think of it like training wheels for meditation. If sitting in stillness is still too difficult for you because your thoughts race or you find your anxiety level rising, it may be helpful to start with a more structured road into the stillness world. I would recommend using guided meditation tapes, attending yoga classes, using guided imagery techniques, or using a mindfulness app. Increasing structure can help you feel more solid.

Let's give you a realistic range of stillness muscle building. I work with some people who can tolerate only thirty seconds of complete quiet (without some guiding instruction) when they begin to learn how to be still with themselves. If you can sit quietly for only a minute, then do that, and add fifteen seconds the following week. Or sit for the length of a piece of music that helps you slow down. Quiet muscles that have never been used are like atrophied legs that have never been walked on. You will need to rehabilitate them slowly and carefully. But what a sense of reward when you can use them!

"Nothing is happening." This is a common statement. Quiet time is not about making something happen. It is not about becoming someone else, or becoming better, or more enlightened, or anything in particular. It is about knowing what is there. It is very basic and sometimes may even seem boring. That is okay. Have you ever heard a little kid talk about their day at school? She goes on and on, often repeating herself, and as hard as you listen you really can't discern a plot or even really understand what happened. This is like sitting with yourself in the quiet place. The point isn't the content of the story. The point is to be present to listen to the story. To hold the experience for the child. What I am asking you to do is hold your own experience. No matter what it is. There is no right way. There is no performance. Over time this will shift. A child who is able to tell her stories gradually gains confidence in her own voice, and it gets clearer and makes more sense over time. This will happen for you as well.

The quiet place is about sitting within a safe, trusted space. It is about building a relationship with yourself. Over the years I have noticed in my work as a therapist, especially with my child clients who live in precarious situations (foster care, etc.), that relationships, like the quiet place, are very basic but not easy. Trustworthy relationships are really about consistent, benign attendance over time. Even the most severe mistrust gives way to this powerful force. Like water or wind wearing away rock. Attendance over time is almost invisible, but it is transformative. This is where the word *practice* comes in. You must find time daily to go to your quiet place. Maybe it is one minute a day. Maybe it is forty minutes a day. There are monks who do this for three years straight—but even they had to start somewhere. So the quiet place is something that you need to create for yourself that is comfortable, allowed to be whatever it is, and practiced daily.

In addition to *the quiet place*, the Preparation phase is a good place to experiment with other activities or experiences you find soothing; you will need to be able to reliably use soothing practices in Unintegration. Marsha Linehan, in her work with dialectal behavioral therapy,[2] talks about how to soothe with the five senses[3]—and this can be a really good way to start experimenting with what you find soothing. What visual images help you feel better? I keep lots of photos on my phone to look at when I need to shift my state from one that isn't comfortable to one that feels better. What sounds or music help me feel better? Some people find that white noise machines or sound machines that play nature sounds help them feel more relaxed. The Preparation phase is a great time to experiment. Play different tracks of music or sounds and notice what effect they have on your body, your mind, your emotions. In this way you get to experiment with what is soothing and your own self-awareness. With the sense of sound, you can experiment with playlists of music or mindfulness tapes or apps. You can experiment with going for a walk with music and without music—which was more soothing? You can experiment with what is soothing to your sense of touch—cozy blankets, heavy blankets, hot baths, or sitting outside in a cool breeze. If you are comfortable, you can experiment with massage or other touch-based therapies to see how they impact your state of soothing. You can see what is soothing for your sense of smell, and what things you like to eat or drink that are soothing. This is all about experimentation and awareness—just noticing what supports you in your work of healing, and what you don't find helpful right now.

This is also a time to experiment with what helps you *show up* in your work in therapy. Learn what helps you show up in the literal sense—practical things like a schedule you can manage, making sure you have someone to watch your kids, or allowing enough time to travel to your appointments. But once you are there, what helps you bring yourself in? This is similar to the earlier conversation about what is soothing, but it is related to what helps you feel more relaxed in seeking help. Earlier I talked about kids needing to talk from underneath a blanket, or clients bringing a spouse with them on the first visit. When I worked with teenagers who had difficulty making eye contact, we used to let them wear sunglasses so that they could calibrate how "seen" they wanted to be as they got to know me. And while this book is geared primarily toward clients, I will say that the most important way a therapist can help a client show up is to meet them where they are—start at their ability to talk, at what they need to bring themselves into the room and into the conversation.

Let them set the agenda. This is not the same as being a blank slate or being completely silent. I once worked with a client for six weeks, and during that time she spoke only one word. Just the word "Word." And I worked with other children who never spoke, or took a year to speak.

They used actual silence to be quiet. Some clients need silence, and they bring it with them. But silence, like wind, comes in all forms. Silence can look like so many things. I have had other child clients who were noisy and chatty and yet they too, really, said nothing. Their families lived with the "code of silence" typical of the neighborhoods I worked in, and their talk, their conversation was a fluent art of conversational silence. It was *as if* you had a conversation, but you didn't. Teenagers are often good at this conversational silence. They are good at answering questions with descriptions like *fine, good, not much, weird, maybe, yeah,* and most telling—*nothing.*

My child clients who lived with the "code of silence" needed some chatter to feel *at rest* in my presence. They needed to not feel so much under a spotlight. I think silence was long taught and understood as a means of not being obtrusive—not interfering in someone's ability to talk. But silence isn't always quiet. It can be blaringly loud if you aren't used to it or if it feels dangerous. People who have stayed away from their fears for years need to gradually approach them—and silence can be like being in a locked cage with their worst fears.

In the field of psychology there is often a lot of discussion of silence—what it means and when it should be used. But I think it is too literally discussed and too literally understood. I think it is important to understand the need for silence—What does it do? What is silence?—and how it can serve healing and growth, whether you are the client or the therapist. When you are the client, silence offers you either protection or space. If you bring silence, you protect your truths—from others hearing them and, usually more importantly, from you having to hear them. Silence in any form means *I don't have to deal with that yet.* And silence can offer you space—space to "just be" without having to be anything in particular. It is a blank canvas—and you can stretch out in it and figure things out.

But the first mistake, I think, is that we think of silence as sound. I think it is more useful to think of silence as *rest*. As a space that you can relax into, like a hammock. Where you feel safe, or calm, or interested—the way babies look when they are happy in those little backpack carriers. I focus on this state of rest because a relaxed brain is a thinking brain and a learning brain. A relaxed brain can gain some perspective. A relaxed brain can heal. Sometimes it is *actual* silence that helps, and sometimes it is something that looks the furthest from silence that helps this. I think of times I have had big writing projects and sought out coffee shops to write in so that my mind could rest on the background white noise of coffee shop chatter. Everyone needs a different way of finding where their brain can relax and be in the state it needs for growth, conversation, creation, or healing. I have found that for people who have lived through trauma, the ability to modulate how you are heard and when you get to speak is not only important but a big piece of the healing.

PART 3

Unintegration

We think that the point is to pass the test or to overcome the problem, but the truth is that things don't really get solved. . . . They come together and they fall apart.

PEMA CHÖDRÖN, *When Things Fall Apart: Heart Advice for Difficult Times*[1]

Unintegration

The two temples at Abu Simbel built by King Ramses II during the thirteenth century BC had to be moved out of reach of the rising waters of Lake Nasser created by the Aswan High Dam in the 1960s. The two temples consisted of the Great Temple, dominated by a façade of sixty-foot colossal statues of the king, and the Small Temple, which has four massive statues of Ramses and two of Nefertiti. In order to save the temples from being submerged by Lake Nasser, a multicountry, multiagency partnership worked together to create a plan. This took much time, planning, and preparation, not unlike the Preparation phase to help to heal from trauma, described in Part 2— there was "extensive geological and geotechnical investigation and determination of internal stresses and locations of fissures in the sandstone."[1] To support the integrity of the temple as they were dismantling it, they placed steady steel scaffolding inside the temple rooms, put provisional landfill in front of each temple façade, and excavated and removed all of the rock above the temple.[2] Extensive drawings were made of the temple from every vantage point so that the moved temple would remain in relation to the cardinal points: the sun would grace the faces of the statues in the same spot at the same time of day. The drawings would allow the blocks to be cut so that their size and weight could be assessed, as well as for the impact of what they were—faces of statues, for example. But once the preparatory work was done, the group worked out a way to cut up both the temple façade and the temple walls into huge blocks. "The sculpted faces were to be left whole when possible and no frieze separated at a place of particular fragility. . . . The sanctuary ceilings, which had, for generations, held themselves together according to the basic principles of an arch would slowly be sliced and stored, taking the arch effect with them."[3] The smallest of the blocks weighed twenty tons. Each block was numbered and stored. After the blocks were moved to higher ground, both temples were reconstructed block by block. It was careful work.

Unintegration is the second phase in the Cycle of Healing Repeated Trauma, following the Preparation phase. I know *Unintegration* is a long and somewhat cumbersome word, but it fits the experience better than any other word I can find. Unintegration is not demolition but instead describes the "coming apart" that is both intended and supported. The temples at Abu Simbel were *unintegrated*. They did not *disintegrate*, nor were they knocked down. They were taken apart, attending to the weak spots in the wall and the vibrational force of the tools. They were dismantled carefully so that they could be put back together again in a stronger state. Each block that was removed was strengthened at the time of removal through reinforcement and was carefully inspected and, wherever required, strengthened again. Unintegration is an important phase—it is about dismantling, but it is also strengthening. So let's spend some time learning about Unintegration—and understanding this important phase of healing.

I first came across the word *unintegration* as a doctoral student reading D. W. Winnicott.[4] Winnicott is famous for his work with mothers and children, and he uses the term to describe a part of healthy development that most infants or children go through. According to Winnicott, unintegration was important because it was a space where the child felt relaxed and safe enough to let go of feeling the need to hold himself together and allow all of the pieces that made up the child, the ones that were solid, the ones that were growing, the ones that were just on a learning edge—all of the feelings, thoughts, experiences—to come together so that the child could experience himself as whole.[5] He describes the typical scene of a toddler resting on his mother's lap. I have such a perfect image of this with my niece Jesse when she was just two years old, sitting on my sister-in-law's lap at the end of the day as all of the adults were talking. She had just had a bath and was wrapped in a towel, her blue eyes looking at the rest of us some of the time, and dozing some of the time. She was held and comforted but not the center of attention. In modern parlance she was "hanging out."

Winnicott defines unintegration as a resting state. Mark Epstein, a psychiatrist who writes about therapy and Buddhism, compares this resting state to meditation—a state of *non-being*.[6] In some ways you can see this resting state as both a state of *being*, that is, being with whatever is, and a state of *non-being*, in that you don't have to *be* anything in particular: you allow yourself to bring all aspects of yourself together in one place. You rest in the hammock of yourself, without *pulling yourself together*. What supports this experience is a *holding environment*.

In the case of a child, that holding environment is a parent or caregiver and the safe space that they provide. In the case of someone healing from trauma, that holding environment is the relationship you have with your therapist, guide, or therapeutic group. As discussed in Part 2 on the Preparation phase, this holding environment is about creating a safe space that can be trusted and leaned on, where the climbing ropes are connected—not too loose, not too tight. It is where, as Winnicott describes, you can *rest* and let all of the pieces come together in one place.

So far, the description of unintegration as a place of rest sounds relaxing. Though it is the state where disparate parts come together, it is an experience of being held and being whole. And this is where Winnicott's description of unintegration in normal development and the experience of unintegration in the healing of trauma are different. The action or activity is the same: lean on a holding environment and allow all of the parts of you to come apart so they can knit together. The experiences, however, are vastly different. In healthy development, unintegration can feel like reverie, but in healing from trauma, most often unintegration will feel like a crisis.

In the Preparation phase, you work hard to solidify the strengths within yourself and within the relationship with your therapist to feel safe. You begin to lean on this safety by talking about the trauma, your feelings, and what your experiences are now. You even spend time talking about what is getting in the way of your ability to talk. And all of this safety, this strong holding environment, allows you to let go of the things that you were using to protect yourself. You may let down some of your walls.

This is the irony of unintegration: it is not a crisis that makes you feel bad. It is the safety. It is the safety that allows you to do the work that triggers (or really allows) the feelings of an *old crisis*. When you allow the pieces to come apart, it can feel like you are falling apart because you let yourself lean on safety. Winnicott contrasts unintegration—a relaxed state of coming apart to reconnect—with disintegration. Disintegration isn't planful coming apart, but falling apart in crisis. Unintegration is the coming apart or falling apart you can experience when you feel safe enough to experience an *old crisis*, whereas disintegration is the falling apart that can happen in a *current crisis* or in a state of overwhelm.

Let's look at real examples of disintegration and unintegration. I'm going to start with disintegration and tell you the story of Stephanie, who came to see me because she was struggling with anxiety and with her schoolwork in college. When we first met, she explained that she had experienced childhood trauma and had worked with a therapist before. She wanted to focus initially on her symptoms of anxiety and her strategies for being more organized as a college student. In the first few sessions we worked together to develop some self-care systems to help with her anxiety and some organizational strategies for her schoolwork. This focus fits the work of the Preparation phase and, given her high level of anxiety and her history of trauma, was the right place to be focusing our energy initially. But the next week, Stephanie didn't show up for her session. She called a few days later and said that she had overdosed on her ADHD medication and gone to the emergency room. She also said she was at risk of getting evicted from her apartment, she had let an old boyfriend move in who was constantly drunk and refusing to leave, and she was worried that she was likely to fail a class. Stephanie was in crisis on at least three different fronts; she was in a state of disintegration because her crisis existed in the present day. It wasn't an old crisis (even if it may have mirrored one), but a current crisis, and thus her work in therapy would not be trauma work but instead the work of stabilizing her life.

Now let's look at Kelly's story to see the contrast with unintegration. Kelly came to see me initially because she had a serious eating disorder. We spent nearly two years working together to help her get her eating and weight issues under control. She often canceled her appointments, but as her eating and weight stabilized, she became more consistent in her attendance and was able to talk about her reluctance to let the relationship with me matter. She was also gradually able to talk more about the issues that led to her eating disorder, including an abusive childhood. Not long after her more consistent attendance and our conversations about her childhood, Kelly announced that she was moving to Denver, where she had a friend who could help her get work. I asked her why she wanted to move and she said that she "just had to get away." Over the course of the next few meetings she was able to talk about the feelings of fear and rage that had started to come up in talking about her childhood: anger at what had happened to her. But not just anger. She was also aware that the closer she felt to me, the more afraid she was that I would leave her the way her father did. She said that she wanted to leave me first.

Kelly had leaned on a healing relationship and let the weight of her protections come off. But then she began to feel the crisis she had lived in as a child. This is an example of unintegration. By sharing her history and leaning on the relationship, she experienced the fear of abandonment that went with her history. This was an old crisis that revealed itself in the present because she was in a safe enough environment to let her walls down, and she was safe enough to let herself feel it. My job as her therapist was to help her hold the old crisis without creating a current crisis. We talked about her plans to move and negotiated that she delay it for one year. Kelly agreed to continue our work for a year, and then make a steady and planned transition to Denver.

The problem is that disintegration and unintegration can feel exactly the same when they happen, and often it won't be clear which one is happening. You came to treatment to heal your trauma and to feel better. And in the beginning you did feel better. But now the harder you work at healing, the worse you may feel. This is the experience that often has people wanting to quit treatment—it can be challenging to work so hard and feel worse rather than better. And in some ways, I wonder if those of us in the psychology field haven't done a good enough job helping people understand the process and what the experience of working through trauma can feel like. So many people feel destabilized when they hit the Unintegration phase and then feel like they did something wrong.

Unintegration doesn't happen because something goes wrong. In fact, it can be a real sign that things are going right—that you have worked hard to create a safe and solid platform in your life and in your relationship with your therapist or group. Unintegration happens because it's safe enough to do repair work on an old crisis. Yes, unintegration can feel like a crisis. But it is a planned crisis, in that you are actually often working very hard to do the things you need to do in order to feel safe enough to fall apart. It is a measured crisis in that you will be looking at the amount of stress you can manage. And it is a supported crisis (I know this sounds like a contradiction) where, unlike the trauma you lived through where there was no help or support, you now have a support network to help you navigate these waters.

But for all of this—the work, the planning, the care, the support—it will not feel good. In fact, often it will feel bad. The feelings in this phase can feel like a real betrayal. Nothing really prepares you for the experience of it. One minute you are walking on solid ground, and the next, *whomp*, you feel like you are in an absolute tailspin. Some signs that you are in this stage: you may feel really uncomfortable or you can't find any way to get comfortable, nothing feels right, you are cranky or irritable for no apparent reason, nothing seems to make you feel better. Just yesterday you felt like you had your bearings, and today you don't. There is little that prepares you for this state. You don't so much choose to enter it as much as it happens to you. It is almost as if when your unconscious feels sufficiently solid and held, it decides to just leap. You won't know when it is coming. This stage can catch you off guard, which, because you are a trauma survivor, is the very thing that you hate.

What makes this experience all the more confusing is that all of your hard work in the Preparation phase may have made your life more solid than it has been in years, or ever. Your addiction may be in remission, you may have a much more quiet and safe life, you may have a new and better-paying job. Your life looks good! You may find yourself asking, *Why do I suddenly feel so off balance?*

The Unintegration phase is like opening the junk drawer of your emotional world. For years you just stuffed whatever you didn't want to think about or feel in this drawer. Now you are opening it, and stuff is coming out. Most often, what comes out are the emotions we fear and aren't good at managing. For many, these are feelings of sadness, depression, vulnerability. For others, they are anger or rage. For almost everyone who has experienced trauma, they are often helplessness and shame. In the Unintegration phase, you slowly and carefully pull each thing out of the drawer.

The state that supports unintegration is similar to the mindfulness practice we discussed in the section on awareness in Part 2. Remember, mindfulness meditation isn't easy for trauma survivors. It's a healing medicine, but it needs to be taken in manageable doses. There is a similarity between the restful state of mindfulness and the restful state within the healing relationship. In mindfulness, you are essentially resting on a relationship within yourself. And in the Unintegration phase, you are resting on the actual healing relationship with others. In both situations you are resting, as if you were in a hammock, leaning on security and calm. Both meditation and unintegration are states where one is exposed to what is there: they are states of stillness within the environment. And as I mentioned about mindfulness, when trauma survivors sit quietly, they are often exposed to the difficult experiences they lived through. For people who have had relatively peaceful lives, the experience of unintegration can sometimes feel relatively pleasant. For people who have experienced repeated trauma, the experience of unintegration, at first, and for a long while, can be very uncomfortable. For some people, when the water gets still and clear, they see starfish; for others, they see sharks.

Understanding Attachment

In Part 2 on the Preparation phase, we talked about connecting with your therapist and guide, and we began the conversation about trust and what it takes to build trust. Now I want to take that conversation a little deeper. When you first start on your healing journey and you get help, it can look fairly simple. *This person is there to help me. I am an adult—how hard could this be?* And actually, that's a great attitude to have. In the beginning it can feel comforting and supportive. But here in the Unintegration phase you may discover that what seemed simple feels complicated. You may experience how difficult it can be to talk or trust. Or, you may be surprised or overwhelmed at how important therapy and the therapy relationship have become—*Why is this person or my emotions taking up so much time and space? Why does trusting someone feel dangerous or scary instead of being helpful?* In Part 2 we talked about the need for safety and how important it was to create the experience of safety in your life and in the relationships in your life and with your therapist. And we also talked about how that isn't as easy as it sounds—how the *experience of safety* and *the feeling of safety* don't always go together when you are trying to heal from trauma. How trust can paradoxically feel unsteady or dangerous. So here in the Unintegration phase we are going to look at how we understand safety and connection in relationships—and how these things have been affected by trauma.

How can you learn or relearn about safety? How can you build relationships that are healthy and feel good? How can you use your connections to others to support your ability to calm, soothe, and steady yourself? Why is a healing relationship crucial to healing from trauma? The answer to these questions falls into the area of attachment. Attachment is its own whole area of research and study and I am not going to cover it all in this book, but I want you to have an idea of where it came from and how understanding the components of attachment can support the work you are doing from healing from trauma.

The study of attachment got its beginnings after World War II as psychologists started looking at the aftereffects of children having been separated from their parents during the war. Prior to this the psychology of child development—how we become who we are—wasn't really studied on actual children but instead in kind of a rearview-mirror way by looking at how adults remembered challenges in their childhood. But after World War II, this new group of psychologists looked at *actual* children and their difficulties and began to understand something fundamental about how we organize ourselves and our relationships and how we understand the world.

One of these psychologists was John Bowlby, who studied children who had been placed in care, away from their parents.[1] You may remember that in England during World War II, parents in London sent their children to live in the countryside with other families or in children's homes. Parents did this for all of the best and most hopeful reasons: because they wanted to protect their children from the dangers and horrors of war. As it turned out, however, the children who were separated from their parents and sent to the country actually suffered more distress than the children who remained with their parents but were exposed to the violence of war. The research showed that there is something both fundamental and essential to our growth, well-being, and capacity to manage stress that we get from our primary relationships—and this began the study of attachment that continues today.

We think of attachments as our relationships or connections—what are commonly called *intimate relationships*. But attachment is much more than that. Attachment is a whole *system* that operates inside us. When I was in high school I took a computer programming class— this was in the dark ages of computers when the room next to the computer room was filled entirely with large mainframe computers. These were not iPads. They were Buicks. We learned to program in BASIC (Beginner's All-purpose Symbolic Instruction Code, a simple computer language) and solve math problems and create rudimentary computer games.

This was in an era before personal computers, and I went off to college with my high school graduation present of an electric Olivetti typewriter. I majored in German literature and didn't think much more about computers until many years later, when I had shifted into the study of psychology and was writing my master's thesis and had to program and run my own statistics for the data analysis. So there I sat in the basement computer room of the college with the two phone-book-sized manuals of SPSS, the statistics program at the time, to write the computer program. Not knowing anything more than the BASIC I had been taught in high school, I found that with basic (BASIC) mental scaffolding of how the computer worked, I could decode any computer program—even if I had to use the help screens to do it. BASIC provided the scaffolding to understand the way a computer "thought" and responded. When something wasn't working, I knew where to look and what command it was looking for. BASIC allowed me to understand the expectations of the computer and how to approach problem solving with it, even if I was unsure of what I needed to do.

One way to think about attachment is that it is sort of a BASIC operating system for humans. It is a relational and emotional operating system on which all of the other systems have been built. And just like your computer, when there is a problem with the operating system, every other program and process is affected by it. If you think about attachment as an operating system, you can see why almost every aspect of your healing work is both dependent on it and affected by it. You can also see that even if some of your more difficult symptoms may be better—you aren't having as many flashbacks, or you are sleeping better—you may also feel like things such as your relationships or your mood are still difficult. Appreciating the central function of attachment can help you appreciate why rebuilding trust and your own system of self-regulation can be so hard but rewarding. Attachment is a series of processes that have functioned throughout human evolution and history as both a system of safety and a system of self-regulation.[2] Ideally, you form a secure attachment system during infancy and early childhood, and this system then forms the blueprint or scaffolding for all future relationships throughout your life, for how you are able to regulate your mood under stress, and for your general worldview.

So how does this operating system of attachment work? And how does trauma affect this attachment operating system? In terms of trauma, at its most basic level, you need to understand that repeated trauma shatters your experience of trust and relationships. Trauma is first and foremost about an extreme experience of helplessness—of being totally alone and without support at a moment of terror, fear, or physical threat. That experience can destroy your trust in other people and what you expect from other people. But trauma can also destroy your own trust in yourself—in who you think you are as a person. This is true even when the thing that is terrifying isn't even another person—when it is a hurricane or a disease. But most repeated traumas are traumas that are perpetrated *inside a relationship*—by other people—whether the perpetrator is an individual or a group. This is the trauma of child abuse, sexual abuse, clergy abuse, domestic violence, gang violence, police violence, genocide, and war. Most repeated trauma is *repeated relational trauma*, and therefore what is badly damaged is your experience of relationships, your understanding of relationships, and your capacity to use relationships to grow and heal. If your trauma happened in childhood, quite often you never got to have an experience of a safe, secure attachment. You may feel like you have to be vigilant about your relationships, always worrying that people will leave you. Or you may believe that you don't need anyone, that you can and must do everything yourself. If your trauma happened in adulthood, quite often your belief in the safety in relationships was shattered or altered. You may feel like you don't know who you can trust. Or you may feel like your trauma has made *you* untrustworthy or that you must hide your experience of trauma in order to protect the relationships that you are in.

Attachment can be affected by things that you might not call "trauma," and these things need not be intentional. The main crux of the matter is whether an infant or child's biological and psychological needs are generally met and he or she is not left in an untenable state of distress. This can be affected as much by neglect as by anything you might call abusive (indeed, sometimes more). And some trauma can also be due to parental depression, illness, or other familial catastrophe that interferes with parental attention of the infant.

And the paradox is that this system—the attachment system—is one of the greatest casualties of repeated trauma, and it is also the main pathway that must be used to heal from the trauma. It is both what needs to be mended and the source of healing, and therein lies the difficulty. The part of you that is hurt, vulnerable, and at times pretty raw is exactly the thing that must be worked with in order to heal from trauma. Some of you may be building a healthier attachment system for the first time, and some of you may be repairing an attachment system that was torn or broken. Either way, you will be working with your attachment system in relationships. Remember, no one heals alone.

WHAT IS THE ATTACHMENT SYSTEM?

The attachment system is a biological, psychological, and social-behavioral system made up of three main factors. It was designed to have you seek out caregivers or social support under stress (proximity seeking); help you experience safety and security that helps you manage and soothe your difficult emotions and increase your positive emotions—experiences that become part of your biology and neurology (safe haven); and help you use this safe haven to feel solid enough to explore, play, and work knowing that you have the support behind you and to return to it if you need it (secure base).[3] The attachment system doesn't describe the entire relationship between you and your original caregiver, but rather the behaviors and experiences that get triggered and managed when you are under stress. In some ways you can think of the attachment system as the most foundational stress response system that humans have.

The best way to understand how to build or rebuild an attachment system is to look at how your attachment system is formed in infancy. I know it can seem like a stretch to talk about the behaviors of infants when you are worried about trauma as an adult—but this is a lifelong system and it will be part of your job to be able to talk about and repair your own attachment system given where you are now. Repairing your attachment system requires that you know how they were formed in the first place.

All mammals are born small and relatively helpless—and human infants, especially, take a long time to grow into adulthood, requiring many years of caretaking throughout their development. When you were an infant you needed a caregiver to protect you from danger and to help you manage all of your physical and physiological states: you couldn't feed yourself, clothe yourself, or change your own diaper. You couldn't calm yourself down or cheer yourself up. Some of you didn't get this, but ideally, all the things that you would eventually do on your own you learned first through your parents or caregiver. Winnicott, the child psychologist who coined the term *unintegration*, also famously said that "we cannot describe the baby without describing the environment"[4]— any infant is actually the sum of the relationship between the baby and caregiver. Everything you know and understand about yourself and the world, you learned first through your first relationships.

There are three main aspects to attachment. The first is called *proximity seeking* and merely means that you seek out your attachment relationships—you seek to be close to them when you need them or want them. When you are young, this means that you want to be physically close to them, and as you get older you seek this closeness in different ways, from physical proximity to a more representational proximity—your wedding ring, for example—or the photos on your desk or phone. The second aspect of attachment is the way the caregiver provides a safe environment and meets most of the infant's needs—both physical and psychological—by calming or soothing an infant who is afraid, upset, or angry. This kind of safety is called a *safe haven*.[5] The third aspect arises when the infant can then expand this sense of security and safety into their environment and explore using the caregiver as a *secure base* to return to. Confusingly, in much of the literature, often all of these simply get called "secure base" and imply the safety, security, and soothing that a secure attachment creates.

As you can imagine, or may have experienced, all attachments aren't the same. Depending on the relationship between parent and child, different attachment styles emerge. Let's look first at what happens when attachment goes well. I want you to meet Lyla and her parents, Jesse and Hans. Lyla is six months old and is busy learning about herself and the world through attachment. Attachment isn't passive. It's active—attachment is work on the part of both the parents and the infant. Lyla is busy communicating to her mom and dad—she lets them know when she's hungry or wet or tired or uncomfortable—with facial expressions, with shrieking, with movement. And her parents, Jesse and Hans, respond as best they can to what Lyla is telling them. Jesse and Hans often have to guess what Lyla is communicating, and they communicate back to Lyla in words and actions in order to help Lyla come back into a state of comfort. In this exchange, Lyla takes in the soothing words and actions from Jesse and Hans. What is getting connected in Lyla's neural pathways is the connection between "I'm uncomfortable" and "I can feel better." "I can feel uncomfortable, and the world can help me feel more comfortable." For now, she needs her parents for this. But gradually over time, as she takes this safe experience in, over and over, Lyla will be able to do this for herself. Attachment is built through repetition. It isn't something that is learned in one instance—it is learned through hundreds, even thousands, of small repetitions. Jesse and Hans's consistent responses to Lyla's needs are building a secure attachment. But attachment is not just about soothing negative emotions, it's also about responding to positive emotions—to the attempts at connection. Lyla is communicating through smiles—she smiles and her mom, Jesse, smiles back. This responsiveness encourages Lyla to keep communicating—it says, "I hear you," "I see you," "You exist to me." This reflecting back of feelings and expressions, whether positive or negative, is called *mirroring*. It is a powerful driver in attachment. It seems so simple, and it is what most people do automatically when they are near infants. Mirroring helps an infant come to know its own mind and understand the minds of others.

So if all goes well, as in the example of Lyla, you get what is called a *secure attachment*. A secure attachment is one in which the child knows to turn toward the caring adult to feel more secure and use him or her to soothe or self-regulate. With a secure attachment a child will use the parent as a secure base—a safe place to venture out from and return to. They will wander off and play, and yet if something becomes stressful, they will turn toward their parents for calming and soothing. In this way the attachment relationship can seem sort of invisible until there is a stressor, and then it kind of "lights up" and you can see the attachment system activate. This is also why you may be confused by your children who were apparently fine all day in school, and then come home and suddenly fall apart about something that happened to them.

We save our distress for our attachment people: we know where it is safe to let go and share our biggest sorrows and struggles.

ATTACHMENT AND TRAUMA

But what happens if it doesn't go well? What if the child doesn't have a safe or consistent caregiving situation, or if there is outright abuse? In these situations, what is built between the caregiver and the child is an *insecure* attachment. When a parent is rejecting, or angry, or frightening, then a child will learn that they can't go to the parent for soothing or security; the child won't seek proximity with the parent and can't use them to help themself self-regulate. An insecure attachment is one where in order to feel safe, the child either feels like they have to be vigilant of the parent—and watch over them to take care of the parent or make sure they won't leave—or they may feel like they have to ignore the relationship altogether or completely detach from it. In an insecure attachment, the caregiver who is supposed to be providing security is the one who is creating the stress and fear.

And now, before every parent reading this section fears that they have ruined their child, what is really important to understand about attachment and healthy relationships is that *it isn't about getting it right all the time*. It isn't about being the perfect parent. For a secure attachment the only thing you need to be as a caregiver is "good enough"[6]—which means simply that *most of the time* you are able to help the child with their needs and you don't leave them too long in a traumatic state of distress. In fact, powerful research shows that both parents who have secure relationships with their children and parents who have insecure relationships with their children get it wrong about the same amount of time (roughly

50 percent): all parents are going to get it wrong at some point. A parent will be too loud or not loud enough. Will bounce the child when the child wants to be still, or not bounce the child when the child wants to be active. *Getting it wrong* is actually just part of what it means to be in a *normal* relationship. So what distinguishes a secure relationship from an insecure relationship isn't about getting it perfect, but about your ability to go in for repair.[7] Parents who have secure relationships with their children keep trying something else in the interaction until they get it right *enough*. Or they apologize for getting it wrong. Or they get it wrong and inquire. And this constant state of "try something—get it wrong—repair" is how we human beings teach each other how to be in a relationship with each other.

Tolstoy famously said that happy families are all alike and unhappy families are different in their own way—and this adage is mirrored in attachment. For attachments where things go well, there is secure attachment, but when it doesn't go well, the attachments are *unhappy* in their own way, yielding three different kinds of insecure attachment: anxious (preoccupied), avoidant (dismissive),[8] and disorganized (fearful-avoidant).[9] Let's look at each of these styles because they will help you understand the impact of trauma and some of what may be helpful in healing from trauma. First, in some ways it's helpful to think about each of the insecure attachment styles as a solution to a problem. Each of these attachment styles was the best solution that you could come up with to cope with poor, inconsistent, neglectful, or abusive caregiving. The style you ended up with has to do with your personality style, the behavior of your parent or caregiver, and the success of the strategy you chose in helping yourself cope with the stress of insecurity.

If you are anxiously attached, you decided to use a strategy of managing inconsistent caregiving by becoming hypervigilant—and anxious.

You want to believe in relationships and you pay close attention to relationships, but you don't believe in their reliability. Children who employ this strategy look clingy or fearful—never wanting to let go, for fear they will never be able to grab hold again. If you are an adult who employs this strategy you may find yourself assuming that no matter what you do, you will be abandoned by the people you love, or that the relationship is too fragile to handle your problems.

If you are a person with a dismissive attachment style, you settled on the opposite strategy—you decided that it was too hard or painful to try to rely on unreliable caregivers and chose to simply "not need" anyone, seeing any of the normal proximity seeking as a weakness; you work instead to protect yourself through self-sufficiency. You often look pretty solid on the outside, but feel disconnected on the inside. Others may feel like they can never get close to you.

And the last category of insecure attachment is called "disorganized" in childhood and "fearful-avoidant" in adulthood—and tends to be the result of the most abusive or neglectful parenting. In many ways it's an attachment style where neither of the strategies of the other two, anxious or dismissive, worked well enough—neither getting close nor staying away was consistently successful—and so you may find yourself alternating between them in what one of my psychiatrist colleagues once described as a "closeness-distance"[10] problem. As a fearful-avoidant person you can find no safe distance. Often the solution is a *false self*. You create a persona that looks good on the outside, but you believe that if anyone knew the "real you" on the inside, they would leave you, which forces you to work desperately hard to make the outside look good, which means that you have to hide your problems rather than seek help. And because you believe that this false self is a fraud, it's hard to let anyone get very close for fear of being found out.

The common element in all of the insecure attachments is the lack of a consistent safe haven or secure base. You don't feel like there is a place of safety you can turn to, and you don't typically feel like you have a solid internal sense of being okay that you take with you. There is no place where you can comfortably rest. The basic premise of attachment is that *fear constricts and safety expands.* Secure attachment and the three types of insecure attachment show how our primary experience of consistent relationships affects our belief in and use of future relationships. But attachment is not just about the blueprint for relationships, it is also the way we internalize those relationships—how the comfort and soothing from a relationship becomes both our biology and the internal framework for how we regulate our emotions.

So how does the experience of attachment become our biology? How does the secure base go from being a part of your relationships and environment to become a foundational coping resource—to being part of your lifelong operating system? Let's look at this in the same series of steps that happen as you develop. The first thing to understand is the simple matter of physical development. Babies who develop inside a secure attachment have healthier physical development and healthier brain development. This physical development and brain development helps an infant be more resilient to stress and creates a healthier nervous system—how we calm or soothe ourselves or how we energize ourselves. So, the first thing to understand is that the secure base of a relationship can become a secure base in our biology through our nervous system: it becomes our system of self-regulation.

Your brain is organized into different parts that have different functions[11]—and is generally seen to have three basic levels of organization. The lower brain—what has been sometimes called "the reptilian brain"—is responsible for the basic acts of survival: breathing, eating, wakefulness, and balance. It maintains our physical homeostasis, such as temperature, keeping us in physiological balance. The center brain, or the limbic brain, is in charge of your emotional and relational world. For the first years of life, your memory and experience is primarily a right-brain experience and memory is stored in your amygdala—the storage site of your emotional memory. The limbic system is the center of our attachment system and the center of our emotional regulation system. The limbic brain is subcortical (literally, below the cortex or upper brain). And the upper brain, or the neocortex and the frontal lobes, is where we store our learning—and where we do our thinking, learning, and decision making. But the integration of these brain structures affects our self-regulation, and the structure of the brain that connects all of the parts of the brain is the prefrontal cortex—essentially a control center for planning and anticipation. The prefrontal cortex sits at the intersection of all three sections of the brain: the lower brain, the limbic brain, and the neocortex. It is the part of the brain that helps us either inhibit behaviors that we don't want to do or initiate behaviors we need to do.

The limbic brain goes through massive growth in the first year of life,[12] and therefore the subcortical areas of the developing right brain[13] are naturally more affected by the environment and relationship to the caregiver. The relationship to the caregiver and the experience of the world as safe or unsafe becomes "memory." But subcortical memory is different from the memory we typically think of. We like to think of memory as a tape recording, and we often think of it in terms of what we specifically remember (I will cover more specifics on memory in Part 4). For the purpose of this example, let's use the metaphor of a song or a dance. It's as if in the first few years of life, you are listening to a very important song and learning a very technical ballet, but you don't actively store the words of the song or the story of the ballet, not in any retrievable way. What you store in your amygdala and limbic system is the melody and the choreography. You remember the feeling of the interaction, not the content. You remember the movement of the dance. This is the way emotional memory is stored and the way it works as part of the operating system. Emotional memory is stored in your cortex and the emotions—the "felt" part of the experience—are stored in our limbic system. This is why situations can trigger an emotion in us, even when it doesn't seem logical and we don't have the words or language to describe the experience.

So with your attachment system you are taking in the choreography of self-soothing, for managing stress and staying engaged in the relationship. While the exact mechanisms for transmission are still being explored, research has revealed some interesting outcomes from secure attachment and its impact on infant stress response systems. This line of research typically looks at cortisol level. Cortisol is a stress hormone that is associated with higher levels of physiological arousal and stress. One group of researchers looked at how infants managed their stress at their pediatrician visits for routine inoculations. They tested the infants over time and found that at first the infants would cry and get comforted by the parents. The soothing from their parents helped them feel better and lowered their cortisol levels. But over time, in contrast to the insecurely attached infants, the securely attached infants were able to lower their own stress—they would experience the stress of the inoculation—and since their previous experience was that a stressful event was paired in a timely manner with soothing, they would begin to soothe themselves on their own. This has been called *attachment as buffer*.[14] The physiology of securely attached infants begins to mirror the actual relational experience that they were receiving from their parents—under stress, once their stress hormones kicks in, their own system of soothing moves in to calm their system down.

So, if you grow up with good enough caregiving, not only do you experience secure attachment on the outside, in the form of a soothing, holding relationship, but this relationship moves inside and becomes part of the way you self-regulate—you learn to bring your system into a state that feels comfortable. This ability to manage the emotional state that you are in—to either calm down or bring your energy level up—is created through your attachment relationships. This system of soothing and regulation, once you have it, acts as a buffer for your entire life. It has even been shown to have a protective effect on people who have lived through trauma later in life; soldiers who were securely attached before they went to war were less likely to get PTSD from their experience than soldiers who weren't securely attached.[15] It's not a perfect protection system—but it seems to help for some people.

In addition, attachment behavior not only decreases cortisol, the stress hormone, it increases oxytocin. Oxytocin is a neurohormone that motivates us to move toward people and relationships and sensitizes us to social perception. It makes us more likely to seek out others. So what happens to your self-regulation system if you aren't fortunate enough to have a secure attachment—a safe environment? What if you grow up in an environment that is frightening, dangerous, or neglectful? Let's go back and look at the attachment system from a biological perspective in a situation of insecure attachment. In secure attachment, a stressor happens and a parent intervenes in a timely manner. In insecure attachment, the young child is left in a state of distress for longer than they can manage. The biggest problem is that since infants depend on adults to manage both their inner and outer states—they don't have very many ways to cope with severe distress—they either ratchet way up, screaming and crying with a system that is overaroused in an attempt to gain the attention and care of a parent, or they completely shut down so as to unhook or shut off from the stress of their current situation.

Going back to the parts of the brain that help us manage our emotions—the limbic system and the amygdala—if you don't get soothed in a timely manner, and you live in a state of distress or shut down, the amygdala, which is designed to assess danger, becomes hyperalert; it creates a state of constant vigilance and looks for and sees danger everywhere, even when the threat isn't currently there.

What is important to understand about the attachment relationship becoming self-regulating biology—or that lack of an attachment relationship interferes with the establishment of self-regulation—is that self-regulation is mostly about managing arousal level: managing how much stimulation or intensity comes in and for how long. It determines how calm we are. Our brains and physical systems function best when we operate in what Dan Siegel calls our "window of tolerance"[16]—the middle zone of arousal, not too high and not too low.

How does this attachment system get affected if you experience repeated trauma as an adult? The good news is that if you came into adulthood with a secure attachment system, you have more protection, more resilience than someone who came into adulthood with an insecure attachment. But repeated trauma will still affect the attachment system. First, your attachment system becomes a core of what you call your *self*. This is the person that you know yourself to be—and repeated trauma can damage your sense of self.

We are selves-in-relation:[17] our sense of self is built inside relationships, and when our feelings about ourselves change through trauma, we can lose our feelings of connection in relationships. Consider a veteran, Mike, who returns from war. On a night raid in Afghanistan he and his team shot an elderly women while her grandchildren watched. It's an image he can't erase from his mind. When he is at home with his wife and mother-in-law, with whom he is very close, he finds that he tries to avoid being in the same room with her. Everyone in the family says that they love him, but he believes that he has fundamentally changed because of the war. He feels like there was a "Mike before the war" and a "Mike after the war." He doesn't want them to know the Mike who killed the grandmother. Though he had solid relationships when he left for war, and despite the support he is currently receiving from his loved ones, Mike can't lean into these relationships. His attachments are now insecure because the self that had built attachments has been damaged.

Attachment is the foundation of how we create relationships and how those relationships become our system of self-regulation. Attachment forms the operating system that is the foundation of our relationships, our worldview, and our ability to adapt emotionally. Repeated trauma affects this basic operating system—and this disruption is a major source of difficulty for survivors of repeated trauma. And not only does the attachment system need to be healed and attended to, it is also a pathway to healing. This requires trauma survivors to wrestle with the fear and mistrust that repeated trauma can cause and begin to repair this basic operating system of attachment.

Learning to Lean

Leaning is what allows unintegration to happen. Leaning on support allows you to take the weight off your old protections. It allows you to let go of the tightness or rigidity of the old rules or the old story. Leaning on relationships and trust challenges your old experiences of relationships and how trauma may have affected them. If you don't lean and take the weight off of what was hurt, all of the old rules and protections stay rigidly in place to splint what was broken. When you lean and take the weight off what is hurt—when you allow what was hurt to be seen without having to have all the protections around it—you begin to actually see it and experience both the protections you used and what was hurt.

Most people learn to lean in small steps—especially people who have been hurt. It is similar to the way people learn to do the "trust falls" popular in team-building exercises. To do a trust fall, you need two people. You have one partner standing in front of the other partner but facing away. The partner in back has their hands up and resting gently on the back of the person in front. The person in back has a solid stance so that they are capable of holding the weight of the person in front. At a mutually agreed signal, the person in front leans their weight back into the waiting hands of the person behind them. Some people can lean back an inch. Some trusting souls can lean all the way back. If we use this as a metaphor, most trauma survivors lean back in the tiniest of increments but it doesn't feel tiny to them. They may lean back millimeters and still feel like they have lost all control.

Leaning is a practice of giving up control, of depending on someone. It is a practice of letting someone close enough to support you, which means that your fear system believes (and has experienced) that someone is close enough to hurt you. Remember that trauma is the act of being caught off guard, and staying in control feels like a way to protect yourself from ever being caught off guard again. Leaning allows you moments of not living in a trauma-organized world—and in the Unintegration phase, it can feel out of control.

Surviving trauma is all about behaviors that keep you safe, and often away from other people; trauma makes you wary, vigilant, mistrustful. Surviving trauma has you holding everything in, holding everything tightly together. And as you lean into the healing process, parts of the trauma can begin to untangle from each other.

The younger you are, the easier this is to learn. I worked with a toddler named Daniel through an early-intervention program many years ago. I will never know what his real struggles were at home, but he would arrive at the school on a bus in a nearly catatonic state: he wouldn't make eye contact, he wouldn't speak, and he wouldn't move. I would pick him up from his car seat and hold him tightly, letting him rest his whole weight on my body. And when he did, he had an unbelievable dead weight—it was as if he had a battery that wasn't charged, and he couldn't move. He would lean his head into my shoulder and just breathe, eyes closed. Typically, he would lean on me for about ten minutes, sometimes longer, and recharge his attachment batteries. And at some point, when Daniel had gotten enough, he would lift his head, say "Down," and climb down and head into class.

The older we are, and the more hurt we have been, the harder this leaning is to learn. Quite simply, it is harder to learn when we can't learn to lean by leaning physically, the way Daniel did. It isn't that simple because the repetition required for learning this kind of safety isn't a onetime experience: you don't lean once to learn attachment, you lean thousands of times. When you have to relearn leaning, or learn it for the first time in adulthood, it isn't literal physical leaning, but instead leaning into other aspects of relationships and attachment. You can lean into the structure of relationships—into their reliability or constancy—and you can hang on them as you would belay ropes in climbing. In order to heal from trauma, you need to unlearn your self-protections that keep you from leaning, and you need to relearn the experience of leaning itself. But you need to do it gradually, at your own pace. And learning to lean is one of those skills that is paradoxical. You can't work harder to lean; you actually have to let go.

I have been thinking about this even more this week because I have been texting back and forth with my friend Laura, whose toddler, Emma, is having difficulty falling asleep at night. Emma was a good sleeper and now in her busy toddlerhood she is suddenly a terrible sleeper—having difficulty settling herself down and getting calm without her mom actually being present. Toddlerhood is an age of exploration and movement—toddlers stretch themselves and search farther and farther out—and their curiosity and enthusiasm pulls them outward. It's like they are constantly pulled to jump into the moving river of life, and then they find themselves overwhelmed when they realize that they have moved far downstream from their mom, dad, or caregiver. "Wait a minute! How did I get here? Where are you? How could you leave me?"

Toddlers are still learning to trust in the constancy of the world and relationships: Are you still there when I can't see you? If you aren't there, do I still exist? Toddlers don't yet have the capacity to hold someone in mind. Out of sight, out of mind. They need to borrow the battery pack of their parents to relax, to slow down, to feel calm. And sleep is so difficult, for both children and adults alike, because you can't put effort into falling asleep. You can't try harder at it because effort actually works against you, keeping you awake. And the more upset you get, the more difficult it is.

Falling asleep is about letting go. And anytime we have the dual task of learning to let go and trust—at the same time—we are challenged by one of the most difficult learning curves we will face. Some of these learning curves come in their normal developmental stages, as with my friend Laura's daughter, and some of these learning curves come when we go back and mend our broken pieces. We have to learn all over again, or even for the first time, what it is like to let go and trust enough to lean and to heal.

Learning to lean and learning to fall asleep have something in common. Both of them are like learning to float. Teaching a child to learn to float is incredibly difficult. First of all, there is no logical reason that anyone should believe in floating at first sight. When you put an object in water it sinks. All small children know this. So when you tell them that you want them to just lie there on top of the water most children look at you like you have lost your mind. Yes, they are determined to learn how to swim, but asking them to just lie there seems completely crazy.

It is a really gradual process. First, you have them lean against you. And when they trust you enough, then they will lie on your outstretched arms with you holding their entire weight on your arms. And then gradually, oh so gradually, you will lower your arms bit by bit and let the water hold them.

It must be gradual. Why? Because the minute the child gets scared, what do they do? They scrunch together and sink and then shoot up and grab your neck—proving their own point that floating is impossible. It is why Laura must put her daughter to bed and stay near enough to be a felt presence and gradually move farther away as her daughter learns to float back to sleep. Laura has to have her emotional arms underneath her daughter enough to be felt.

I loved teaching kids to float because it was so tangible. It was easy to physically hold a child and let them feel your presence and trustworthiness. It was easy to feel how much they could tolerate floating on their own before they needed to be held again. It was so empowering to the child as they learned how to float and feel that this substance that felt so dangerous before actually could hold them up—the pride that they could master it, and the bliss of floating.

So often as a therapist I wished that this process of learning trust could be as solid and tangible as learning to float. Learning to emotionally lean on someone is the same process, but it is so much more incremental and so much more difficult. It is not easy to be an adult and feel so vulnerable. It is hard for adults to learn to swim and float, and it is hard for adults to learn the kind of trust it takes to lean on someone emotionally.

Learning to lean as an adult, and learning to lean as an adult who has been hurt often, relies often on the ritual of repetition and gradually stretching yourself. You learn to lean on the safety of reliability before you can believe in or lean on the safety of relationship itself. You lean into a schedule of meeting your therapist, relying on the constancy of the both of you showing up. You lean into how conversations start or end. You lean into rituals that help you settle down or find your strengths like mindfulness or gratitude or physical exercise. You lean into the practice of saying how you feel and letting someone else witness it and reflect it back to you.

And slowly you let go and you begin to lean, and you feel a moment of safety, or minutes or hours—and while you may feel good, or feel relief, it is also true that leaning on help begins the unintegration process. And this is the paradox of safety in healing: it can hurt. Sometimes I liken it to the experience you have when your foot or leg has been asleep and suddenly you get feeling in it again, and it is tingly and painful. The power of the Unintegration phase is the pace at which it happens. Much like the example I described earlier of the temples at Abu Simbel, the process needs to be slow and deliberate. It needs to take into account the weight of what must be dismantled—the bigger the trauma, the longer the trauma, the more attention needs to be paid to the size of what gets unintegrated at any one time. But it is my experience as both a therapist and a client that if you trust the process of leaning and allow safety to guide the process of uncovering trauma, it will generally unfold in a way you can tolerate and sustain.

Container: Managing the Emotions of Unintegration

The process that you are entering with unintegration is usually what we call *regression* in children. In infant and child development, when a baby is about to make some developmental shift, say, learning to stand or walk, they usually have a week of falling apart. They had been sleeping through the night and now they are crying again. They had been getting along well and now they are continually fussy and irritable. Before and during the transition to the new developmental step, they are uncomfortable; they have to let go of their current ability in order to take in and then integrate a new ability. We see this as normal and necessary in infants and children, and we see this as a shortfall in adults. T. Berry Brazelton, a pediatrician who has written extensively on child development, refers to these developmental periods as *touchpoints*.[1] Development requires effort and energy, and there are necessary periods of backsliding in development in order to make the leap forward. I am here to tell you growth is impossible without regression, without some undoing or unintegration.

Regression is an experience. It is not necessarily a way of life. You don't need to completely give up all your capacities all the time (going to work, for example) in order to change. But you do need to have times where you can let yourself unhinge enough to shift. The problem with uncomfortable experiences is that it is hard to remember that they are temporary. This is made worse by our notion of the diagonal line of growth. We are eternally climbing up this steep hill, and the feeling of any backslide terrifies us; after all, gravity having its say would have us careening back down that diagonal line, as if life were a game of Chutes and Ladders. You are going either all the way up or all the way down.

What can hold you while you are having this experience of coming apart? The Unintegration phase can stir up some big emotions—emotions that can knock you off balance—and you need a way to hold them, and hold the work you are doing so that it feels manageable, so that it *is* manageable. And what can make it manageable is creating a container.[2] In the previous sections on attachment, I talked about attachment creating a secure base—and that is essentially what I am talking about with a container. The container of relationship is made up of trust and the behaviors that increase trust. The attachment system is set up to create a secure base within relationships and to create a secure base and emotional self-regulation system inside your physical and emotional self. So the container I am talking about is both within the healing relationship and inside yourself.

What I know now about creating the container in the healing relationship is that a lot of it has to do with respecting the size of the container—how much it can hold—and the pacing of what is talked about: how much to let in, how long to talk about things or experience things, how frequently you meet, how intense the conversations or sessions are. A lot of these decisions, especially early on, are made by the therapist or guide, but I believe that if you understand the role of the container and how to be aware of your own levels of arousal or stress, you become its co-creator, making the container a much stronger and safer place.

How do you do this? It's simple but not easy. You start by being aware of the state you are in—what you are feeling, what you are thinking. You do it by having basic conversations: What is your experience of the conversation? Is it too much? Do you need to slow down? Take a break? Switch topics for a moment? How are you experiencing the relationship—what needs to happen for the container to feel more secure? For you to feel safe? To feel free to speak?

But creating the container between you and your guide requires that you understand your own internal container, your *window of tolerance*,[3] because this outer container will help you strengthen the one inside you. You do this by paying attention to your physical self and what it is telling you, and to your emotional self and what it is telling you. This is where you will get your information about what is too much, what is not enough—whether you feel like you need to slow down, stop, or move things along.

What is the window of tolerance? Each person has a window of tolerance: the boundary between what is too much arousal or stimulation (too much anxiety, sadness, rage) and what is too little arousal or stimulation (feeling completely shut down and numb). Inside our window of tolerance we function better, our brains work better, and we can learn and interact better. Inside our window of tolerance we feel in control of ourselves and our world. Many things can affect our window of tolerance: being tired, hungry, sick, or stressed, and previous experiences that are positive or traumatic. Trauma survivors tend to have narrower windows of tolerance because trauma can make our system hypersensitive to anything that reminds it of the trauma—and therefore, trauma survivors find that there is very little space between too triggered and too numb. This small window of tolerance can make you feel like there is no freedom of movement in your world—where all of your energy is focused on keeping away any memory, any experience, any feeling that connects to your trauma. Much of the work of healing from trauma involves expanding this window of tolerance. You do this by coming into contact, in small manageable doses, with emotions and aspects of your trauma history. As you build your capacity for self-regulation, self-management, and soothing—through mindfulness, stress management techniques, and self-talk—you are able to briefly be outside your window of tolerance without experiencing wild anxiety or shutting down and going numb. And each time you are able to stretch your window of tolerance and still feel safe, your container gets bigger and more solid. You are able to hold more of your experience.

We have discussed mindfulness and awareness as methods of slowing down and soothing. Let's look briefly at self-talk. Self-talk is inner speech—the conversations and mostly coaching we do with ourselves. Inner speech is good, it is necessary, it is required. Self-talk supports both learning and action. As much as we sometimes hate the voice in our heads, without it we would be handicapped; people who lack the capacity for inner speech have severe learning and memory difficulties, and they often lack the capacity to control their behavior. Inner speech helps us learn through the repetition of instruction, and it supports action through the narration of what we need to do—it helps us anticipate, plan, and complete.

But one crucial thing to understand about inner speech is that all inner speech, all self-talk started out as "other talk."[4] We learned to speak to ourselves through the language of others, through the tone of others, across our life span. Self-talk always begins as a part of our attachment relationships. What our early caregivers said to us becomes the first inner recordings, and then other important voices were added to the internal chorus. The ability to take in the voices of others makes us adaptive as a species—in one generation we can shift the learning if we need to, and it also makes us better at living in communities; we literally have a community voice to help us navigate the norms and rules within groups.

Your own inner speech will be the most frequent voice you will ever hear in your life. It began as outward speech around age three and moved to a silent inner speech by age seven. And it has been a constant presence ever since. The question is this: Is it serving you? Serving your learning? Serving your healing? Serving you in your relationships and your work? Because once you are in your adulthood, your inner speech becomes yours to edit and revise. Inner speech tends to be short and instructive. So as you are going through this process of healing, it may be important for you to have some statements to help yourself heal—"I'm okay" or "I can do this" or "I can ask for help" or "It's hard but I am strong." Inner speech helps you build emotional muscles, slowly and carefully.

Another aspect of the container in the work of healing from trauma is the fact that healing from trauma is not the only aspect of your life. It can feel like it at times. It can feel like the only thing in your life that feels real is the work you are doing in your healing. It can feel frightening that suddenly therapy is so important, and it can seem like the old life you had fades into the background. But it is important to remember that there is more to you than just being a trauma survivor, and there is more to your life than just healing from trauma. While you are healing from trauma, you must hold the multiple aspects of your life: the life you are currently living and the aspects of your life that need to be healed. During treatment you need to let the two tracks of your life run at the same time. Once you have gained some solid ground in the Preparation phase, you will be engaged in your life: you will be going to work, doing things with friends and family, doing errands, participating in your community—you have a whole, full, messy life. At the same time, you will be doing work in therapy or group, which will be stirring up old stories and feelings, which may feel destabilizing and make you feel as if your life is falling apart or as if you are coming apart. These two different aspects of your life can feel really far away from each other—and each can make the other seem not real.

This is where you need to hold the two tracks and let both experiences of your life be true at the same time. Your current life is moving along with its typical ups and downs. And at any given moment you can be hit hard by feelings of the past or grief long unattended to.

One way to think about treatment is to look at it like a second job or intense pastime. I had a friend who worked as a chef during the day but spent every night renovating his old house. His work doing carpentry every night didn't negate his skills as a chef, nor did his skills as a chef negate his capacity to do carpentry. Both sets of capacities were aspects of who he is. While cooking he often thought about the next set of projects he needed to do at home, what materials he would need, and what he needed to pick up at Home Depot on the way home. While working on the house, he often thought about the next day's offerings, what he might make with the ingredients that were coming in.

The capacity to let two tracks run at the same time does a number of things. One is that it allows, even encourages, you to continue on with your life while you are getting better. There is often a wish in this work to be able to disappear to some treatment center and come back "fixed."

But fully engaging in and living your everyday life is important not only for the necessary reasons of safety, shelter, social connections, and income—but also, perhaps more important, because you get to experience your strengths, your resiliency, your healthy side. You need to feel, on a daily basis, that you are more than your trauma history. You need to see that not only have you survived, you have created a life for yourself; you are capable of strength, caring, persistence, generosity, patience, and humor. You have people who care about you, who love you and whom you love. You are able to contribute to the world with your talents and effort. When you are healing from repeated trauma, attaching this anchor line to the present is one of the most important safety actions you can take. Healing from trauma can trigger difficult emotions and memories, and these can feel very real, sometimes more real than the life in front of your eyes. But they are both real—the present and the past are both true.

"But isn't it lying to feel one way and act another? Am I being dishonest with people around me if I don't tell them how I am feeling?"

There is no simple answer to this except to say that at all times, both can be true. You can feel awful: anxious, sad, devastated, detached—whatever gets stirred up by your trauma history. But these feelings are old feelings—like a soundtrack to a movie that has already happened. Sometimes these feelings drown out the current soundtrack. It is hard to hear the present over the past. But you have to remember that the current soundtrack—your current life—is real. Your old feelings are real, because you have them, but they aren't about the present, and if you can let both soundtracks run at the same time, gradually the old soundtrack will fade.

Holding two tracks at once is a difficult skill, and if you can't do it you will have a much harder time healing. So I think that it is a skill worth learning and practicing. When you are in the process of healing from a physical injury, it is often important to pay attention to pain management and the kinds of physical adjusting or compensating you would need to do in order to both heal and live your life. And the same is true when healing from trauma. You need to engage in emotional pain management and make the necessary adjustments in order to continue the work of healing, but also to live your present life to its fullest.

Dismantling Defenses

Trauma is what happened to us, but trauma is also what we did to survive. Our defenses, our protections, are part of our trauma story, and even though we created them to protect us from the impact of the trauma, those defenses can keep us locked in a world that feels like the trauma is always about to happen again. And it can feel really difficult to stop these old protective behaviors. It can feel really difficult to imagine that there is a different world where you wouldn't need these same protections. The Unintegration phase is where you begin to really see these protections and wrestle with taking them apart. Let's say that one way you protected yourself when you were young was to imagine that you were more in control of the situation than you were. You imagine that at age seven you really should have been able to protect your mother from your father. You blame yourself for the violence that occurred and you create a defense of being vigilant about control. The current story you have about the trauma is that you should have been more in control and you should have been braver. This story protects you from the feeling that this could happen again, because the problem wasn't that powerful people could be violent and out of control, which could make anyone helpless. The problem was that you were not brave or vigilant enough to stop the violence, which means if it ever happened again you imagine you could stop it.

In the Unintegration phase, as you talk about your experience of getting help and what happened to you, you run up against your old story. In many ways you can't see your old story until it gets challenged in the present. This old story of "I must be brave and protect everyone" becomes the defense or rule that "I must be vigilant about any negative emotion that may lead to violence" and "I can't say anything that may hurt or frighten anyone." In the Unintegration phase your old rules, your old story, your defenses get challenged because in therapy and in life, these rules of extreme protection no longer make sense. Your therapist reminds you that actually it's not your job to take care of her. Or she points out that in your story of trauma you were only seven years old, and in no way is a seven-year-old supposed to be in charge of an adult's safety. Or, she says simply that talking about your feelings isn't going to be harmful for her or for you. All of these statements challenge the protections that organize the way you live in the world.

Unintegration is where you have the ability to come apart or, really, have your defenses come apart enough to begin to heal. The experience of surviving repeated trauma is different from surviving something awful that happened only once. If a trauma happens once, the event will break through your natural defenses, but if something difficult happens repeatedly, you protect yourself from it. You build defenses, protections, and these protections become a part of who you are; they become your habits and how you see and understand the world. Defenses are the thoughts, beliefs, attitudes, or behaviors that you use to protect yourself from being overwhelmed by your feelings of anxiety, fear, rage, sadness, helplessness, shame. Defenses aren't bad or good. They are part of what it takes to function as a human being. It is absolutely necessary to have defenses; they help you manage and modulate the amount of stress that can come at you at any one time. It is important to have access to the proverbial turtle shell so that when necessary, you can retreat inside it and find safety. The most important thing to understand about defenses is not that you shouldn't have them, but that they are best when they are chosen: when you can choose when and how you use them, rather than operating on autopilot and feeling like you have no choice at all in how you feel, think, or behave.

Unintegration needs to be done incrementally and slowly. Small shifts in behavior allow us to stay in an emotional range that may be uncomfortable but still tolerable. They allow us to both stay in and expand our window of tolerance. It is no different than physical therapy for a physical injury—you want to be stretching the muscle so that you are increasing its range, but if you go too far it will tense up or get injured again, so you must balance this need to push yourself to stretch, but not stretch so far that it interferes with your healing.

Unintegration doesn't happen because you try to take things apart. It happens because you challenge old defenses or protections with new behavior. You lean into the relationship with your therapist or guide, challenging your old stance of self-sufficiency. You begin saying what you lived through or was true for you, challenging your old rule of silence. What is important here in the Unintegration phase is how it feels, because the sentences that come out of your mouth may sound very similar in Unintegration, Identification, and Integration. For example, you may say, "My father dragged my brother down the stairs," which sounds like you are telling your trauma story, but your experience of saying this sentence is very different at each phase of the healing cycle. In Unintegration, you may get the sentence out, but you aren't hearing your own story, or hearing the story as if it belonged to you. Trauma fragments our memories and our experiences—we are miles and miles away from our stories and our emotions, even if we can utter the words.

One of the effects of repeated trauma, as discussed earlier, is that you come to protect yourself from everything as if it were the trauma you actually experienced. You wrap yourself up in whatever protections worked at the time: avoidance, obedience, defiance, imagination, recklessness, or control. You come to believe in these protections the way one believes in gravity: without them, you would literally fall over, become unglued, cease to exist. These aren't just protections, they are your laws of nature, the rules that govern your world. And like those laws of nature, you don't see them until you challenge them, until in the Unintegration phase you do or say something that requires you to not follow one of those sacred laws. And then it feels like your whole world is coming apart.

On my kitchen refrigerator hangs a yellowing newspaper photograph of a Buddhist monk in his saffron robes standing in the middle of the street, defiantly, in front of a row of young military soldiers. The soldiers are standing in a row, with gray shields and gray helmets, rifles slung over their shoulders, carrying clubs. They are holding their shields up in front of them as if the monk had a weapon he could shoot them with, though the monk is weaponless. The monk is simply wearing a saffron robe blowing in the breeze. He is protected only by his faith and convictions. I have kept this photo because I think it is the best illustration of defenses that I have ever seen. We think of defenses as being strong and powerful. When we encounter our own internal defenses, they can seem stubborn and unyielding. It can be hard to see them, hard to get them to put down their weapons, and the instinct is to try to overpower them—muscle them into submission. Our internal defenses are these young soldiers, and this photo tells us everything about them. In the photo you can't see the monk's face, but you can see the faces on the soldiers. The soldiers have all the weapons and protections. But for all the outward protections they have, they do not project strength. The look on their faces reveals their fear. Up against actual courage and conviction, they don't look like they want to protect anything so much as they want to flee. The power of the courage in front of them is bigger than they are, and they know it.

Even when you want to change or see how important the change is to your life, your relationships, your work—even when you can see how much you need to change—you can find it difficult to change your behavior. This is where you can understand your defenses as *resistance*. Resistance has been defined as "the motivational forces operating against growth or change, and in the direction of maintenance of the status quo."[1] The psychiatrist Martha Stark simplified this description even more to a tension between "yes" and "no":[2] "Yes, I want to change" and "No, I want to stay the same." She states that if you lean more in the direction of talking about or working with the "yes"—wanting to change—you will feel more anxious and uncomfortable. And if you lean more in the direction of avoiding change or not talking about it, your anxiety will go down. So in some ways if you aren't feeling at least a little bit uncomfortable, anxious, or awkward, you know you probably aren't doing anything different—you probably aren't stretching away from your old defenses. As we discussed earlier, in thinking about the window of tolerance, this is all about balancing your ability to stretch into new behaviors and tolerate the feelings that go with them and backing off from the hard work to recover a bit. Learning to titrate the amount of tension or anxiety as you work with growth and change is one of the most important skills in healing from trauma.

All of these things are you, and when you are trying to talk about it, they can feel like disparate parts, and the inconsistency of the conversation can make you want to speed up, to be one or the other: the one who was hurt or the one who is protected, and not both, and not all the feelings in between. The incongruity of the conversation, the overwhelming emotions, and the embarrassment of not being able to coherently tell your story can make this phase really uncomfortable. You are taking all of these risks—you are brave enough to dive over and over, and for a long time, there is no tangible reward. In working to become whole, it is helpful to have someone there to be the lifeguard, to watch you dive over and over, watch you come up for air and encourage another dive. And each dive, each small conversation brings up another piece that you will use to make your mosaic—another piece that will eventually be part of your whole trauma story.

Cages, Reenactment, and Flight

When I was in college I had a dream about an injured eagle.

I am swimming in a lake and the sun is shining on the water. There are other people swimming in the water. I look across the lake and I see a large cage sitting on top of the water. Inside the cage is an eagle. I swim quickly toward the cage because I am worried that the cage will sink and the eagle will drown. I am not sure how it is possible that the cage is just floating on the water, but I am sure there isn't very much time left before it will sink. As I get closer to the cage I see that the eagle has a wounded wing—it is askew and there is an open wound. I want to get to the cage and open the door so that the eagle can get out and fly away before the cage sinks. I swim toward the cage and reach toward the door, but when I do, the eagle begins to hit its wounded wing hard on the bars of the cage. While it hits its wing on the bars it stares straight at me. I back off for a moment to let the eagle settle down. I reach toward the cage, and again, the bird hits its wounded wing, injuring itself further. I feel scared and frustrated. I want to help this bird, but my helping provokes it to injure itself. I am not sure how much time I have before the cage sinks, and I don't know how to make the eagle understand that I don't want to hurt it, that I want to set it free. Each time I reach toward the cage, the bird hits its wounded wing on the bars. It never takes its eyes off me. Every time it reinjures its wing I worry that it won't be able to fly if I can get the door open. The eagle is watching my every move, and each time I signal that I am moving to the cage, it raises its wing to hit it again. Finally I can't bear the anxiety anymore and I wake up.

If you have ever tried to heal from trauma or help someone else heal from trauma, you might recognize the eagle with the wounded wing—the part of ourselves that views safety and helping with the counterintuitive response of fear. This dream was incredibly instructive. I have never found a better illustration of what it's like to confront the dilemma of wanting help and not being able to tolerate it or believe in it. Trauma wants to be healed. Sometimes I picture trauma as archaeological shards that rise to the surface through the wearing away of the topsoil that covered them over. The most ancient of our injuries will eventually start poking their edges out. The shards will out. The truth, not THE truth, but your truth, truth with a little *t*. But the problem is that this truth does not always come back in the form of words or a coherent story. Repeated trauma is typically not digested in words, and therefore instead of a story, trauma can often come back in the form of action. The story can come back as behavior. It comes back when you hit your injured wing, again and again, when something in your life tries to shift and help you as you begin to heal.

From outside the cage, from the vantage point of helpers and people in your life who love you, you can see all the possibility. For those of you literally swimming in safety, you can't possibly understand the allure of the cage. You can see that it's only a small cage. You know that the world is big and once you are out there is nothing that you can't do or have. For those outside it looks like all you have to do is open the cage door and fly out. It looks so impossibly easy, and it's easy to judge harshly those who remain in their cages.

From inside the cage, the view is entirely different. The cage is what is known. The cage, even though it may mean imminent danger, feels like the only safe place in the world. Safe relationships, the people who want to open the cage door, seem more dangerous and hurtful than the pain of an injured and reinjured wing. Our human systems depend so much on the experience of equilibrium: once something feels set, we don't want to shift it, even if the set point is false, even if the set point is killing us.

I'm not sure why, but words often don't feel as real as actual trauma. They just don't. There is always something lost in translation. Some of this may be because as a trauma survivor you have such good protections that you can't feel your own words. Or maybe your trauma never was put together with words, so the trauma and the words that describe it don't feel connected to each other. But the truth is, telling someone a story about being scared often doesn't feel as real as creating a scenario where you make them feel scared. Communicating by making someone feel what you felt, rather than explaining how you felt—this is the constant dilemma posed in healing from trauma.

Part of it is the wish to be understood—which is a reasonable wish. It can be so hard to believe that anyone can understand what it was like.

Showing them—hitting the wing in front of them, having them be as helpless to help you as you were to help yourself or anyone else during the trauma—communicates so much more than the sentence "I feel helpless." Or at least, it seems that way. In the section titled "Trust and Ropes," I talked about a client, Jim, who took months to trust me enough to come in for his first session. He would not show up at his appointment, and when I called to find out where he was, he would reschedule; he did this each week, until finally one day he showed up. But when he finally showed up, his test of my trust took a different form. On that first day of meeting with me, he walked into my office, sat down, and pulled a paperback collection of horror stories out of his backpack. He opened it up to a certain page, handed it to me, and said, "Read this out loud," so I took the book and began to read.

I didn't know what I would be reading. I didn't know whether what I was going to read would make him feel better or worse, or whether it would hurt him or help him. I didn't want to be another abuser for him, but I didn't want to have him think I was afraid of scary stories because from his chart I knew he had suffered horrific abuse. I wanted him to know that I could take anything he needed to tell me. But in that one action of handing me the book, he let me know what it felt like in his world. He brought me into a world of horror and fear, where there were no easy choices and no safe moves. I had waited months to meet with him, and this was his test of me in the first minutes of our meeting— this was a high-stakes moment, and he was helping me understand that his whole life had been one of these high-stakes moments.

In psychology we call these actions *reenactments*. Reenactment is the telling of the story through action rather than through words. Sometimes a client will reenact their trauma stories in the world almost literally. I worked with many teenage girls who had been sexually abused and who would put themselves in dangerous situations again and again where they would get sexually assaulted and relive their original trauma. And sometimes, like Jim, clients reenact the experience in a different way; they will act in such a way that either they, or I as the therapist, experience the trauma in some way.

As someone who has lived in trauma, is related to people with trauma, and has worked with people with trauma, I can tell you that there is a strong pull to reenactment, almost an undertow, and this experience needs to be understood. It needs to be seen. Reenactment needs to be honored and worked with. In the Preparation phase, there is a break from this pull. Hope and optimism and energy open the cage door and give the eagle the idea that he might fly, or if he flies, the idea he doesn't have to go back to the cage.

But as the Unintegration phase starts, you can find yourself in the cage again. You put yourself in the cage again. And when people try to help you, you start hitting your injured wing and staring straight at them. The problem is that going back in the cage looks different for everyone who has experienced trauma. In order to heal from repeated trauma you need to have a healthy respect and understanding for the false safety of the cage. You need to understand that there is this riptide, this undercurrent that will show up when you think you are swimming toward safety. Unintegration is the phase where things shake loose.

Early in my own work of healing I became overwhelmed with images of razor blades—cutting my wrists, slashing my throat. For years I couldn't stop these images. I didn't understand them. I am not a self-destructive person, so it felt alien to me to have these thoughts and images. They were constant, but they weren't unfamiliar. My mother in her many suicidal tirades would threaten to slit her wrists. She would lock herself in the bathroom and threaten to swallow razor blades. My dad would scream at her from the outside, sometimes breaking the door down to stop her. The images that came to me seemed to be some sort of a communication. They happened more when I tried to talk about the trauma I experienced. They happened more when I had negative feelings like anger or shame. They happened more when I thought I was being abandoned.

I didn't even tell my therapist about these images for a long time. They seemed too real, and I was afraid that in talking about them I would be doing to her what had been done to me: holding her hostage with fear. I thought by saying *I can see myself slitting my wrists*, it was the same as doing it. But holding on to the images by myself didn't work either. The constancy and power of them meant that I was living in a world of violence. I bought razor blades. I kept them in my bag. It felt oddly reassuring to have the real thing until I realized that I was entirely too comfortable with the idea of action. I frightened myself enough to talk to my therapist. I walked in and handed her all of the razor blades.

Handing them over was a relief, not so much to have the dangerous things gone, but because the tangible object felt more real than words. I am a therapist. I was working as a therapist at the time of this episode. I believed in the power of words but I had no comprehension of the power of reenactment. I couldn't understand why it felt so much better to hand her the razor blades than to say, "I feel terrified." But I admit it did. I hadn't jeopardized anyone's life, but words can initially feel like such poor messengers of experience. I think it's important to know that and to not give up on talking about the trauma anyway. Over the years I have learned that talking about trauma is more like learning to play an instrument than having a conversation. The story of your trauma is music; it's complicated, and when you start putting words to it, it will sound like the first feeble attempts to play a flute or a saxophone. It won't sound like anything. It won't move your emotions, and you will feel awkward and silly because you are learning to play an instrument in front of someone. And you want them to understand you. But over time you will get better at playing. And the notes, the words, they will sound better for the practice, and the songs will come together and have meaning. I promise this is true.

The problem with being in the cage is that you can't see the cage. Instead you see the world outside, distorted by the bars. Somehow you can't see that you are in a bad place—you think that's just the way the whole world is. When I was struggling with the self-destructive images, I believed them to be my truth—in the sense that I believed that they were trying to tell me something, that I was really that self-destructive. The images were vivid enough to make me think I should act on them, and those kind of images can be disturbing enough that they start interfering with your judgment.

When I finally could talk about them, I could start to get a sense that these were images I was given, like pictures burned into the brain with emulsion. These images weren't mine. And in finally seeing that, I could let them go—so that each time they showed up I could say "Not mine" and let it go. I want to be clear that I am not recommending reenactment as a treatment modality; as both a client and a therapist I value the work it takes to turn feelings, memories, and experiences into language that can be shared and then stored in your own memory as a coherent narrative. This is important, brain-changing, heart-healing work. But I think it is also important to acknowledge that our stories of repeated trauma don't always come out in neat chapters. And as we lean on help and dare to allow others in to help us with our broken wings, we need to be able to talk about and work with the stories that come to us through actions and behaviors.

Helpful Practices for Unintegration

So what are some practical ways that you can support your healing work in the Unintegration phase? Unintegration can really affect your feelings of stability and wreak havoc on your mood, so any practices that help you with self-regulation—that help you both stay within your window of tolerance and gradually expand it—will help you feel more solid during this phase. Unintegration also demands that you work on aspects of trust and leaning into relationships that help you dismantle old protections, so you also want to work on any practices that help you strengthen your trust and communication in relationships.

One concrete thing you can do for your work in the Unintegration phase is to make lists of what supports you—lists in black and white that you can put on your fridge or in your day planner or in your phone so that when the worst disorganization and disorientation hits you, you don't have to rely on your brain or your emotionally charged thinking—you have at the ready a list of things that are helpful. You can make lists of things that help you feel calm, that make you feel loved or grateful, or that help you get going again. In this way you can use your brain at its best to support you when you have days when your brain and your emotions are at their worst. On really bad days you can create a schedule of the whole day. You can just take out a white piece of paper, write the hours of the day down the left-hand side, and then schedule out your day so that you know what is happening next. This is what vacation tours do to help people feel relaxed and calm about their time—we are more calm when we know what is going to happen next without needing to make decision after decision.

Unintegration is also about unlearning old habits and defenses, and this isn't a selective process; that is, when you stop using a defense in one area of your life, you stop using it everywhere—while you are trying to unlearn it. For example, if you are trying to learn to be less vigilant and controlling in your relationships, you may also find that you are less vigilant about your belongings—that your autopilot of "needing to know everything" is down, and that you lose your keys or you forget appointments. It's important in the Unintegration phase to pay attention to your vulnerabilities or the smaller signs of disorganization in your life. It's often due to letting go of some old habits, but it's also a chance to figure out whether the trauma work is going too fast or whether you need to put in more supports for yourself. Even simple things like writing yourself Post-it notes about what you need to remember, or having a new routine of always putting your keys in the same place.

Also important for the Unintegration phase are practices that help you reach out and communicate, especially when you are in distress. For most people who have experienced repeated trauma, the ability to reach out under duress is a limited and unpracticed skill. The hallmark of trauma is helplessness, and when you have experienced repeated trauma you often just give up on the idea of help altogether. When you are doing the work of unintegration and difficult emotions arise, part of the un-learning you need to do has to do with the assumption that there is no help in the world. Some people find it helpful to have a way to check in each week with their therapist with something as simple as a 1–10 scale—"how distressed are you this week on a scale of 1–10"—so that you don't have to find language for everything you are feeling yet, but have a way to describe the emotional experience the way that pain patients describe their pain. You may want to establish some protocols or plans for what to do when your distress levels are at a 5, or a 4, or a 3—when and how should you reach out for support? What works for you? When do you need to call your therapist? Email or write your therapist? Text your therapist? When would journaling work and when wouldn't it? Who is on your social support team? Sometimes it is helpful to let the people on your team know why you would need support and what would be most helpful from them, and ask them if you can reach out to them, the way that AA sponsors can be supportive when an alcoholic is feeling an urge to drink. And sometimes it can be simply supportive to be around people and not have to talk—to just be part of the everyday conversations of relationship and not have it be about the trauma at all.

One of the things that I found extremely important during the healing process for myself as well as for some of my clients was the ability to acknowledge the emotional difficulty in the Unintegration phase as a form of flashback—as an emotional flashback. This shift has been called an "amygdala hijack"[1] by Daniel Goleman, Richard Boyatzis, and Annie McKee or "flipping your lid"[2] by Dan Siegel. What it feels like from experience is more akin to the transformation of a werewolf. One minute I am having a normal discussion as an adult, and the next minute I fall down some emotional rabbit hole that feels like a bad mix of blind rage and panic. There is a part of my brain that can see, from a distance, that what I am experiencing is not connected to what is currently happening, but like watching a movie, I feel too distant to be able to do anything to stop it.

When these happened to me, I referred to them as "werewolf brain." When you get emotionally triggered you may feel like you have completely and totally become a crazy person because the feelings you are having and the words you are using to describe them are not ones used for a mundane problem—they are used when your life is in danger, when everything you have might be lost. When a war veteran dives under a parked car at the sound of a car backfiring he is experiencing a war flashback; it is logical and lifesaving behavior in the wrong context. In healing from trauma, these werewolf moments are emotional flashbacks—and it takes both courage and practice to find and use the words that describe what is happening inside you. It takes courage to admit that you turned into a werewolf, that your experience is so wildly out of control inside you. It takes courage to sift through the words and find ones that say how you feel, not how you wish you felt, and not how you think other people think you should feel. And it takes courage to say these things out loud. But courage isn't enough. You will need the patience to practice this over and over. In healing from trauma you will fall down this hole many times, and each time it happens you will believe that this time you are never getting out. You will believe that this transformation into a werewolf is the final proof that you aren't getting well, that it is hopeless. You cannot predict the future with a brain that is living in a traumatic past. You can't believe the rantings of a terrified person. Your job is to say what is true and to bring yourself back into the present with care and compassion. So one of the most important practices to help you is actually, when you feel able, to make a conscious shift to identification—to take those feelings and fragments and begin as best you can to put words to them.

PART 4

Identification

I had less and less control over my history each day. . . . It should have been easy to trace: this happened, I was here, that happened next, all of which led inevitably to the present moment. . . . I realized, as I stood there in the church, that there was a sharp distinction between what was remembered, what was told, and what was true. And I didn't think I'd ever figure out which was which.

KEVIN POWERS, *The Yellow Birds*[1]

Identification

Many years ago, one of my child clients wanted to put together a thousand-piece puzzle. We settled on a puzzle that depicted emperor penguins and their baby. We started the puzzle project by setting up a folding table near a window in my office so that we could work on the puzzle and leave it there, safely away from where the toys and games were—so that other children coming to see me wouldn't harm the puzzle in its ongoing fragile state of assembly. Setting up the table mirrored the Preparation phase—creating a safe space to put the puzzle together. Next, we opened the box and dumped out the pieces. This act mirrored the Unintegration phase—letting the old container (defenses) come apart enough to let the pieces out. And then we sorted through the pieces and started to figure out what pieces went together to make a whole picture—this is the Identification phase.

In putting together a jigsaw puzzle there is a significant amount of time and effort between when you dump all of the pieces out on the table and when you are sitting with a finished puzzle with the complete picture. You think because you have all the pieces that putting it together will be relatively easy. My client and I thought we could start by finding penguin pieces or just building a corner, but actually many of the pieces were indistinguishable from each other. Was that white puzzle piece part of the ice or part of the sky? Was the black puzzle piece part of the ice or part of the penguin? It turned out that before we could put the puzzle together, we needed a system to sort the pieces, then try to identify them more accurately, and then try to put them together in small, experimental configurations. And these three tasks of sorting, identifying, and experimenting with how things fit are the crux of the Identification phase. With our penguin puzzle we began by finding all of the edge pieces. And then we sorted by color as best we could. And then we started to experiment with pieces to see if we could build small pieces that would help us identify even more.

Sure, a thousand-piece penguin puzzle wasn't easy to sort, but trauma and traumatic memory are even more complicated. There isn't just one picture or one story. With repeated trauma you don't even have one puzzle. What you have instead are thousands of puzzle pieces all mixed together from dozens and dozens of puzzles. Some of these puzzles have all of their pieces, but most of them do not. Some of the pieces are clearly visible, and some of the pieces have been so damaged that you can't decipher what they might be. We don't need a simple jigsaw puzzle as our metaphor; no, we need perhaps the most complicated jigsaw ever assembled—the Dead Sea Scrolls.

The Dead Sea Scrolls[1] were so named because they were discovered in the Qumran caves about a mile away from the Dead Sea. The fragments of the scrolls were discovered in eleven caves over a period of years from 1947 to 1956, and a twelfth cave was discovered in 2017.[2]

The Dead Sea Scrolls are considered the second-oldest surviving texts of the Hebrew Bible that date from the last three centuries BCE to the first century CE. Some of the texts were intact, but most of the texts were fragments—over 100,000 fragments that made up 15,000 pieces of over 900 different manuscripts. Some of the manuscripts are copies or various versions of the same stories—multiple versions of Genesis, for example—and the scrolls are written in three different languages: Hebrew, Aramaic, and Greek. Some of the pieces were damaged or illegible. It was a massive task to put the pieces together, but a crucial one; this was not just a treasure trove of history, it was a key to understanding the origin and trajectory of modern religious belief, and this information had possible implications for religious belief and behavior going forward.

How do you put together a puzzle made up of over 100,000 pieces and 900 different manuscripts? You begin much the same way my client and I did. You begin by sorting. By trying to understand and identify each of the pieces. The Dead Sea Scroll fragments were initially sorted by the material that they were written on—leather parchment or papyrus. Then they were sorted by the language and the handwriting, by the spacing of the lines, and by the stories themselves. They were sorted and put between glass plates to protect them and to organize them into categories to see what pieces belonged to which stories—to be able to see if their initial sorting held up as they tried to put the manuscripts together.

Sorting isn't a linear task—in putting together a puzzle as easy as the penguins or as complicated as the Dead Sea Scrolls. There were many pieces that my client and I sorted and then had to sort again later—pieces we believed to be penguin that turned out to be ice, or pieces of ice that turned out to be sky. The sorting process—the identification process—requires that you try to figure it out over and over. You give the piece or fragment a name—ice, sky, parchment, Genesis—you guess its category, and you attempt to have it make sense in some context. When we are talking about healing from trauma it can be a bit more confusing to talk about, but it's fundamentally the same process. It's more confusing because we take the fragments of experience, or emotion, or visual image and we put language to them—we tell a story about them—but it isn't the full story of the experience that we will have in the Integration phase, where all the pieces come together in one place, where we have made meaning of the experience and can feel it and know it as ours and feel the impact of that. It's just the first attempt at trying to know what the pieces are and how they might fit together. It is the first attempt at telling one of the stories of what happened.

Researchers in Israel[3] looked at how a trauma survivor creates the story of his traumatic experience over time. This study looks at how a person responds to a single incident of trauma, not repeated trauma, but this example offers a way for you to understand how the identification process works, how the process of working with your traumatic experience allows you to make meaning of it and understand how the trauma connects with your identity and your life. In this study, the researchers followed five men who had survived a terrorist attack when they were on their way to a holiday gathering. The researchers interviewed the men when they were admitted to the emergency room following the attack, and then at multiple follow-up points, having them answer the same questions about their experience of the traumatic event at each meeting. The researchers focused on three factors of a narrative that are important for how a person copes with trauma—continuity and coherence, creation of meaning, and self-evaluation. They noted that the first attempts the men made at describing their

experience in the emergency room immediately following the terror attack were fragmented and only partial accounts. Over time, the men
were gradually able to recount more cohesive stories that were less fragmented and helped them make more meaning of the event. What was
most striking was how their stories shifted over time. The researchers
reported that

> this survivor described himself in the first week as hysterical,
> and said he screamed loudly at the horrible sights. At the inter-
> view one week post trauma, he blamed himself for terrifying the
> other survivors and frightening everybody. But as time passed,
> he attributed a different interpretation to his screams, and, at
> four months, he spontaneously said that maybe his screams
> actually saved everybody, because they were heard by the sol-
> diers who hurried to help.[4]

One of the fragments that this survivor had of the trauma was his
experience of screaming. The identification process was his attempt to
tell the story of his experience and how the screaming was a part of it.
The first pass at identification was "I was hysterical." The second pass
was "I scared everyone with my screaming." And much later, "I saved
people because I screamed." This research so clearly showed that it's
not just "what happened" or the objective reality "We were attacked
and I screamed"—it is the subjective experience of what you as a
survivor lived through and the way you construct reality as you are
sorting through the traumatic experience.

The preceding example was a single incident of trauma and the processing that occurred afterward. The processing of repeated trauma
is slightly different—in part because the ongoing trauma interferes

with the ability to revise the original story over time. At best what happens is that you create the first story from the fragments of experience enough to make sense of it, survive the trauma, and attempt to gain some sense of control from the helplessness that trauma creates. So the first story you have is not so much a story about the trauma as a story about protecting yourself from it. And in some cases you don't even have a protective story, you have just the unintegrated fragments of the traumatic experience. And then the fragments or the protective story gets buried under the weight of the next traumatic experience, where you do the same thing: you create a protective story or bury the fragments and move on.

So you show up to therapy and start to tell your trauma story, and it can seem like it is your story; it has coherence—that is, a beginning, middle, and end—and it has cause and effect. But the story isn't what actually happened, or it doesn't take into account the context. For example, I had a client who was sure that when she was little it was her fault that her uncle molested her. She can tell this story in the Unintegration phase—it is a trauma story, and she believes it—but it is also a story that is really a defense, because it protects her from the feelings of helplessness that she felt at the time and the rage at being unprotected. She makes the trauma her fault so that she can believe that she has the power to protect herself in the future. She tells this story in the Unintegration phase, and her experience in therapy (she feels protected, maybe for the first time) and the feedback/questions she gets (do you really think nine-year-olds are responsible for an adult's behavior?) start poking holes in her story. The old story starts to fall apart. And this is the Unintegration phase. So she is back to the fragments of the story—the images she has of it, the emotions—some of them new because the old story protected her from them. And now in the Identification phase, she starts to try on different ways of understanding the story—finding different ways to explore the emotions, or different vantage points to see what happened.

The goal is that with each new time she tells a part of her story, she is building toward a place where she can finally see herself in a more realistic way as a kid who lived through something terrifying. As she tells the story from each fragment she has about it—what she saw, what she heard, how she felt, how she feels talking about it now, what she understands about what children need—she can come to understand that she was actually a kid who needed protection, and now she has to rethink how she takes care of herself and create new assumptions about what is and isn't her responsibility. When the story has shifted to hold the person she is now and the kid she was then—and she can feel and hold all the feelings that go with it—then she makes the shift into the Integration phase. Identification is the work between the old story or the fragments that come up when the old story crumbles and when all the pieces come together to hold the you that experienced the trauma, and the you as you are now, and the impact holding this information has on you going forward.

So even something as straightforward as a penguin puzzle takes multiple attempts to identify the pieces in order to put it together. You may pick up the same piece a dozen times not knowing exactly what it will be or how it will connect with the whole picture. And the same was true for the fragments of the Dead Sea Scrolls. It took multiple attempts at identification—in fact, it sometimes took DNA testing or infrared technology in order to read a fragment. The first attempts to put the manuscript together actually impeded later work of assembling the documents, not unlike my trauma story of child abuse being my fault impeding my ability to have a complete narrative of the trauma and how it was integrated into my life. In the early 1950s, as scholars were initially putting the Dead Sea Scrolls together, they used newly invented adhesive tape—not knowing that the adhesive in the tape would eventually cause massive damage to the document and require decades of conservation work to be able to read the fragments again and put them together correctly.

With a jigsaw puzzle the pieces are visual, part of a visual scene; with the Dead Sea Scrolls the fragments were both physical objects and written words. With trauma, the different pieces exist in many different forms. They are visual—what we saw or what we imagined seeing.[5] They are verbal—sometimes you are starting with an old story. The pieces sometimes have sound or smell. They can be physical—the sensations in your body. They can be protective or disorganizing. The pieces can be emotions, or a piece you pick up can trigger layers of emotion. The Identification phase is where you pick up each piece and do your best to talk about it. Sometimes you are talking about this piece for the first time. Sometimes you are talking about this piece for the thirtieth time. Sometimes you have a piece you can see clearly—you can see the scene in your head—but you can't bring words to it. You can feel the emotion, but you have no clear story to tell. In the Identification phase you just keep picking up the pieces and trying again—picking up the piece and telling the story you can tell, and then seeing what else connects to it. How else you understand it. Let's look at an example of how the identification process can work in therapy.

One of my clients initially came to see me for an evaluation for bariatric surgery. Her evaluation revealed that she was struggling with emotional eating and bingeing, which can be dangerous with bariatric surgery. It was decided that she would first participate in an eating awareness group and gain some sense of control over her eating so she would be better able to manage the strict diet that is required of bariatric surgery patients. She was disappointed that she would have to complete the group before she could be cleared for the surgery, but she went to the group and when the eating awareness group ended, she asked to come back and see me for individual therapy because she realized that she needed to work on the issues that arose in the group. She realized her eating and weight issues weren't going to change solely with surgery—and that her issues of childhood trauma, which she thought she had put behind her, were still bothering her.

In doing the eating awareness exercises in group, she began to connect her eating and her weight to her history of childhood trauma. In the five-phase model, her participation in group began her process of preparation, and as she leaned on the support of the group and experienced the exercises, her old story and protections began to come apart. The story that she had about her eating when she began the group was that she was unable to control her eating—that she was out of control and surgery was the only way for her to be in control because after surgery she would have no choice but to follow the strict diet. She believed that she was "broken" and surgery would "fix" her. In group she was able to see that this first story didn't make sense in terms of her life: she believed she was out of control, and yet in her role as a charge nurse, she was excellent at being in control—she had no trouble setting limits and being disciplined about her work. Her old story wasn't holding up anymore. She was experiencing unintegration and she didn't know what was true about herself anymore.

So this is where the shift from unintegration to identification can begin. We started with her first puzzle piece about her eating and the feelings she had about that—and this first puzzle piece was her first story about being out of control. So we started with that piece to see what it might connect to, and what those connections could help us understand of other pieces. What did being out of control feel like? Were there other times she felt out of control besides her eating? How did this piece about feeling out of control when eating connect with how she felt as a child? When she first reported her experience of overeating, she did it in a rote sort of way—sort of businesslike, without much emotion—the same way she had answered the questions she needed to answer for the bariatric surgery survey. So sometimes when you start to pick up the pieces, you plan to tell new pieces of your story, but when you try to talk about them, the old story is what comes out first. That's okay. It's your starting point. You just pick up that piece again.

Gradually as she talked about feeling out of control with her eating and her experience as a child, lots of different emotions surfaced. At first, the emotion she was able to identify was the shame of being overweight and not being able to control her eating. Even though she was trying to tell her story of her childhood, the initial conversations were her experience of being in the present situation and talking with me about weight and her fear of being judged. Many different emotions can come up when you are trying to put words to your story. Sometimes they are the emotions you experienced during your trauma. Sometimes they are the emotions you couldn't experience during your trauma. And sometimes they are *secondary emotions*—the emotions you have about having an emotion. I might be angry that I shared something that made me feel vulnerable, or I might feel shame in revealing that I am angry—these are secondary emotions. When she was able to talk without feeling shame, she talked about feeling scared. That even though she wanted the surgery, and she wanted to lose weight, she was afraid not to have food to comfort her, and she was afraid of being more visible if she lost weight. She felt that her weight made her invisible, and this made her feel safe. This was a big shift in her story—food went from being something that made her feel out of control to something that she could also acknowledge made her feel safer. So then we spent time on the puzzle piece of safety—and this is where she talked more specifically about the trauma—about her mother's boyfriend abusing her younger sister and how she would sleep on the floor of her sister's room to protect her. And now more and more pieces were being identified and described: the feelings of being out of control, the feelings of shame, the feelings of fear, the wish for safety, the abuse of her sister. Each of these aspects were discussed separate from each other—not intentionally, but because they hadn't yet integrated into a whole story.

Memory

With short-term trauma it can sometimes be enough to remember the story itself and tell it to a caring witness, although even with the example of the men who witnessed the terror attack, the story went through multiple revisions. But with repeated trauma, there are always the three different forms of trauma: the trauma that did happen, what you did to survive and the protections you used, and what didn't happen because of the trauma. The middle phase of healing allows you to work with and talk about all of these forms of trauma because you are not talking about just history but also your experience in the present, your experience of what it is like to be on your healing journey, and what is getting in the way of the conversation.

In the Unintegration phase you start to wrestle with your defenses, the protections that keep you from feeling or keep you from feeling out of control—you stretch them enough so that you can talk about what did happen and what didn't happen. In the Identification phase you wrestle hard with your memory. You wrestle with the things you do remember, the things you don't remember, and the memory that you will come to understand as your basic operating system: your survival as memory, your worldview as memory. Why is it so difficult to pull up information? What makes everything seem so disconnected? Why is it so hard to tell your story? Why is it so hard to talk? All of the information stored in our brains and bodies is memory. Our history is memory. Our identities are memory. Our abilities are memory. The way we are in relationships is memory. Our coping skills are memory. Our experience of trauma is memory. And the trauma we experienced impacts memory at *every point*: the way you take in information, the way you store information, and the way you retrieve information. Without understanding memory, you really can't fully understand or have compassion for your response to trauma, or the way you have protected and continue to protect yourself from trauma, and why it is so hard to heal from it.

Driving up Route 128 outside Boston last summer, I passed the Polaroid headquarters being demolished. It was an eerie sight. Wires and rebar and concrete falling at odd angles juxtaposed with the rainbow sign. It looked like it had been bombed. Days later, it was gone. In my childhood, Polaroid was the symbol of the future—and now it was being removed from the landscape. It was somewhat ironic that the icon of memory was being erased. The future and the past—destroyed at once? When the Death Star was blown up in *Star Wars*, the force it held was destroyed all over the galaxy. Would the destruction of the Polaroid building release the power of the chemicals that created all those images? Would people open their photo albums from 1978 and see blank pages where middle school graduation had been?

The phrase may have been "a Kodak moment"—but a Polaroid picture literally captures memory as it is happening, and you take it away with you, tangibly, in hand. While the encoding of memory in your brain is different, there are some useful parallels between what occurs as you take a Polaroid picture and what your brain does to capture the memory.

Point, shoot, and click! The bottom of the Polaroid film contains packets of photochemicals. The rollers through which the film is sent break the packets of chemicals and spread them across the film and through the layers. This starts the chemical reaction. A reagent is spread across the film. Once the chemicals meet in the middle, the reagent starts to turn clear. As it turns clear, the image you captured slowly appears and you have a developed photo. Much like Polaroid film, memory in your brain is one big chemical reaction. How, what, and for how long we remember things is a chemical process; this chemical process is highly sensitive to trauma, and the process itself can change through trauma.

But before we get to the complexities of chemicals and brain structure, let's look at the main components of memory. We come into contact with information from the world voluntarily or involuntarily; in order for this information to become a memory, it must be encoded into the language of our brains. It must exist long enough to get consolidated into long-term memory, and ideally it should be sufficiently categorized—like a well-labeled manila folder in our file drawer—so that we might be able to retrieve it when we want to. Memory can be affected by the conditions of each of these areas: how we attend to incoming information, how the information gets encoded, how it gets consolidated, and how we are able to retrieve it. Traumatic experience, especially, affects each component of memory. And if we go back to the distinction we made at the beginning of the book—between single-incident trauma and repeated trauma—even traumatic memory may differ in how it ultimately affects memory, or our ability to hold, understand, and heal from trauma.

But to understand traumatic memory and the impact of trauma on the way we think and remember, it is helpful to understand the components of how your brain works and how memory works. Healing from trauma is a lot about healing memory—not changing it, or burying it, but helping your brain make connections between things that have been blocked or things that were never connected and need to be. Healing from trauma is about learning and growth, and learning and growth are really forms of memory.

In order to understand how memory works, you need to understand how your brain communicates. So let's start at the beginning in understanding your brain. The basic building block of the brain is the neuron or nerve cell. Your brain has at least 100 billion neurons making 100 trillion neural connections or synapses.

So how does information get into our brains? How do we "download" the world? The world comes to us through our senses: we see something, we hear something, we smell something, we taste something, and we feel/touch something—and often in combination. The nerve cells or neurons in our sense organs—our eyes, ears, mouth, nose, taste buds, and skin—connect to other neurons in our brain to bring the information from the outside world into our brain.

As I write I have a hot cup of mint tea next to me. I lean down and smell it, and this triggers the receptors for my olfactory nerves to communicate with each other until they reach my brain. Sensory input has a couple of different pathways through the brain: the high road, through the hippocampus and cortex, and the low road, through the amygdala. What is the difference? Why are there two roads? The low road is really your emergency broadcast system. It is a quick-and-dirty relay system to make sure that any incoming information doesn't spell imminent danger. Since mint tea doesn't trigger my amygdala to suspect danger, it is my hippocampus-cortex that enjoys naming the smell and thinking of the associations I have had with it. I drank a lot of mint tea studying for finals in college. I studied in the politics lounge in an old academic building that had its own hot plate and teakettle. The smell of mint tea can bring me right back into that room.

But what if the incoming information were unclear or ambiguous? What if I didn't know what I was looking at? If something dark veers into your peripheral vision, chances are you will jump away, even if that thing is a leaf and not something that could hurt you. This is because the visual data coming in is relayed along the low road to the amygdala, which is *fast (That looks like danger, tell legs to jump!)*, and then relayed to the high road, the hippocampus-cortex, which in neural terms is slower (*Hmmm . . . what is that? A bird? No. A plane? Wait, no, look, it's a leaf . . .*). But too late. Your amygdala already told you to "JUMP!" long before your cortex identified the object as a leaf. When we aren't triggered to imagine danger, it's the hippocampal-cortical route that presides, but the amygdala always gets first dibs—it gets to call the initial shots ahead of your "thinking and remembering" brain.

In fact, you don't even have to consciously remember something in order for your amygdala to respond. In my neuropsychology seminar I learned about a woman who had been in a terrible car accident that caused her to be in a coma, and after she woke up she had complete amnesia about the event—had no memory of the car accident at all. But when she was driven through the intersection where the accident occurred, she experienced all of the physiological reactions of stress: higher heart rate, higher respiratory rate, and anxiety. Her sensory data from her eyes seeing the intersection went to the amygdala, which had stored the data of this intersection as a dangerous place, even though no corresponding long-term memory of the accident was encoded in her hippocampus or cortex. Her thinking brain didn't know about the intersection or the accident, but her emotional brain did. The amygdala pulled the emergency alarm for the body.

The amygdala and the hippocampus are both part of the limbic system we discussed in the section on attachment: they are part of the main system of encoding information in our brains. Your amygdala stores your emotional memory and much of your memory for the first two years of your life.

The hippocampus, to oversimplify, is used to encode knowledge—the kind of learning you *know that you know*: people, places, events, objects, information. This kind of memory, memory for knowledge, is called explicit or *declarative* memory.[1] It allows you to answer questions like these: What is the capital of Wyoming? Where were your parents married? What was the name of your elementary school? How do you say *hat* in French? Information goes into the hippocampus, which communicates with the cortex, the vast sea of nerve cells that store our information.

The other memory system, also oversimplified, is the implicit or *procedural* memory system. This system is made up of the amygdala as well as the striatum and cerebellum, which are used to encode emotional memory and motor memory.[2] This is the learning that you know, but don't always know how you came to know it or how exactly you do it. It is the memory for motor skills like whistling, tying your shoes, or riding a bicycle. It is the memory of our emotions and habits. It is the memory from the preceding example of the woman knowing the intersection was dangerous without a conscious memory of the experience. It is our unconscious memory system that runs in the background.

It is a memory system set up for speed and efficiency. Your ability to do motor tasks like walking, writing, or driving are not supposed to take up a lot of cognitive space. When you first learn something, your thinking brain is engaged—remember learning to drive? You had to consciously pay attention to everything—your hands, your feet, the road. And then once it is learned, your motor memory takes over and it becomes automatic—reflex. I learned to drive on a standard car with a stick shift, and there are still days when heading into a turn, I reach for the shift even though I now drive an automatic. The motor memory of shifting at turns has remained in my system.

I sometimes think of procedural memory as either a blueprint or a computer operating system. It is a grid that we use to operate in the world, and we don't typically question it because we are unaware of it. We can only see its effects by observing our behavior. It is our habits, our reflexes, our biases, our assumptions. A growing body of work by attachment theorists and psychologists categorizes our understanding of relationships and attachment as a form of procedural memory: implicit relational memory.[3] Implicit memories operate more like blueprints than objects—they tell us how things work, what paths to follow, or what to move. Because implicit memories operate more out of our conscious minds and with less language, especially once they are learned, they are more difficult to consciously retrieve and describe. They are our autopilot.

This distinction between explicit and implicit memory has huge implications for traumatic memory. Because the low road through the amygdala is our emergency broadcast system and is the first place that trauma gets tracked, much of trauma gets encoded through procedural or implicit memory. This means that our fear-alarm systems operate at a level that is largely unconscious and therefore more difficult to work with directly. One way to understand the attachment styles we talked about in Part 3 is to think of them in terms of procedural memory: secure attachment is an unconscious memory system that organizes itself around safety, and insecure attachment is an unconscious memory system that organizes itself around fear.

So now the information gets in through our senses, and it gets routed through either the low road (the amygdala) or the high road (the hippocampus-cortex). And once information comes in, it needs to be encoded—to be "written" in a language the brain understands so it can be stored and remembered. Here we make a distinction between short-term memory and long-term memory. *Short-term memory*, also called *working memory*, is the holding area where information stays when it first comes in: someone tells us their phone number and we repeat it back, keeping it in working memory. Short-term memory lasts minutes. *Long-term memory* lasts days, weeks, years, or forever.

There are three possible ways for information to move from short-term memory to long-term memory: urgency, repetition, or association. *Urgency*, with the release of stress hormones, creates a powerful wash of chemicals that strengthens the connection between neurons or synapses. And, as we will soon see, urgency also determines how and where the brain encodes the information into long-term memory. So while urgency can create a very long-lasting memory—after a single exposure to a threat, the amygdala is capable of retaining that memory of threat throughout an entire life span—the ability to recall or retrieve the memory can be more troublesome and not under conscious control.

Repetition is a familiar learning tool (you have all memorized facts or vocabulary words by repeating them, or improved free-throw shooting through practice), and it creates long-term memory by eliciting strong chemical interactions between neurons at the synapse. Repetition is our strongest form of learning, and most learning, both implicit and explicit, relies on repetition. This is why it is so hard to make behavior change, because the new behavior must be repeated for so long.

Association is the ability of a piece of information to tap into a neural connection that already exists. If I read a list of nine numbers out loud to you and asked you to remember them and repeat them back to me after a couple of minutes, you would typically find this task very difficult. But if those nine numbers also happened to be your social security number, then the task would be easy, because they are numbers you have already memorized and stored to use. You have simply attached another label to the folder already labeled *social security number*. And if I asked you a year later what the numbers were, you would still be able to give them to me because they were already part of a previous neural connection. Association is also why it is important to look for strengths and behaviors across your life that you may be using in one place, like work, and perhaps weren't thinking of as a strength to use at home or in your work of healing. Once something is already learned, it can be easier to transfer that learning to another domain than to have to learn something new.

TRAUMATIC MEMORY

When you are trying to do something or remember something, the strongest memory, the most overlearned memory, will be chosen first. It is your memory that guides your behavior. Our brains are designed for this. And this fact predisposes the most urgent and most practiced information to be easily retrieved.[4] This is why traumatic memory is so efficient in its ability to embed itself in our brains. And it is also why traumatic memories and the protective habits we created to survive trauma are so difficult to unlearn.

What happens in memory when trauma occurs? In the beginning of the book we talked about the difference between acute trauma and repeated trauma. Let's look at memory for acute trauma first. When I was five my father was a volunteer fireman and had been called the night before to the scene of a train crash. The experience was remarkable enough for him that he got us in the car the next morning to go see it. The image of that scene is still vivid today. At five I wasn't prepared for what I would see, and I was overwhelmed by the devastation of the wreck. It had been a freight train and the wagons were all over the ground, and many had been consumed by fire. The wagon nearest us had carried books and they were scattered all over the ground—some burned, some intact. I think some of the overwhelm came from a five-year-old's understanding of the world—all objects are somewhat anthropomorphized, meaning they have a human quality—and looking at this destroyed train made me think it had died a horrible death. Also, books were my best friends, and seeing all the books all over the ground was too much. I was very frightened and asked to leave. I can still see the image clearly with photographic quality. The onetime experience fixed the memory in my mind before I could find a way to protect myself from it. Some information comes into our system with a dose of extra stress hormones, which break through our normal defenses of attention, and the information gets encoded fast. Therefore, the memory of the traumatic event or experience is stored as an extra vivid memory. And these memories have incredible longevity.

Repeated trauma is very different in terms of how memory is stored. The same year as the train crash, my parents had some very serious and violent fights. I know they happened because of other things that occurred afterward and stories I have been told by multiple sources, but I have only hazy, fragmented images of the memories of these fights—unlike the train wreck—even though my parents' fights were much more frightening and traumatizing. But witnessing the fights was different from witnessing the aftermath of a train wreck. The fights were a repeated trauma. By age five I had already developed ways to protect myself from experiencing the severe stress of acute trauma by not taking all of the information or experience of the fights into my memory.

Remember, memory is affected by the following areas: how we attend to incoming information, how it is encoded, how it is consolidated, and how we retrieve it. Long-term, sustained trauma affects all of these. First, we stop attending to traumatic information the same way that I attended to the aftermath of the train wreck. At the sight of the train wreck I was fully aware—my eyes were wide open and I could smell the fire. During my parents' fights I was not. I was either numb or in a dissociated state—that is, paying attention to my imagination and not what was actually happening. Being numb changes the way you take in information. If your hands were numb from cold and someone told you to close your eyes and handed you an object, it might be hard to know what it was. If I wrapped a microphone in a blanket, the incoming recorded sound would be muffled. When we numb our senses, the incoming traumatic information isn't recorded as clearly or in as organized a fashion. It is registered as noise, and it likely reinforces the neural pathways of previous trauma, but it isn't remembered as a discrete event or as discrete information—it is stored as an emotional memory, a motor memory, as the "practice" of trauma.

Children are especially known for defenses that protect them from taking in repeated trauma. Adults do it too, but because children have fewer options at their disposal to protect themselves (they can't run away or leave), they have to use the brain's ability to limit incoming information. The first defense, which I just described, is numbing. The second common defense is dissociation. Dissociation is often described as "leaving the body" or disappearing. It is the capacity of the brain to have the current situation not be happening to you. Many people describe traumatic situations where they felt like they were watching the traumatic scene they were living through from above; they could see it happening as if they were watching from the ceiling.

The thing about dissociation is that it creates a state of being that feels like "not-me." At its most extreme, dissociated states can become organized personalities that are part of what was once called multiple personality disorder (and is now called *dissociative identity disorder*), but all dissociated states are split off from the memory function and the learning function of the everyday working brain of an individual. It's the memory equivalent of having a separate hard drive or a separate set of computer files in a different computer language to work from during trauma. The memories of trauma essentially are stored in this separate hard drive, and it protects the other hard drive from having to manage the trauma. You don't so much choose to dissociate as you either are just able to do it or not—people have more or less capacity to dissociate. From my experience of working with trauma survivors, the people who lived through repeated trauma and didn't have the capacity to dissociate were more likely as teens and young adults to use drugs or alcohol as an alternative means to reach a protected or numbed state. But whether you used drugs or experienced dissociation, which involves an increase in endogenous opiates (narcotic-like drugs the body makes itself)—the altered state affects the way you attend to and then encode incoming information.

In addition to releasing chemicals in the body to numb or alter the state of consciousness, stress also shifts the way incoming information is routed or encoded. The same chemicals that are released when we are under stress heighten the activation of the amygdala,[5] making it more likely that the memory will be encoded as a procedural memory—a memory of something you know, but don't know you know. To make this even more likely, high levels of stress hormones shut down the neural networks of the hippocampus-cortex circuit—effectively taking our memory for knowledge "offline," which means that the details of the memory, the story of the memory, and the context of the memory are not properly encoded.[6] The memory is there, your brain recorded the information, but the information was stored without any meaningful labeling or description.

Even more striking is the loss of language during and after trauma. During trauma, and even recalling trauma, there is reduced blood flow to the parts of the brain that process language, which hinders your ability to use language to store or retrieve memory.[7] The fact that trauma interferes with our language capacity is important to understand because it will help you have compassion for yourself as you try to find words and language for your experiences of trauma. When you experienced your trauma, the parts of your brain that process language were essentially offline. The brain, during trauma, tries to be efficient and sends its blood flow to the parts of the brain that are most needed in a crisis. So your experience isn't remembered in words, and that's why it can be hard to remember the story in words. This is why it can be so hard to find words to describe what you experienced—and why you spend so much time in the Identification phase working to bring language to your memory and trying to tell your story from different vantage points of understanding.

Finding Your Path

If its interest in truth is linked only to amnesty and compensation, then it will have chosen not truth, but justice. If it sees truth as the widest possible compilation of people's perceptions, stories, myths, and experiences, it will have chosen to restore memory and foster a new humanity, and perhaps that is justice in its deepest sense.

ANTJIE KROG, *Country of My Skull*[1]

The work of identification is repetition. It is picking up a piece, a fragment, a part of the story over and over again. Annie Dillard tells a story about a student who goes up to a famous writer and asks, "Do you think I could be a writer?" To which the writer responds, "I don't know. Do you like sentences?"[2] In the Identification phase you don't just have to *like* sentences, you have to *love* sentences. You have to love sentences, because sometimes sentences are all you get—and it's more than the single word you started with. You have to love sentences because they are a piece of your story. And sentences are great because you can repeat a sentence as often as you need to in order to keep going. It doesn't matter if you have already said it; say it again. You can grasp on to the last sentence you spoke to find your way again—like the handholds and footholds of a climbing expedition, or like the stone cairns that mark the trails above the tree line.

In her waiting room, my therapist had a flat basket of small rocks and stones. When I first started in therapy I thought this was awesome because I was a therapist (in training) who also had a flat basket of small rocks and stones in *my* waiting room. I took this as a sign of validation (*Look! I am a cool therapist too!*). And the similarity and familiarity gave me the hope that I could feel at home there. The rocks in the flat basket in my office were stones I had picked up from the coast of Maine—all different shapes and colors; most were different colors of granite and many had a big stripe of white in the middle, rocks that my nieces and nephews called "lucky rocks." The rocks were something that the teenagers who came to see me could take with them if they wished—reminders of the work that they were doing or talismans to give them strength. The stones in the flat basket in my therapist's office were more polished, but there was one larger flat rock that I quickly decided to use as the base of a small cairn.

Now, cairns are traditionally piles of large rocks usually placed along trails as trail markers. I saw my first cairns hiking in the White Mountains when I was a teenager. On the first day, in the bright sunlight of a summer day the cairns looked totally unnecessary. The trail ahead seemed obvious; it looked like there was no need for a giant pile of stones every twenty yards to mark the way. But when I woke up the next day to fog and rain and couldn't see more than twenty-five feet in front of me, the purpose of the cairns was bright and clear—cairns are beacons. Hiking from cairn to cairn was the only possible way forward.

If you are a writer, you have to love sentences, and if you are hiking in the White Mountains in fog, you have to love cairns. That summer I traveled for two whole days above the tree line only ever seeing the way to the next cairn, which taught me the lesson that you don't have to be able to see the whole path ahead of you in order to keep going—you just need to be able to see to the next cairn.

There were times over the years in my therapist's waiting room that I would pick up a rock and place it on the flat rock. Then I would put one more small rock on top and sit down in the waiting room chair, pleased with my effort and my miniature cairn. I never said anything to my therapist about them. Actually, there were times I barely said anything to my therapist about anything. There were many times that I found it really hard to talk. As someone who had failed self-control in second grade because I couldn't stop talking, I was stunned to find myself unable at times to find words—any words at all. As Bessel van der Kolk says, "As long as you keep secrets and suppress information, you are fundamentally at war with yourself. . . . The critical issue is allowing yourself to know what you know. That takes an enormous amount of courage."[3] And what I found was that it takes an enormous amount of bravery, effort, and patience to keep working to find the words that may help you remember. There were many times it felt like I didn't have words. But on those days I had those stones. And with those stones I built cairns to find the path forward.

The cairns in the basket of rocks were a source of play—they gave me the feeling that I could move forward and not feel stuck, the way I felt stuck with language. Sometimes I would come into the waiting room and the stones would have been moved. It felt like a conversation—a back-and-forth—without any of the pressure to know words. Over time, the play with the stones in the basket made its way from the waiting room to the office—with metaphor, with poetry, with art. And all of these cairns slowly helped me find my way forward, to words and to myself. Cairns are a perfect reminder that the whole way forward doesn't have to be clear. You don't have to see the whole path, you just have to be able to make it to the next cairn.

The Identification phase is about moving along the path from cairn to cairn, sentence to sentence, memory to memory, forging a trail that you can follow. Sometimes the markers are small, sometimes they are big, and sometimes you have to go over the same parts of the trail again and again. Robert Moor, in his book *On Trails*, states that "every trail is, in essence, a best guess." [4] Even in the situation of the most primitive trail making, an ant or animal finds food—something that they want to return to—and leaves a preliminary trail. The next ant or animal behind them will take a different, usually slightly smoother route, cutting off some of the sharper edges or turns. Over time, with many passes along the same route, a trail is made that one can consistently follow. "Trails," explains Moor, "extend backward—and paths extend forward." [5] The trails we are creating or re-creating are our history, our full trauma history—and by creating that trail, we can locate that history in the past, where it belongs. Trauma may have happened in the past, but until it is integrated, the trauma tends to exist in an ever-happening present. Trauma obliterates the past and the future and leaves you in a state where it feels like the trauma is always currently happening or you are always trying to protect yourself from it happening again. Healing gives you back the full range of time, but you have to do the work first of clearing the trails of the past so that you might find the openings to the paths of the future again.

What helps you tell the different aspects of your story in the Identification phase? What gets in the way? One thing that trauma survivors struggle with is finding words, or telling their story and worrying that it's not some perfect form of the truth. Sometimes it can be hard to put into words what it is you are trying to describe—the words can seem too small for the emotions that you are describing. The words *true* and *truth* can sometimes feel too big. I like to remind myself and my clients that when I use the word *truth* in terms of healing from trauma, I am talking about truth with a little *t*, not a capital *T*. When you are trying to tell your story, you are not on a witness stand—even if it can sometimes feel like it. You are not trying to tell everyone's truth, or some version of an objective truth, a truth that everyone would agree on. You are trying to say what is true for *you*, in this moment as you tell it. I have found that the most important work of the Identification phase can be saying *one true thing* at a time. One true thing to get you started. One true thing as the cairn. It can sound small, but it isn't. It can sound easy, but it isn't—saying one true thing can be really hard.

If you have experienced repeated trauma, you know that you couldn't say the truth out loud. Sometimes it was outright forbidden, sometimes you were trying to protect others, and sometimes you didn't say it because you didn't want to know what you lived through. For people who have grown up under brutal regimes—whether in your own home or in a foreign country, or whether you have lived through any long siege of trauma or grief—you were rarely permitted to say what was true. You had to say what was expected of you or what you and others needed to hear in order not to get hurt. Most narratives of repeated trauma are told by the aggressors who perpetrated the traumas. They are told by the people who had the power—the people who did the damage. During and after trauma, those in power often control the message: they control what gets printed, what gets said, and what gets heard. Quite often the story you have, the story you start with, is the aggressor's story, and it is this story you have mistaken for your own. As Milan Kundera said, "The struggle of man against power is the struggle of memory against forgetting."[6] It is the old story that begins to crack in the Unintegration phase. And it is your story that you are working hard to remember in the Identification phase. I have yet to meet a trauma survivor who hasn't felt the truth catch in their throat. Who hasn't started to speak and found that the words dissolved as they came close to moving to their tongue. One second you can see the horror, can feel the fear, can see the image clearly, and then when you go to describe it with words, everything disappears. Your brain is blank. You have gone numb. Where did the story go?

And almost every trauma survivor I have met has doubted their words, has believed one thing above all: they would not be believed. This is the difference between putting together a jigsaw puzzle and putting together the story of your trauma. When you pick up a piece of the jigsaw puzzle and hold it up, you don't imagine that there is someone who wants you to believe it is anything other than you think it is. But speaking the truth about trauma tends to conjure the image of someone who is judging you and your words. Each little piece of your puzzle is subjected to the most glaring scrutiny, with the judge demanding, "Are you *sure* that is the way it happened?" And this truth can feel like a double-edged sword because there is a part of you that, when you get your truth out, desperately wants to be believed. And there is another part of you that wants that truth about your trauma not to be true—is afraid that the act of saying it out loud will actually make it true. I know of war veterans afraid to tell their stories because they can't feel the truth of the stories as they tell them—instead they only can feel the truth of the story when they see the look of horror on their listeners' faces. A soldier tells his therapist that he had to kill a child, and he watches the look on his therapist's face and fears the horror that may be reflected in her facial expression. It is a double-edged sword to be understood. Remember that stories happen in social relationships, and this interpersonal act helps us hold our stories, helps us hear our stories, and ultimately helps us make our stories whole again.

Helpful Practices for Identification

So what is the work of the Identification phase and how do you support it? The work of the Identification phase is anything that helps you take what you are experiencing on the inside and bring it to the outside so you can bring language and meaning to it—so that you can share it with another and have it witnessed. It's the work of gathering all your aspects of memory—the memory you have of what happened, and the memory that has become part of your behavior or your beliefs, your survival behavior as memory—and giving that memory language in as many layers as you need to feel like you are telling your full story. So what helps you get your experience and memory from the inside to the outside? What helps you stay engaged in the challenge of working with your memory and combating the difficult emotions and frustration that can arise as you work with telling your story?

One thing that I found helpful through the process of healing was to think of the Identification phase in the same way that I think about writing. When I was struggling through long stretches of the Identification phase, I was in graduate school and writing a lot of papers. And so I found it helpful to use Anne Lamott's book *Bird by Bird* as a training manual not just for writing but also for healing. Lamott explains that writing doesn't happen in a neat or linear way. She states that "the only way I can get anything written at all is to write really, really shitty first drafts."[1] Shitty first drafts are where you have to quiet all the voices of judgment and perfection and just write—no matter how it comes out. Using the frame of "shitty first drafts" in the Identification phase of healing helps you talk yourself down from feeling like you have to have the perfect description or the absolute truth. The idea of the shitty first draft helps you keep at the struggle of talking—helps you see the act of conversation as practice and not performance, as a place where you learn, repair, and restore. So the first thing that you really must embrace is the idea that the work in the Identification phase is *practice* and that you will have a lot of shitty first drafts on your way to having your full trauma story.

What helps to support you in your ability to stay with the idea that healing requires practice? In my own work of healing I learned this from watching small children. Children are the gurus of learning. Their whole being is driven by and oriented toward learning. They are shameless in their pursuit of new skills and new knowledge, and nothing so small as falling down, dropping something, or spilling something will get in their way of learning. They will practice things over and over and over. They are not embarrassed by what they don't know and not slowed down by what they can't yet do. Watching them, I found that I was insanely jealous of the children I observed. I was jealous of their lack of self-consciousness and their shamelessness. In my healing I often felt so much shame at showing what I didn't know or couldn't do because I believed that I already should know how to do it—that it shouldn't require repetition. I believed that talking about my experience shouldn't be as difficult or awkward as it was, or take as long as it did.

The truth is that I actually understand hard work and repetition. I rowed for four years of college and then spent a few years after college trying to make the U.S. women's rowing team. For nearly seven years I trained six to eight hours a day. Given that rowing is really the same stroke over and over again, I was a master of repetition. I was really good at trying it, and then trying it again. I was good at working my way through things, and patiently (or not so patiently) getting better at something. But healing was different. Healing so often wasn't about working harder. I often felt like I was running at the same wall over and over again—and in rowing that worked, and in healing it didn't.

For a long time I could only see what I couldn't do when I watched the children, and yet when I slowed down and got quiet enough to really observe the children learning, I realized they weren't just using repetition and perseverance. I observed that they were using something completely different from me—they were using play. Play was their technology for learning. We don't think of play as technology, and yet play exists in every species and every culture as a primary and powerful means of learning. Sometimes the learning is about the actual skill, but as it turns out, play is much more likely to help us learn about our capacity to engage with the unknown, with what is difficult in the world and inside us, than about any particular skill. Play is more an attitude than any particular activity. After all, play is completely subjective—I might find gardening fun and playful, and you may find it to be an absolute chore, and you may find mountain biking playful, whereas I find it to be terrifying.

One of my favorite examples of how practice can also be play comes from my time as a waterfront director at a Girl Scout camp in New York State. The waterfront was on a lake that had one fixed dock and a floating dock out in deeper water. In the afternoons the girls would come down to the lake for free swim, and the most important activity of free swim was a game called Rate My Dive. Girls would line up to dive, and it was my job as the lifeguard to play the role of dive rater. Each girl dove into the water, and when they came up for air they would turn and look at me and I would announce their rating. The rating system was made up and broken down into ridiculous increments: "That dive was a 3.56." They hung on their ratings and earnestly got on the dock to try again. Play is what helps us practice—helps us come into contact with the things we fear and overcome them. And Rate My Dive was exactly this kind of play. Diving is a difficult and frightening skill for kids to learn, but doing it repeatedly with the distraction and fun of the rating gets them to practice. They focused on the rating and what they could do to improve it. The repetition of learning takes a lot of patience and the ability to keep going in increments.

So let's first think of play as a stance, as a way of approaching the practice that you need to do in order to heal. Healthy play is spontaneous—there is openness and freedom of movement. Games change, the endings of the story change, and anything can happen in the course of the play. Children working out the stress of starting school may play school, but it can take many forms and they often switch roles—sometimes they play the teacher or sometimes they play the brilliant student. They play "jungle school" with their stuffed animals or make their parents be students so they can experience the power of being the teacher. Traumatic play is different. Traumatic play is grim and repetitive.[2] Children who have been in a car crash will play "car crash." Each episode of play is like the one before. The ending never changes. They just reenact the car accident over and over. There is no sense of mastery—there is only repetition. Play is integral in the healing of trauma. But traumatic play won't heal on its own; traumatic play needs intervention and support from the outside to shift and work with the story. And if we return to the example of Rate My Dive, we can see that playful practice is about repetition and play, but it is not repetition and play in isolation, or just with peers. Rate My Dive serves another crucial purpose: I was required to witness each dive—to really *see* them dive. The combination of repetition and being held in awareness creates the ideal environment for growth, and especially for healing. As the author M. R. Montgomery states,

> There is this thing that happens with children: If no one is watching them, nothing is really happening to them . . . if you are very small, you actually understand that there is no point in jumping into the swimming pool unless they see you do it. The child crying, "Watch me, watch me," is not begging for attention; he is pleading for existence itself. They will remember. They will hold it, keep it, make it true.[3]

In the Identification phase, you are not just telling your story, sentence by sentence. You are having your story, each piece of it, witnessed. As you pull up each piece of the puzzle, your words are witnessed, as is your brave work of finding those words and sharing them. Your therapist or your group can act as the lifeguard, witnessing your story and holding the pieces for you as you dive in and come up with pieces of your story over and over.

So what does it mean to hold the stance of play or playfully approach the practice needed in telling your story? How do you find words or language for the feelings that you have, for the images you have, for the memories you are trying to piece together? Identification is the phase in which any therapy that helps you connect your experience with language may be useful to try. Expressive therapies—art, music, and dance—can all help expand your ability to take your internal experience and add another dimension that can help you bring language to something that you couldn't reach otherwise. Metaphor can be helpful in finding language, and expressive therapies offer an intermediate space between experience and language. You can take a fragment, an emotion, a part of your story that you can see or hear but that feels too difficult to describe out loud—or for which you can't find the language—and through other forms of expression you can make a first pass at it. You can draw it in a picture or find a piece of music that describes it. And you can bring language to this: you can talk about the picture or the music and how it relates to the piece or the fragment. You build a vocabulary—you find how the piece connects.

An example of using art to bring language to an internal experience is when I decided to try a body tracing. The exercise for a body tracing can be used for many things—all you need to do is have a long length of paper, like butcher paper, and then lie down and have someone trace the outline of your body. I took the tracing of my body, taped it to the wall in my kitchen, and made the rule I could do whatever I wanted—but I had to do what I felt, not what I thought. For reasons I didn't understand, I felt compelled to rip multicolored construction paper into small pieces and glue them on, mosaic-like. I filled in the entire tracing with all of the tiny pieces of paper in various configurations of color—like an abstract mosaic. And the finished product surprised me. I had been looking for a way to talk about how fragmented or disconnected I felt, and here was a picture that helped me have the conversation. I could talk about the pieces of paper on the tracing and how they didn't connect with each other, and I could talk about the pieces of my experience and how I couldn't feel the connections yet. It was a relief to have some language for my experience and to feel like I could be understood. I have used body tracings as both a therapist and a consultant—it is a way to help people bring their whole self into the conversation. Most people who have experienced trauma tend to protect themselves by disconnecting from their bodies and living in their heads. As they work through the Unintegration phase, this often begins to shift and a lot of emotions and sensations occur, and they can experience great difficulty in talking about it. Using the body tracing is a way to talk about their body at a slight distance away from it.

Body tracings are only one way of many to explore something difficult through the use of an object—whether art, music, writing, or dance. Using an object or an action that allows you to work with difficult emotion or feeling at a slight distance is called *displacement*. You are displacing the internal experience or story from something difficult to an easier, more acceptable or immediate substitute. This can all sound very clinical, but having something concrete to look at and speak to can be immensely helpful in many everyday situations. I often have my corporate clients sketch their organizations and where they see connections or disconnection between the various people or roles. Getting it out on paper allows them to get more information down about the situation than they typically would if they were talking, and it allows them an extra bit of distance from the experience—they are both a part of the chart they just made *and* outside the chart talking to me about it.

Metaphor is the verbal version of displacement. One of the easiest methods to use, from kids through adults, is to ask this question: If your feeling/problem/struggle were an animal, what animal would it be? Describe the animal and then talk about what this animal is thinking or feeling, and what it needs and wants. This is a way to play with the language of feelings or needs—and then you can gradually see if it helps you tell your story. As a client I have used displacement as a way to take in the safety and care of treatment. My job has required a lot of travel, which has been difficult for me in therapy; I don't like leaving, because I fear being forgotten or left behind. Over the years I have used displacement in a number of ways. Perhaps the first time I really noticed its impact was when I was going on a trip to Romania. I had recently been using the metaphor of a bear to describe my feelings, and so when I left on the trip I asked my therapist to watch this metaphorical bear. We discussed where he would stay (in a pen in the backyard), what he liked to eat (fish and, oddly, candy), and what he needed (stories). During the trip, we occasionally had contact through email and she would update me on the status of the bear—how he was doing, what it was like to watch him. And miraculously, I felt, for perhaps the first time ever, remembered—even though I was away. What is really important to understand is that we had had the regular adult conversations about the trip. She had said directly, "I will remember you." I could understand each word and cognitively understand, but I couldn't absorb this message—like a nutrient that can't get across the blood-brain barrier, the message could not get in directly, because my protective walls were still too high. Through displacement I could actually feel the words. I knew where we were eventually headed, and it gave me hope that I could feel it for myself at some point, even if, right now, I could just feel it through the metaphorical experience of the bear. The metaphor allowed me to put into words what I was feeling, but it also allowed me to receive information in a way that I could hear it.

This is the magic of displacement—it allows for playfulness to support difficult information and difficult feelings. And what may be surprising for people with trauma histories is that the difficult feelings may very well be positive feelings like love, care, attention, support, and reassurance. Working in displacement is play because it enables you to take something you are feeling and separate it from yourself just enough to not feel stuck or trapped by it. You have enough space, suddenly, to move around something that has been really difficult and look at it from more than one perspective. Sometimes you can find your own metaphors—they will come to you as you are trying to describe your experience: "I felt like I was in a boat that was stuck on a sandbar" or "It feels like I want to jump into the pool, but it feels like there is no water in it." And sometimes your therapist or someone in your support group may offer a metaphor. And sometimes you may borrow the images, examples, or words of others that you find in fiction, film, or poetry.

In the Identification phase, poetry can be a great way to find language for your emotions and experience. And it can be a great way to honor the fragmented nature of how traumatic memory is stored and restored. Poems are by their very nature fragments, but beautiful fragments, whose sole purpose, it seems, is to bring language to experiences that defy language. When you are trying to talk about experiences that don't make sense to you, or trying to find words to match feelings, sometimes poetry can be a great place to start. I had a stanza from Adrienne Rich's poem "Integrity"[4] taped inside my day planner for a while— "Anger and tenderness—my selves / And now I can believe they breathe in me as / Angels and not as polarities." I was struggling with the feelings of anger that were coming up, and the idea that feelings of anger and tenderness could work together—both the image and the idea—allowed me to talk about my anger and how I understood tenderness, and what both of these emotions meant to me as I healed from trauma. *Tenderness* seemed to be a word that could single-handedly create an internal environment for healing—just saying it or hearing it softened my heart enough for it to take more in. It reminded me to be gentle. It reminded me to be kind. I borrowed this line of poetry and the words, and they helped me start conversations for myself—and helped me piece together parts of my story.

Other people's words can be important as starting places for your own ability to tell your story. I remember reading the opening line in Barbara Kingsolver's *Poisonwood Bible*—"Imagine a ruin so strange it must never have happened"[5]—and feeling such relief because this was *exactly* the way it felt to try to talk about trauma: that it was this ancient ruin, but it was so difficult to describe this ruin that the impossibility of description made it seem impossible that it had happened at all. The relief at finding metaphors and images in poems for emotions you couldn't quite name or describe—or finding other's people's words, phrases, or stories to support your ability to talk—feels like finding edge pieces when you are putting together a puzzle; you suddenly have something a little more solid to lean on while you figure out what goes together. Other people's words and stories can help you while you are finding language and ways to talk about your trauma. Don't worry about using them. You will use them until you find your own, and you will use them to help you find your own. And as you move on in your healing you will know these fragments of poetry and writing as the dear, kind friends that they are. They will always remind you of the places on the trail where you have been.

PART 5

Integration

Once again I had found myself in the presence of a truth and had failed to recognize it. Consider what happened to me: I had thought myself lost, had touched the very bottom of despair; and then, when the spirit of renunciation had filled me, I had known peace. I know now what I was not conscious of at the time—that in such an hour a man feels that he has finally found himself and become his own friend.

ANTOINE DE SAINT-EXUPÉRY, *Wind, Sand and Stars*[1]

Integration

As we approach the Integration phase, let's review how we got here and what the transitions between the phases are like so that you can know where you are, and you can recognize the phases when you are in them again. Keep in mind that the journey of healing from repeated trauma is a repeating spiral—you are moving forward, but you are constantly cycling around. You began in the Preparation phase, where you worked on strengthening your external resources (the supports you had in your outside world—work, home, family, friends) and your internal resources (your capacity for awareness and mindfulness). And you also worked to strengthen your relationship with your therapist and create solid communication and the foundations of trust. You practiced leaning on the trust that you built within yourself with the work you did in the Preparation phase, and you also leaned on the trust in the relationship with your therapist.

And as you leaned on the trust and safety you created in the Preparation phase, you entered the Unintegration phase. Remember that unintegration happens because you lean on support—not because you try to knock down your defenses, but instead, you work on risking behavior that is different than the behavior of what you did to protect yourself. It is an important tenet of this book that defenses are dismantled slowly and carefully. Unintegration is the process of unlearning your protections—of not living in survival mode—so that you can gain access to more of your self, your story, your experience. Perhaps your way of protecting yourself was to hide your feelings and be numb, so you were not overwhelmed with feelings. Or maybe your way of protecting yourself was to endlessly take care of other people, obscuring your own needs—and now in the act of getting help, you are beginning to lean on someone else and experience the emotions that come up for you when you feel vulnerable.

During the Unintegration phase, these pieces of your history started to come up—things you had pushed aside during the years that the trauma was happening—and it was uncomfortable. The Unintegration phase can feel disorienting and disorganizing, but you can make the shift into the Identification phase. You can gradually bring language to your feelings, to your experiences, to what did happen, and to what you used to survive. You can bring language to the memories and begin to know what belongs to you—and maybe what isn't yours to hold on to anymore. Perhaps your initial story was that you believed that you didn't protect your sister, and for most of your life you have felt that it was your job to protect people. As you look at pieces of this story, you decide what your actual responsibility was given your age and the circumstances. You look at the assumptions you have about what it means to protect someone and whose job it is. You look at whose rules and beliefs these were. How do they serve you now? What makes sense? And in your work of sorting and talking about the pieces, you begin to see and feel the complete picture of an aspect of your trauma. You do all this work in the Identification phase, identifying pieces and talking about them, and then one day you have that conversation and something shifts—all of these pieces come together and you can see a whole picture and you "get it" in a new way. This is the Integration phase. Integration is where you acknowledge what happened and make meaning of it, which allows you to get a sense of the devastation and loss. And because your story is witnessed and can be held in a healing relationship, you can get a sense of safety and freedom you may have never experienced.

But what does it mean for something to come together into an integrated whole? A nontraumatic example of integration is my experience of learning how to do an Eskimo roll in a kayak—where you roll over and come back up in one move. I spent one summer working at camp, and every day during my break that summer, my friend Connor would work with me while I tried to master the Eskimo roll. To learn the Eskimo roll you have to learn the separate parts of the roll and master each part. But being able to complete the whole motion—roll forward, spin over, and twist up using your hips—all at once—that took me all summer. The mastery of the whole motion was integration. It wasn't enough to know or master the pieces. They all had to come together in a continuous whole in order to work. And just because I did it once didn't mean I had it down completely. I still needed practice with the parts, and I still needed continuous practice with the whole motion.

There's a couple of things you should know about the Integration phase. One is that, at least initially as you move through your healing journey, the transition can feel abrupt. The fragmenting that happens with repeated trauma has kept you protected from seeing and feeling the whole picture. And in the Identification phase you keep talking or doing whatever you need to get your story out. You may repeat yourself and tell the story from different aspects and relate it to different parts of your life now, and then there is a day where suddenly some aspect comes together in full view, and you get a sense of the whole. And this can feel big. This is an iterative process—sometimes the pieces that come together form one memory of one event, and sometimes they help you see your trauma experiences as a whole. It is different for everyone, and it is different at different points in your healing journey. The transition to the Integration phase can often feel sudden. In the Identification phase we talked about the analogy of putting a puzzle together—and with trauma it's a little like putting together a puzzle you don't have a picture for.

Sometimes the Integration phase starts with a state of shock. Your whole view changes and you sit there, stunned, looking around. In the spring of 2013 there were a series of very dangerous and destructive tornadoes in Oklahoma. One of them was nearly 1.3 miles wide, covering a 17-mile stretch. This EF5 tornado had wind speeds reaching 210 miles per hour. Witnesses described this tornado as a "black wall of destruction." The photos that emerged from this tornado were of complete devastation. Homes and elementary schools were flattened—just piles of rubble and twisted metal. All that was left for miles were the cement slabs where the homes once stood and piles and piles of debris. Yet scattered among the rubble would be a closet-size space with concrete walls, or a doorway angled up from the ground. These safe rooms or underground shelters were the only things left intact in all of the destruction. The Integration phase is a lot like emerging from the safe room. Even though you knew there was a storm, and you knew some of what you might see, it's still a shock to open the door of your shelter and take in the whole picture.

The next thing about the Integration phase is that it can be really tiring. It overtakes you and even though you are a person with a ton of energy who never naps, you find you need a nap every day. Or you can't say yes to everything that you used to. It can feel like a huge effort to do mundane tasks. It can feel like you are on your last raw nerve. Both the grief and the new learning that emerge in this phase take a lot of energy, and you will find that even simple things can feel like a major task. There is a slowness, deliberateness, or quietness that goes with this phase. Sometimes this slowness can feel exhausting and heavy, the way it feels hiking at high altitude where you have to work hard to take each step. As Ed Viesturs, an Everest climber and guide, states, "The last 300 feet to the summit you would think is only 300 feet but at these altitudes (at 28,700 feet) the amount of effort that you need is exponentially increasing in difficulty. . . . The last 300 feet take one to two hours to climb. . . . You breathe six to eight times and then you take another step and then you breathe six or eight times. . . . You can't look at the whole ascent. You have to break it down into small sections and into tiny little steps."[1]

The Integration phase shares a stance, an environment, an experience with the Unintegration phase. Both unintegration and integration require a letting go, or a state of relaxing into safety. In the Unintegration phase the old pieces come apart as you let go, and in the Integration phase, there is enough space and safety for the pieces to come back together. You need to create "transitional space"[2] for these shifts to happen. The hard work is actually in the "not-doing." What I mean by not-doing is if you hold tightly, if you work too hard, if you push ahead, there isn't enough loosening for things to shift. The image I have for integration is what it takes fractured bone to heal—the stillness that a splint or a cast provides. The fragments must be in contact with each other and the whole limb must be still enough, long enough, for the parts to be able to mend. Integration is a very tender time. It is a time that requires a bit of stability as you allow the pieces to come together and mend.

What is more difficult to explain is exactly how this happens and how long it takes. Integration is about healing, mending, growing. Integration is new sustained learning or development. It is a repeated learning, and when it occurs there is a shift—a shift that changes not only how you feel but how you understand: how, as the psychologist Robert Kegan would say, you make meaning of something.

The Integration phase is the place where all three aspects of repeated trauma come together: what did happen, the protections that aided survival, and what didn't happen. It is also where the fragmented parts of traumatic memory—the story, the feelings, the experience—all come together in one place. You understand what happened in the context in which it happened. Integration allows all of the pieces from the Identification phase to make contact with each other, to sit in the same space, to knit together. The two biggest pieces of work in the Integration phase are *mourning*[3] and *new beginning*.[4] Mourning is facing the impact of what actually happened and grieving what did and didn't happen—grieving the years you needed to protect yourself. And new beginning is the ability to understand and practice new behaviors of the missed learning and growth, in order to seek out ways to have those experiences. The word *integration* comes from the Latin *integratio*, which means "renewal." And in bringing the pieces together you not only re-create your history, you renew your sense of yourself as a whole. The pieces combine to become something greater because in healing there is growth.

Integration is this something greater—it is an "aha" experience. It's not learning in the sense of knowledge of facts so much as it is finally understanding the entirety of something, the meaning of something, or how things are actually connected. Integration is a shift of worldview—it transforms not just *what* you know but *how* you know. I sometimes refer to these moments as "Helen Keller Water Moments." In the story that most people know from the film *The Miracle Worker*,[5] Helen is a young child who loses her sight and hearing to scarlet fever and is lost in her own world. She rages and fights and struggles to make herself understood, and she can't connect to the world around her. She has experiences, feelings, and sensations—but no way to put these things into language. And then her teacher, Anne Sullivan, comes along and begins to teach her that each thing in the world is paired with a word. And in the beginning, since Helen is a smart child, she is able to memorize words and how to spell them, but it is an exercise, it's all intellectual. She hasn't quite connected the idea that there is language—a way of taking what is on the inside and having it make sense not only to yourself but to someone else as well.

When I first started in therapy and my therapist would ask me, "How do you feel?" (as therapists are wont to do), I didn't have the connections inside myself to answer this question. I couldn't feel the feelings, and I hadn't yet connected words to these feelings. My experience was still unintegrated. Instead, I would think, *How would she imagine I would be feeling about this?* I tried to answer the question from the outside looking in. Slowly, over time, I began to notice the experience inside myself and put words to these experiences. And like Helen, slowly, I paired feelings with words. I would rummage around inside myself and try out words: Sad? No. Angry? No. Anxious? Yes! I had a word that went with a feeling! And someone else could hear it too and suddenly understand where I was. It was the building of a whole new vocabulary, not of different words, or words I didn't intellectually understand, but a vocabulary of experience that connected these words to my actual feelings—not what I thought other people wanted to hear or what other people would understand. This action of connecting the feelings and words and my experience is what makes the experience mine.

Helen's breakthrough comes after a big fight where Helen throws the water pitcher at dinner. Anne decides that Helen must refill the pitcher, so she drags her out to the water pump in the front of the house and puts Helen's hands under the running water and signs the word *water*. And something clicks. Helen, who had a bit of spoken language before her scarlet fever, connects the signed word *water* with the spoken word *water* she once had, and gets it: the water she feels is the same as the word *water* in her head and the word *water* her mouth wants to make. All of these things connect. This is the experience of integration.

In real life the Integration phase of healing can happen in minutes, hours, weeks, or months. Integration can have a feeling of heaviness, of deep mourning, and it can also have a feeling of lightness—a freedom of movement or experience that you have never had. Integration is a transformational shift. As you integrate pieces of your history, your ability to understand them is different, and your vantage point in feeling and understanding the story is different. Here's an example from Mark, who had witnessed domestic violence as a child. When he first began sharing his experiences, he talked about a very difficult and scary experience when he was eleven. When he first told his story he was very judgmental of his eleven-year-old self; he seemed to hold himself to adult standards of behavior. He seemed to view himself as simply a small adult. For Mark there was, in some way, no differentiation between the past and the present. As he told his story, it was all happening for him now as it had then, and he had no view of it as the past, and no view of himself as a child. He told it from the first person as if he had just lived it—and he talked about his behavior from the vantage point of being an adult. But in his work in therapy over time, and in telling and retelling the story, he began to be able to see the situation from the view of an eleven-year-old child, only a year older than his ten-year-old son. He began to understand how young he was, and he could understand the impact of that night on him, and especially when he thought of his own son, he could see how that would affect any child who was that young. When his ability to hold the many pieces of that experience happened, when he could hold himself as an eleven-year-old and the feelings, memories, and impact all in one place, the story shifted from continually happening in the present to something that happened in the past. The story became part of his history. That is the gift of integration. It shifts the trauma from eternally happening to where it belongs: in the past. When the trauma makes the shift to past tense, you get to see that you already survived it: it already happened.

Mourning

Why does the work of the Integration phase sometimes start as a shock? Partly because the fragmenting that the trauma does keeps you from being able to see the whole picture, and partly because trauma survivors engage in a sort of relentless hope. A hope that things could have been different. A hope that it didn't happen. A hope that if they don't talk about it, maybe it's not true. Integration has such a big impact because when you accept that the past is the past, you also accept that the trauma really happened. It sounds simple and obvious. But it's not. This relentless hope has been called a failure to grieve. And it is. But one way to understand this relentless hope is that it is a kind of internal pain medicine that allows you to keep functioning despite the pain of a deep wound. With very painful losses this relentless hope is not uncommon. In her book *The Year of Magical Thinking*,[1] Joan Didion describes her fear of getting rid of her husband's suits, even a year later, after his sudden death. She stated that she didn't want to get rid of the clothes because if he were to return, he would need them. She knew he was dead, but there is a relentless hope that can go with any massive loss or trauma. She describes this period as "the year of magical thinking," and it is: it is magical because it isn't true, but it is also magical because it is so powerful and protective.

Following the violence at Sandy Hook Elementary School, there was a *Washington Post* article about a family that was grieving the loss of their child who was killed in the school shooting. The child's mother talked about using a strategy of pretending for a few hours each day that her son was not dead, but instead he was away on a play date. She would tell herself that for the afternoon, her son was just away from the home, and he would return later.[2] The "magical" hope of this fantasy allowed her to regain some of her energy, which allowed her to participate in her life—answer email, make dinner, do laundry. Magical thinking or relentless hope can be a powerful analgesia (relief from pain). And for acute loss this is crucial. Analgesia allows combat soldiers to walk on broken legs to safety and car crash victims to get themselves out of their seats despite multiple injuries. It can be lifesaving. And truthfully, it can go on for years. This relentless hope is sometimes the last of the big protections to let go enough to heal. Sometimes it can take a long time to get to safety. It can take a long time to build the muscles and have your heart grow big enough to bear the pain. It can take a long time for the sharp edges to wear down. But thanks to your hard work on this journey of healing—all the work you did in the Preparation phase, the risks you were willing to take in the Unintegration phase, the brave conversations you had in the Identification phase—you are ready now to bear your story and the pain that may come with it. Sometimes this pain is a clear view of what did happen, the trauma you experienced or witnessed. And sometimes this pain is a clear view of what didn't happen—the care or protection or help you didn't get.

When I say that mourning is an iterative process, I mean that it is not an event. It happens in fits and starts. Grieving doesn't happen in healing from trauma the way it happens in the movies as some cathartic event. This kind of "big emotion, big event" grieving moment is one of the bigger myths of healing from trauma and loss. It happens that way in the movies because they only have an hour and a half to tell a story. That is the way we wish grieving would happen—in one big burst of emotion. But that's just not the way it works. Grieving happens the way trees take in rainfall. It happens over time, absorbed little by little. We absorb the truth, we absorb the grief.

Children are masters of intermittent grieving, and they are so good at it that many adults fault them for not properly grieving at all, saying things like, "Look at Susan playing, she doesn't even seem sad about it." But children are very effective grievers, they just do it in pieces. When my best friend's son was nine, he experienced the loss of his grandfather. He was very close to Poppop and felt the loss keenly. But as a nine-year-old, he would get connected to whatever he was doing— playing, reading, talking with his brother. And then he would get hit visibly with a wave of sadness and lean on one of his parents in tears— connecting with a big hug. This wave would hit him, he would get help, and then within minutes he would move on to the next thing. I think that if most of us tracked our experience we would more often notice the intermittent nature of our grief. Yes, it can sometimes feel like a lead suit, weighing you down all the time, but most often it feels like you never really know when the full weight will hit and when suddenly it will disappear, and sometimes, in the middle of grief, I can't tell which is worse.

When I feel the full weight of grief, it is painful, but there is almost the company of something tangible—there is a presence. It is as if the loss and the thing you lost were still present. With pain there is a presence, not an absence. I find that with the intermittent quality of grief I can sometimes be more thrown off by the days when the sorrow lifts. It can mean more energy and more productivity, but I can feel alone and lost, without my bearings. I feel the absence of something so greatly that I feel like I will become untethered from the earth.

The loss from repeated trauma is complicated. It is not just the classic loss that we know from dealing with death—the loss of someone we knew and loved. Or the loss of a home that we lived in. Or the loss of your limbs or your sight. These are huge losses. These losses may be a part of your story. But with repeated trauma there is the loss of things that often defy description: safety, innocence, trust, hope, agency, identity, or worldview. You may be aware of these losses at the start of your healing journey, but often you are not. For example, if you have never experienced safety, you might not know that this was something that was a loss. Through your experience of healing—of experiencing *what didn't happen*—you come to feel the loss and the grief of what you didn't get.

Don't mistake your inability to see all the loss for simple denial. Think of it more like smart packing. Mountain climbers don't pack up all of their gear in one trip. They make multiple trips with small loads. Carrying everything at once would be too hard, indeed dangerous, and, depending on the terrain, even impossible. Not taking in all of your trauma history isn't a conscious desire to "not-know"—it is a brain that is smarter than you are about what you can manage. This process usually gets put into place when you are younger—when your brain has fewer capacities and more need to put any available resources toward brain development and survival. Taking in the full weight of what was happening or what had happened to you would have crashed your system; it would have been too much, too hard. So you postpone that realization—sometimes months, years, or decades. You postpone taking in the full story until you can't anymore or until not-knowing is more crazy-making than knowing.

The mourning process can feel like sadness or sorrow but can easily reach to anger and despair. It can feel impossible to hold the sheer vastness of the loss because repeated trauma is always a compounded loss—a loss across time. It was the years that the trauma occurred and the years that you survived and the years that you have taken to heal. All of these are part of the landscape. It can seem impossible to hold the full weight of the loss and hang on to your hope at the same time. Hope depends on the possibility of a future, and traumatic loss can really knock out a capacity to see a future.

This is an important time to lean on your therapist, guide, or group—when you finally survey the wreckage, you want your own personal Red Cross on your team, people who know you and have hope for your future even if you can't have it for yourself at the time. My friend Beth and her family had their home in Pensacola destroyed by Hurricane Ivan. A couple of years ago she drove me by the site where it had stood near the ocean. She told me how her family gathered after the storm had passed—her grandmother, parents, and siblings, all sorting through the debris all around the neighborhood. Combing the debris for the small items and the treasures of their former lives. Beth's grandmother found a family ring. Beth talked so gratefully about how the Red Cross came four times a day during that time, making it possible for all of them to be there and keep working. The Red Cross brought MREs, water, rakes, and gloves. They brought toys for the children.

Local restaurants rallied and brought dinner trucks through the neighborhoods. This consistent and safe support allowed the family to move through their loss. It is astonishing how able the human brain and spirit are at borrowing hope. No one who sees the full measure of the devastation can really take it in and plan their future at the same time. It needs to be done in stages. You need others to help you stack the sandbags, to hand you water, to imagine a better future. One needs to take in the loss before it is mourned and cleaned up.

But I want you to really appreciate and honor the complexity of these losses in their intangible forms. What does it mean to lose the identity of who I am? If as a soldier I participated in the killing of grandmothers and children, how do I recognize myself? The self who I believed could never do that? Who loved his grandmother? Who loves his children? How do I mourn the loss of the self that never got to grow old in its innocence of death and destruction? How do I mourn the loss of a view of the world that doesn't have that kind of violence? How do I hold myself as a kind, loving person *and* as someone who could inflict and endure a violence I couldn't have imagined? These are the tough questions that come with repeated trauma. How can I hold my identity as both lovable and damaged? How can all these pieces that other people get to hold apart live together inside me—without killing me? How do I mourn the loss of all the years that I couldn't speak, couldn't ask for help, couldn't let anyone in? All the years I lived in the storm shelter and not in my life, not with the people who tried to love me?

There are no easy answers to these questions. Some move through quickly, some more slowly. Some traumas require the movement of a group or a system or a country to move with you—and sometimes the timing is all your own. It is unlikely that some of the healing that happened in South Africa would have happened without the Truth and

Reconciliation Commission process, though that process was designed to heal a nation and not particular individuals. The journey of healing helps you articulate the questions—to hold each piece of your loss as treasure that survived your particular war, and be able to mourn and honor the loss.

The smaller cycles of healing that you have done along the way have helped you build the stamina for this phase. You have been working toward this part of the climb throughout the whole healing process—and though it can be hard to trust that everything is going to come together, you can lean on the work you have done along the way, and the people who have been working with you and supporting you.

New Beginnings

The worlds of repeated trauma require vigilance. They are a place where you are always afraid of making the one wrong move. They are worlds where you survive by making rules and rigidly living by them. The rules make sense in the context of the original trauma: "Don't make noise, you will wake up Uncle Charlie." But you carry that rule with you into the present, even where it no longer makes sense. You only knew that if you followed the rules, whatever they needed to be for you, you survived. And you believed, and still believe, that if you stop following the rules, something bad can happen. In the movie *Room*,[1] the characters Ma and Jack are held hostage and live in the confines of a shed. Ma creates a world of imagination and rules to help Jack survive and grow up in this traumatic situation. When they have finally gotten out and are in a hospital recovering, they are taking showers and Jack starts listing the rules they had for a bath and how they lived and Ma says, "There are no rules out here, Jack." Jack looks perplexed and is playfully engaged by

Ma into trying something new. And then we get to hear as he narrates about all the things that are different outside the "room." For a while Jack follows the old rules, even outside the "room" where they lived in the shed, but gradually he unlearns the old and opens himself up for the possibility of the new: he tries new foods, he plays with a dog, he plays with a friend. These new experiences are new beginnings. When you integrate your trauma, when you are able to narrate your story and your experience, the trauma can move from the present to the past. And this movement means, suddenly, that you don't have to protect yourself from the old trauma. Suddenly there is the possibility for something else.

These new experiences are what I call *new beginnings*. I first came across this term while reading articles by a Hungarian analyst named Michael Balint who was one of the early psychoanalysts (Balint's teacher and analyst was Sándor Ferenczi, and Ferenczi's teacher and analyst was Sigmund Freud). Balint recognized that people who had been very hurt needed something different from the treatment that was accepted at the time.[2] He believed that people who had been hurt or lived through trauma didn't need insightful interpretations—they needed a place to mend or heal what he referred to as "the basic fault." The basic fault was a fault line in the self that had broken or shattered in response to some experience in their life. This basic fault is what was in need of healing, but even when it was healed it would always leave a scar. He described allowing his patients to lean on him and the therapeutic relationship—to use the support of actual connection or attachment to heal, not just the interpretation, insight, or words. He called this work *regression*, but it wasn't about going backward. That's where our lexicon and our mythical belief about healing can get in the way of understanding. Healing isn't just about going back into the past, to what did happen. Healing is also about looking at what needs to be learned or strengthened—it is also about what didn't happen. Healing required a new experience of something. Healing requires that you experience new emotions and feelings. It requires that you risk speaking up and speaking differently, and that you practice new behaviors that you either never learned or couldn't practice while the trauma was occurring.

In the Integration phase pieces come together: you have let go and let the pieces come up and out. You have sorted those pieces and described them, talked about them. And you have put the pieces together and taken in a piece or even the totality of your story. Most often this experience initially leads to grieving, to mourning—for what you lived through, for what you lost. But there is a step beyond this experience of grief. Because when you walk beyond grief, you can get to a new place: "Now what?" Or, "What might have been?" Or simply, "I don't know this place. I don't know where I am." You get to a place you don't know because you are suddenly living entirely in the present, without the rules that you used to survive trauma and without the vigilance that protected you.

Integration is not unique to healing from trauma. It defines the process of development and growth. The developmental psychologists Robert Kegan and Jean Piaget both describe a constant shift of moving from one state of knowing—undoing it—to a new state of knowing. As Kegan writes, "growth always involves a process of differentiation"—of moving from "what I have been" to "who I am now." Kegan continues, "Piaget calls this 'decentration,' the loss of an old center, to 'recentration,' the recovery of a new center."[3] The shift from a coherent self to a more fragmented and incoherent self and then back to coherence is the normative developmental route. And this process requires support.

During our growth we need someone to hold both the *me that I was* and the *me I am becoming now*. Good parents hold both aspects of growth and allow their children the ability to grow. Support allows you to make the leap—to risk letting go of the old parts of yourself enough to let the new parts of yourself emerge.[4] And in trauma treatment, it is the three middle phases of healing—Unintegration, Identification, and Integration—where this shift occurs and where you also need an outside other to hold your coherence for you.

The experience of new beginning in the Integration phase is actually a conscious and intentional reengagement of this normal developmental process of growth. If anything defines repeated trauma, it is the absence of growth—the shutting down of the normal processes in favor of a focus on survival and vigilance. In the years of repeated trauma you get older, and you may get taller, but your internal growth stops—you adjust to the trauma and maintain a coherence of knowing that is based on survival, not on a coherent sense of self. And what is so important during the process of healing—and the need is different in each phase—is the support necessary to negotiate the new challenges of growth.

New beginnings are like the stem cells of psychological growth or development that appear more and more in moments of the Integration phase. Many years ago, as I was leaving a therapy session, my hand hit the door, and I turned around. I just wanted to look again, make sure everything was okay, get a reassuring smile, take in the kindness one more time. I looked, and she smiled, and that was it. It was a moment, but it was big. It was a moment of new beginning for me. Letting myself reach out for something. Letting someone see my need and meet it. It lasted seconds and I can still feel the sensations of solidity and connection in my body as I felt them then.

These moments of new beginnings are often a surprise. Sometimes they can be exhilarating. You catch yourself and your long-standing protections off guard, like a toddler who has ditched his parents and is suddenly running free through the supermarket. There is such a feeling of freedom. New beginnings are moments of freedom, moments of possibility, moments of wonder—where you really do *wonder* what will happen next. This is the crux of the new beginning because in trauma you never actually wonder what will happen next because your entire brain and nervous system is wired to *know* what will happen next: you always assume that the trauma will happen again, and you always believe that you are protecting yourself from what will happen next—the trauma that happened before.

So the freedom of wondering, of stepping out into the world or even into a new conversation can feel exhilarating, but it can also be scary. It can be scary because you are used to knowing and planning, and being surprised isn't what you were hoping for. If there is one thing that trauma survivors usually hate, it is being caught off guard.

New beginnings defy categorization into "good" and "bad." They just are. New beginnings offer a wide range of feelings, experiences, and sensations, but because they are new, they occupy a different space. They are the thing you never had the opportunity to experience, the thing you need to mend the fabric that was torn; new beginnings tend to have a developmental quality that often makes them tender and precious. They are surprising, sometimes scary, sometimes embarrassing— but almost always because they can make you feel vulnerable because you are aware of both *the self you were* and *the self you are becoming*. New beginnings mean that things are fundamentally different. There is a saying that "you can't unring a bell," and new beginnings can feel like this: that they ring inside you and become a new part of you, part of how you organize yourself and connect to the world. Once you have that new experience, you can't go back. This doesn't mean you don't ever go back to old habits. But now when you do go back to the old habit, you notice that it never feels comfortable again. It becomes something you might keep using out of habit or routine or as a crutch, but even this begins to annoy you. You don't so much change the habit as become tired of it—leaving it behind like something that no longer interests you.

New beginnings can happen in moments. Usually they come up as a surprise—but there is no right emotion. I have had clients who had never been able to cry before, and that was a new beginning. I have had clients who had never taken charge of their own appointments, and that was a new beginning. And I have worked in countries where it had been years since groups were able to peacefully meet and talk about their issues— and that was a new beginning. So sometimes new beginnings just show up as part of the work, but other times they need to be helped along.

In the Identification phase we talked about how play was helpful for practicing the act of talking or finding language for inner experiences. In the Integration phase I have found that play or a playful stance can create the perfect environment for new beginnings—mostly because new beginnings are about *wonder* about *not-knowing*, and creating this space is what play does best. A writing game that I used with child clients was something that my therapist brought into our work one day when I was really stuck with how to talk. The game is simple. One person writes a word or a sentence, and then the next person writes a word or a sentence. And so on, until you decide to stop. You can write about serious things, or you can create a story. It doesn't really matter. I remember the experience so clearly of writing something, and handing it over, and realizing that I had absolutely *no idea* what she was going to write next. And that experience of sitting in a space of *no idea* was brand-new. I realized that

I had never felt safe enough to just have *no idea* at all—to not anticipate the next move as if I were playing a life-and-death game of chess. Experiences of new beginnings are as physiological as they are psychological: you don't just know, consciously, in your head that something is new, you feel it in your body. It can feel electrical, like suddenly all of the nerves in your body are connected in a new way. Or it can make you feel really, really awake. Or it can completely knock you over, like the experience rushes at all of your circuits at once, overwhelming them. It can hit as excitement, calm, sadness, tiredness, or grief. But over time the new beginning feels more and more like open space.

Holding Both

War is hell, but that's not the half of it, because war is also mystery and terror and adventure and courage and discovery and holiness and pity and despair and longing and love. War is nasty; war is fun. War is thrilling; war is drudgery. War makes you a man; war makes you dead.

TIM O'BRIEN, *The Things They Carried*[1]

The definition of *integration* is to blend or connect into a unified whole. Given that the universal effect of trauma is that it shatters, the goal of healing from trauma is integration—to create, and really, re-create, rebuild, a unified whole. What is crucial is that the whole you are creating is new. You are not going back to the self you were before. You are creating a whole that integrates the *you* you were before the trauma, the *you* that experienced the trauma, and the *you* that has grown and healed through the trauma.

The process of healing follows the same trajectory as the normal path of growth and development. You will experience things or choose things that will bring about change and cause you to grow and shift identity.

For example, you may get a new job or a promotion, or have a baby, or get a divorce. These are typical adult experiences, but they require something more of you. These challenges prompt you to integrate the *you* you were before the change, the *you* that just had a growth experience (new job, new baby, loss of spouse), and the *you* that grew through that change. These kinds of challenges and the resulting integration happens throughout your life. In my work as both a therapist and an executive coach, I have seen that even these smaller and often happy challenges (new job, new baby) can be disruptive. They can require a big shift in your understanding of yourself and the willingness to grieve the loss of who you were before or what you have lost. But the process of growth, even if it is bumpy, is generally organic—it comes from the work of your everyday life without a conscious decision for growth. These changes in your life prompt you to do the work of integration, and your daily environment supports you in that growth. You often don't know you are actually doing it until the work has been done.

This is not true of integration with repeated trauma or traumatic loss. Integration of normal developmental milestones is a long walk at sea level. Maybe the Catskills. Sometimes the Rockies. But integration of the shattered pieces from trauma is hiking at 28,000 feet. Yes, it is the same process, just as walking at sea level and walking the last 300 feet on Everest's summit require the same walking motion: putting one foot in front of the other. In normal development the aspects of the *me* I was before my new job and the *me* I am with my new job are different, but they are close enough that I can hold both aspects in myself at the same time. The gap between aspects of myself, the meaning I make about it, my worldviews, my identities—these are close enough, even if it is a stretch, for me to hold them both and bring them close enough together to integrate them without too much trouble. And often when we struggle in our lives it is because this gap between aspects of ourselves is just a bit too far for us to bridge on our own. We seek out support, whether family, friend, or professional, when we need a hand or a rope to make it across that gap.

In healing from repeated trauma, the task of integrating aspects of self is the same as normal growth and development: hold both aspects. Let the pieces, learnings, memories, and aspects of self make contact with each other and integrate. Repeated trauma is a more difficult act of integration than normal developmental integration. It is harder to hold both. With repeated trauma the *you* that you were before the trauma can feel so vastly far away from the *you* that experienced and lived through the trauma, and the *you* that you are now. The gap between these aspects of yourself may well feel like the Grand Canyon. In fact, as we have seen, the defenses created around trauma essentially create a Grand Canyon. You make sure that the disparate parts of yourself stay on different rims of the canyon to keep them away from each other. This canyon protects you from knowing and from feeling. But contact isn't contamination. Contact is healing. Contact is growth. Contact is wholeness. And wholeness—bringing together the disparate parts of yourself, your story, and your experience—is the goal of healing. With wholeness you have access to all of your strengths and learning. You have all of your access to your experience—even if it is difficult.

Holding both requires an important but simple word: *and*. Not *or*, or *but*. AND. "I was hurt" *AND* "I am lovable." "I have a hard time with my emotions" *AND* "I am able to slow myself down with help." "As a soldier I had to behave in ways I am ashamed of now" *AND* "I am a loving husband and father." "I can feel really embarrassed" *AND* "I can trust that our relationship is okay." The world of trauma is often a black-and-white world: it makes things look like this *OR* that. Not this *AND* that. Holding both requires you to say *"and."*

Holding both means you have to hold each thing with its strengths and weaknesses, its upsides and downsides. There is a branch of psychology called Gestalt psychology—*gestalt* means "whole" in German—and its focus is on bringing together disparate pieces and understanding relationships between things. Gestalt psychology focuses on polarities[2]—its term for holding both. You take two things that seem to live at opposite sides of a pole—for example, "being seen" and "hiding." And then you explore what it feels like to experience each end of that pole—what are the benefits and costs for each pole? What is good about being seen, and what feels bad about being seen? What is good about hiding, and what feels bad about hiding? By holding both at the same time and holding all of your strengths and weaknesses, you can find the container in yourself to hold all of it: you can find that both of them live inside you and serve you at times in different ways. You get to feel that the disparate parts of yourself all belong to you. These disparate parts are all a part of your identity—and it helps you integrate them and work with them.

Another good example of holding both is Marsha Linehan's work on dialectical behavioral therapy. She talks about dialectics—another term for holding both—and targets specific cognitive-behavioral interventions to learn how to hold both. Linehan has what I think is one of the best examples of what it can look like to experience the integration of two polarities. She teaches clients about the use of their thinking mind and the use of their emotional mind—and she calls the integration of these two aspects of mind *wise mind*.[3] By being able to hold both—the thinking mind and the emotional mind—you actually get something that is bigger, a whole that is new and capable of something more. In holding both you aren't deciding whether one thing is better than the other thing, whether thinking mind is better than emotional mind. You are holding both so that you can have the integration of them: you can have wise mind when you hold both.

Holding both lets the pieces make contact with each other. As I said earlier, you can't force these two things; you have to create the environment, create the conversation that holds them safely, just like setting a broken bone. You need to hold both pieces calmly and steadily and trust that doing this over and over will yield something new, or support the mourning of something old. Integration is about holding both and making contact. In many ways, the goal of integration is not just to hold both but to hold all. With the experience of repeated trauma, there are rarely just two pieces or two dichotomies to hold. But you can't hold all at once. By learning to hold both, you build the muscles to hold all. You begin to experience the "something more" as you hold both the upsides and downsides of each piece.

In each pass through integration, you grow more and you integrate more. When I was a kid, my grandmother's husband, Aubrey, was building an airplane out of wood. He and my grandmother lived in a town house in suburban Maryland, and Aubrey had turned one of the bedrooms into a woodshop. Twice a year, when my brother and I visited my grandmother, we slept in the woodshop on mattresses on the floor. Lying on the floor was an amazing vantage point to look up at the walls, which were covered in pegboard. And this pegboard held dozens and dozens of small pieces of wood glued together—curved pieces and round pieces and arched pieces—and some of these pieces had been glued together to make even larger pieces on a different pegboard. You could watch the growth of wings in various states of assembly along the walls. He started with the smallest pieces and glued them, and then connected these pieces. I watched over the course of years as the whole wings took shape. Healing from trauma is so much like this. It is an iterative, cumulative process. Each cycle through, as you integrate some piece or aspect that was shattered, you build a small piece like Aubrey did with pieces of the wings. At first you can barely tell what the piece is; it looks unimportant. It certainly doesn't look like something that could support your weight or get you off the ground. But the pieces add up. The pieces come together. Eventually they take shape and you are able to go to places you couldn't have imagined.

Holding both, holding all also allows you to hold aspects of trauma that other people may not understand, but may be important to you. In an article in *Vanity Fair* on PTSD in the military, Sebastian Junger highlighted an important problem with recovering from the trauma of war:[4] there are parts of war, or parts of ourselves we found in war, that we don't necessarily want to give up. Yes, soldiers experience trauma, but they also experience camaraderie and courage. As one soldier described it, "There was horror, there was beauty, both co-existed." Many soldiers experience closeness with their fellow soldiers that is hard to find anywhere else. I have heard similar statements from siblings who grew up in abusive families and relied on each other to survive. With the trauma, your identity and your survival become intertwined. The trauma can have you experience the best of yourself and the worst of yourself. And healing from it can be tricky because it's not so easy to untangle them from each other. Fear of losing the good can make you not want to let go of the bad.

Trauma can make experiences feel more real than any "normal" life. Trauma washes any experience in an intensity that can be harder to recover from than any violence. And when violence was shared with comrades, as in war, a family, or even a gang, the experience can be especially hard to let go. Not because you want the war back, but because you miss the closeness. You miss mattering that much. You miss having someone's back, and you miss someone having yours. In any long-term or repeated experience of trauma, your life was rarely a single experience. Even with repeated trauma there were good moments, beautiful moments, and funny moments. There were brave moments and strong moments. And all of it belonged to you. It is always a mix of experiences.

And it's not only the trauma that produces these mixed experiences. So does healing from it. The good with the bad cuts both ways. Sometimes in healing you have to hold the bad experiences to keep the good ones. You have to be able to hold the memories of war to hold on to the memory of yourself as a loyal friend. Holding both aspects of the memory allows you to be whole. And sometimes you have to hold the difficult emotions, like grief, when the good parts of healing happen. Healing doesn't happen in simple sound bites where the experience is just one thing or another. It barely happens in sentences or paragraphs, where there is one line of thought. Healing really happens in poetry—where the paradoxes are written in emotion and contradiction and metaphor. Where all things can exist. As Rainer Maria Rilke says, "Take your well-disciplined strengths, stretch them between the two great opposing poles, because inside human beings is where God learns."[5]

Identity

Will I lose myself entirely if I lose my limp? How can I explain
that the two unmatched halves used to add up to more than
one whole?

BARBARA KINGSOLVER, *The Poisonwood Bible*[1]

When trauma shatters our lives, it often first takes aim at
the developmental milestone we are in the middle of
mastering. If you lived through repeated trauma as an infant or toddler, the shattered developmental milestone was *learning basic
trust*—it can be hard for you to believe in constancy or safety in relationships. And it can be hard for you to have a sense of agency—an initial
sense of self that "I can control my own actions." If your repeated trauma
happens in later childhood and early adolescence, when you are learning
to master skills, learning how to learn, and learning how to be a part of
groups, then you may have more trust or ability to seek out supportive
relationships, but lack confidence in your ability to learn or be good at
anything. And difficulty connecting to peer groups means that you don't
get knowledge outside your family system or the social rules that can

help you navigate adolescence. And if your repeated trauma happens in late adolescence and early adulthood, your developmental milestone is identity. Identity is the summation, the latest edition, of "I am the kind of person who . . ." and when trauma shatters this sense of identity you feel a tremendous loss for the person you were.

The rate of suicide for returning Iraq and Afghanistan vets has been staggering. More vets are committing suicide than died in actual combat.[2] People are shocked. "But they made it home, why are they killing themselves now?" But that's the problem of war. As Gay Bradshaw states, "away from events, when the survivor is released from these circumstances, the traces of his trauma may seem to an outside eye to be gone—normal life is resumed, families are reengaged, work is performed, holidays are celebrated—but appearances can be misinterpreted."[3] Trauma is almost always viewed as an all-or-nothing situation. Either it is happening or it isn't. People who haven't lived through trauma, or who see you living currently without the old trauma, assume that it is over. Yes, you made it through the war, your abusive relationship, or your abusive childhood. The end of the traumatic situation means that healing can start. But the trauma itself isn't gone yet. When people see you on the outside, they see you living your life without the old trauma. But they can't see the inside—where you are working hard to heal and integrate what you experienced.

In my high school in the early 1980s in North Jersey, there was a girl who was one of the "Vietnamese boat people." She didn't speak much English. She wore the same outfit to school every day, a blue skirt and a white shirt. And in the gauntlet that is the American high school lunchroom, she sought refuge at our end of the lunch table my freshman year. She chose well, since we were geeky freshman girls—we did the *New York Times* crossword every day—so we were basically harmless. But one of my regrets is that I wasn't actively kind, just passively benign. We never reached out, we just let her sit there. In my work in Cambodia and Southeast Asia I have since learned about the journeys families like hers made, and if I had life to live again I would love to be able to offer her more than just a place to sit.

But my naïve view at that time was that she was now safe. She got out—she was living safely (I imagined) in our town—so she was fine. It was a simplistic view, and the way most movies end: you make it through the ordeal and live happily ever after. It is a magical thinking of a different sort—and it obscures the work that needs to be done when safety is reached. Reaching safety doesn't mean the hard work has ended—it means it can now begin. What I didn't know in high school about Vietnamese and Cambodian refugees was that after surviving a war and finally getting out, they risked their lives on small fishing boats in the ocean with little food and water only to be taken hostage by Thai pirates, which meant that many of their belongings got stolen, the women and girls raped, the men beaten or killed. Yes, they got safely in a boat only to endure more repeated trauma. Then they landed in the United States.

This view of finally being in safety as the end rather than the beginning parallels the problems that I have seen in postconflict countries. Everyone assumes that a peace accord marks the end of the peace process: life can return to normal. As John Lederach, an expert on peacebuilding, states, "actually the inverse is true. . . . In reality, peace accords mean that a whole new range of negotiations, often more arduous and difficult, are just beginning."[4] A peace accord means that the work can start. This is true of countries, and it is true of individuals.

The problem that you face as an adult who lived through repeated trauma is that you are treated like an individual and not the divided country that you have often become. You went into trauma—war or an abusive relationship—and you had an identity intact. You went in with one identity, and you hung on to that self as long as you could. But then the circumstances of survival required you to behave in ways that countered your identity. You could no longer hold just to the old identity because now you were *also* the other identity. And your old self would *never* have approved of this new self.

But during the crisis or war, it's okay to embody this new survival self. You can leave that old self behind. You can pretend it doesn't exist. You can imagine it is actually gone. But then you return home or you get away and you can see the old self reflected in the eyes of the people who missed you. You see it in the familiar places you lived—in the family photos, in the well-intended welcomes of friends—your old self and your new self: two identities, now sworn enemies on either side of the demilitarized zone of your heart. The standoff begins.

Your loved ones try to help you. They tell you that they love you. That you are okay now. They see you safe on this shore. They think that your war is over. That since you made it back you are okay. They don't know that the real work is just beginning. That you still have a peace accord to work out between the two different selves you carry within you: that you have to start with a truce, not end with one.

Edward Tick notes: "Veterans know that, having been to hell and back, they are different. We expect them to put war behind them and rejoin the ordinary flow of civilian life. But it is impossible for them to do so. And wrong of us to request it." As one veteran Tick writes about notes, whenever he is asked when he left Vietnam, he usually answers, "Last night."[5]

When you hear the stories of people who were traumatized as children, you most often hear about their need to find a self: they never actually grew one. They lived in an "as if" self, waiting for more stability before trying to actually create a sense of self. When you hear stories about those who were traumatized as late adolescents or adults, you often hear the term *soul death*. Instead of feeling like they never lived, like the people who were abused as children, adults who were traumatized feel like a part of them died. They feel like their old self, their inner soul, died. Soul death is like the phantom pain of PTSD. It is a real, experienced pain that others can't see, which makes it really hard to get what is needed to start: validation of the loss, of the pain, of the experience of living as a divided country, as one whose soul has died or who is still in a coma.

Trauma fragments. It can fragment memory, experience, and parts of the self. And this is especially true when what was shattered was identity. The task is once again *holding both*—the *me* I was and the *me* I am. Holding both so that they can come into contact and you can be whole. I know that there are parts that you don't want to own, parts of your story or behavior that you don't want to know to be true—parts you wish you had left behind, parts you thought you *had* left behind. When you hold both, you will experience grief—grief for what you lived through, for what you lost, for the self you were, and for the things you did. You will have grief for a life that is now not possible, the one you thought you would live. But grieving the loss—integration—comes with possibility. You will also have moments of new beginnings. You will see who you are for having lived through your ordeal. For having faced the demons outside and inside. You will expand to *hold both*; indeed, through your work of healing, you will expand to *hold all*. Not only will you heal yourself, but you will have the capacity to sit with others' pain and support them.

Helpful Practices for Integration

What supports your work here in the Integration phase? First, anything that helps you slow down and helps you stay present and connected to yourself and the relationship with your therapist or group. Slowing down helps you tell and absorb your story. In the Integration phase you need space and time to take in the entirety of your experience. While the recognition of the whole can be an "aha" experience that happens quickly, the work of integration is also the slow work of letting this recognition sink in and become woven into the fabric of who you are. This takes time. Remember that in the Integration phase you are building on the work of the previous phases—many of the practices that you used earlier were building the muscles you needed in that particular phase, but you were also building the muscles you need now in the Integration phase. Given the grieving that occurs in the Integration phase, this is a good time to use the practices from the Unintegration phase that helped you soothe yourself and manage your emotions. In the Unintegration phase you worked on being aware of and expanding your window of tolerance, and the practices that helped you there will continue to strengthen your ability to hold your story and the grief that can come with it. So now it may be helpful to review what helped you manage your emotions during the Unintegration phase so that you are aware of what helps and what you can do.

Integration is a great time to revisit your practices of mindfulness and self-awareness. The process of integration is a big shift in perspective. You go from an experience of trauma that is fragmented and often ever-present in some way, either through intrusive memories or the protections you continued to use—and integration creates a shift in perspective to a space where the trauma moves to the past, where it has already happened. Mindfulness helps you strengthen your capacity to observe, which helps you take in what you see. It helps you connect what is going on in your mind with what is going on in your body; this integrative aspect of mindfulness helps you hold more of your story and your experience. And this aspect of mindfulness and holding your experience is not just for the trauma that you are able to hold now, but also for the experiences of new beginning. Being able to find time and space and awareness to hold these new experiences and allow them to be a part of your thinking and your physical experience is a big part of healing.

Music may be helpful during this phase as a way of acknowledging your whole story. You can make a playlist that holds all aspects of you or speaks to the integration work you are currently doing. You can listen to this playlist and simply take it in and reflect on the aspect of yourself and your story that it speaks to. It can allow you to hold parts of your story and your whole story in a different way. If you are more visually inclined, you can make a collage of what is coming together for you at this time and hang it up where you can see. While journaling supports your work in the other phases, in the Integration phase you can focus on using it to capture a more coherent version of your experience and your story. Writing your experience down helps you strengthen the connection between your emotional experience and your verbal experience. Writing can be a private and slow way to absorb your story, and it gives you a chance to read and reread it so that you can really take it in.

Outside of therapy, this is a good time to slow down if you are able. During any important time of grieving or growth, you need more time to rest and take care of yourself. Rest and self-care look different for everyone because everyone has different needs for energy and rejuvenation. All the way through this journey, it has been important to take care of yourself, and in the Integration phase it becomes crucial. In some ways, this act of self-care and rest is part of the new beginning; it's part of a different way of experiencing the loss of trauma and coping with it as a loss and not as something to be buried and ignored or something to just survive. You know how to live through something difficult and move on. But through the process of healing you get to learn what it's like to live through something difficult and take the time to heal, get support, and take care of yourself. I have worked with clients in this phase to find experiences and images that allow them to truly feel the rest, care, and safety that they have worked so hard to create. Their images ranged from remembered landscapes to imaginary retreats—and they worked to make some of these images real by putting up hammocks in their backyard or cleaning up a reading corner in their den.

It's not always possible, of course, but when it is, the Integration phase is a good time to clear your schedule of extra work or volunteer projects. It's a time to let yourself get a passing grade in your daily life instead of trying to get the gold star. Having time for self-care and reflection is important, but more space and time means you get to reduce your overall stress level and pace of life. Integration is supported by slowness, stillness, and a chance to move more deliberately and slowly. This is a good time for long walks where you get to practice your observing skills in nature and your awareness skills of your own body through movement.

PART 6

Consolidation

The difficulties of attaining a durable peace in contexts of protracted violence suggest we know more about how to end something painful and damaging to everyone but less about how to build something desired.

JOHN LEDERACH, *The Moral Imagination*[1]

Consolidation

I travel a lot for work, but this fall I decided to take a day and pause between cities. I stayed an extra night in Austin before moving on to New York City. With my open day I chose to visit the Lady Bird Johnson Wildflower Center, a 284-acre wildlife preserve. Lady Bird Johnson's mission was to create, conserve, and restore native landscape for plants and wildlife. I got there early in the morning with my map in hand, and I started walking the various paths. The first path I chose wound through beds of wildflowers that were covered in butterflies. I turned to a man standing next to me and said something about there being so many butterflies. The man was holding a camera with a large lens, and he explained, "This is nothing. Come back at noon, when the sun is out and it is hot. You will see thousands of them." This seemed odd to me at the time, because I mistakenly put butterflies in the category of other animals who seek shade during the noonday sun. But after reading up on butterflies I found out that they are most able to fly at an internal temperature of 82 degrees Fahrenheit. In fact, they can't move their wings at all if they are too cold. A butterfly's wing muscles must be warm in order for it to flap its wings and fly. This is why you see butterflies basking in the sun. They are the gurus of knowing how to stop and absorb energy. They perch on a flower, absorbing the energy of the sun, warming their muscles, and preparing for flight.

So even though I didn't believe that there could be even more butterflies than I was seeing, I did as the man said and returned at noon for the most spectacular display of butterflies I have ever seen. There were thousands of them, and they were mesmerizing. In fact, I couldn't really stay away from them. I would head off to walk on other trails, and then wander back to the wildflowers to stand among the butterflies again. It was my day of rest, and here were thousands of teachers for me: basking in the sun and getting the strength to fly.

Healing from trauma requires its own phase of gathering energy. The Consolidation phase is a quiet place where you can rest. This phase can seem veiled, invisible, weightless. It can be easy to miss this phase when you are in it. It can take a while before you recognize the landscape. When I hit this phase I know that I *should* recognize it for its feeling of calm and rest. But I don't. I am always looking for the next thing. So when I am first in it, I feel antsy to be back in the work that I left. And then I get convinced that I am now in preparation mode again, when I am not.

Rest is the paradoxical requirement of hard work. Rest is a requirement of building both strength and learning. One of the first areas in which researchers discovered the need for a rest period in order to get stronger was in the domain of sports. In sports there is a model of training called *periodization*,[1] which "involves progressive cycling of various aspects of a training program during a specific period of time." The regimen is designed to help an athlete to get progressively stronger.

Before the discovery of periodization, athletes often overtrained and injured themselves. They would work harder and harder at an attempt to get stronger and faster, but the hard work wouldn't allow their muscles to repair or recover. Gradually over time, instead of getting stronger, the muscles would break down. What strengthens muscles in training is that hard work causes small tears in the muscles, and the rest periods allow the muscles to repair the tears, making them stronger than they were.

Like the Preparation phase, the Consolidation phase can be underattended to and often ignored altogether. For long stretches of trauma work, the emotions, the story, the struggles are the only things that you can really pay attention to. As you work through the pieces of grief in the Integration phase, you suddenly find yourself feeling nothing in particular. For those of you who typically go numb under stress, at first this can be disconcerting. Am I just numb again? But you aren't numb. You are actually experiencing peace—calm. You are feeling the absence of distress. It is the difference between not feeling pain because you are on a painkiller, and not feeling pain because the area has healed. There is an odd openness in the Consolidation phase. I say *odd* because it will likely feel new; for people who have lived through repeated trauma, feelings of openness or freedom are rare. You may not recognize them.

Consolidation is a state without yearning or seeking. It is a place of rest. I believe that this is where your body, your system, your brain absorbs the changes it has been through. It is a state from which you can grow.

When I can't feel the struggle, I assume that I am back in preparation mode. I look around for what's next. But the Consolidation phase isn't Base Camp, it's Advanced Base Camp—it incorporates both the work of consolidation and the next work of preparation. Consolidation is solidifying the work done so far—letting it settle in, letting yourself relax into the new muscles, new thoughts, new ways of being. And then preparation takes on the question of "Now what?" What's working, what needs work, what needs to shift based on the work so far?

This is why periodization was such an important training invention. Athletes are good at knowing how to push themselves really hard— they know what that feels like. There is an inherent satisfaction in the hard work. But it turns out that athletes are pretty bad at knowing how and when to rest. Left to their own training plans, athletes tend to over-train. They push too hard and too long, causing the muscles to break down over time, and their health and performance suffers.

Consolidation shows up on its own. It seems to naturally follow the Integration phase, and it tends to last the length that it needs to. In the Integration phase you began to work on slowing down and taking in your trauma story, and here in the Consolidation phase you are allowing all the work you have done up until now to settle in and become a part of what you know about yourself and can draw on. Depending on the work being done, it can last days or weeks. As both an athlete and a client healing from trauma, I would have trusted the rest periods more if I could have seen something happening. I wished for a visual aid of some sort—where I could have watched a battery symbol get full, the way it does on my iPhone when it recharges. It would have helped me feel like something was happening. And in both athletics and therapy, I often got in my own way by not allowing these periods of rest. I often fought against them. I would push through so that I could feel like I was doing something. But I would push myself to a place of exhaustion and then need to recover. I would force the rest period, but it would take that much longer to recover because I was now in need of repair.

All learning requires rest—which actually may be one of the primary functions of sleep. As we discussed in the chapter on memory, we have two main memory systems: one that is fast (short-term memory, which relies on the hippocampus), and one that is slow (long-term memory, which relies on the neocortex). It appears that rest is a big contributor to moving information from short-term memory to long-term memory.[2] We need a system that can pick up information quickly and use it if necessary. But we also need a way to weave the old information and the new information together—and rest is when this happens.

Consolidation is not only different for everyone, it is different each time you go through it, which is another reason it can be hard to recognize. Not unlike its physical counterpart in athletics, different forms of active rest or total rest are needed, depending on the work that is being done in the work periods. I have spent consolidation periods sleeping a lot, and I have spent other consolidation periods working at an intense job overseas. In both cases, the trauma work was visibly on hold, but the mending was happening in different ways. Sometimes it feels more like you need total rest: sleeping, reading, watching TV, spending time in nature. And sometimes it feels like you need active rest—focusing back on your life, experimenting with something new, taking the opportunity to stretch the muscles you have been growing. As you move through the Consolidation phase, you will gradually reenter the Preparation phase. The longer you do the work, the shorter the Preparation phase becomes, partly because it will naturally begin as you come to the end of your rest period.

Fine

Recently my therapist told me that I needed to spend more time in *fine*. Since I was feeling like if I was "fine" I would be left alone, I was wary of *fine*. As in, now that I was feeling fine, my guide could move on and help other people and I would be ditched. Or, since you are fine, how about helping me now? Was *fine* the emotional ice floe? Was it like Chutes and Ladders—step on the *fine* square and slide all the way back to the beginning? Or would I get so used to *fine* that I wouldn't have the patience for the healing work I still needed to do?

Here's the thing about life—you don't have to worry that things are going to be fine all the time, or whatever your opposite of *fine* is. Life rolls in on its own waves. There can be storms, hurricanes, tsunamis. You need to appreciate the calm days, the fine days. I can remember a Vietnam veteran friend of my parents whose job it was to train military dogs. He talked so lovingly about his time with those dogs—and showed me a picture of him feeding them. He was a gruff guy who played softball with my father; he drank a lot of beer and was loud. But he talked about the dogs and sunsets in Vietnam. He found fine moments, even in the war. And the same is true of peacetime. Find the moments of fine. Work your way up to minutes, hours, even days of fine.

My neighbors had a 45-rpm record of the Byrds singing "Turn! Turn! Turn!" with the famous Bible verse that has been reminding people for thousands of years that "to everything there is a season, a time to reap and a time to sow." Consolidation is the season to reap. The season of *fine*. The season of peace. *Fine* doesn't negate the trauma. It's not "Since you are fine, then it never happened" or "Now that you are fine, you have to remain fine and your healing is done." It's the time to take a break and build some capacity to relax into *fine*.

This is actually more necessary than you imagine. Keeping the principle in mind that neurons that *fire together wire together*, spending time in *fine* builds neural networks of peace and calm. For people who are healing from repeated trauma, so much time has been spent in terror or fear or anger or numbness. The neural networks are set up for those emotions and for the cognitions that go with them. But there is now the need to balance that out. You need to build the neural networks of *fine*. You need to build the neural receptors capable of taking in the positive: positive sensations, positive facial expressions, positive words. Do you recognize these things when you feel them, see them, or hear them? In the section on the Preparation phase, I talked about the practice of gratitude—taking time at the end of each day to reflect and then write three things you were grateful for. In the Consolidation phase you could switch that practice to being able to notice and take in the positive. Each evening, reflect and write about the ways that you felt cared for, the smiles you noticed, the good feelings you experienced. Train your senses to become aware of them.

Because trauma is familiar, because it is what is known, it can wrongly feel like the safe place. And *fine* can ironically feel unsafe. When I hit the Consolidation phase, often I simply find myself there— and I can go along for a while enjoying the experience. But if I bring my awareness to it I feel like Wile E. Coyote when he suddenly notices that he has run off the cliff. He was fine running until he notices that he is no longer running on solid ground, and then *poof* he plummets and grabs desperately for the rock wall. When I suddenly notice I am in *fine*, I forget to put my head back and float—often I start thrashing around, looking for something to grab on to. I need to constantly remind myself that I am indeed fine. I can float. I can swim. The water isn't all that deep. I can even get out and sit in a beach chair.

Taking in the positive can take as much practice as learning to manage the difficult emotions. This is the mistake that is made in larger systems after country-level conflict and postwar reconstruction. As soon as the emergent issues seem to be in place, help often pulls out. They move on to the next crisis or switch to the issue that has greater funding. With the danger averted, and with minimal infrastructure in place, helpers assume that the country can simply build the rest on its own. But as history has shown us, more often the countries with the most support through bad and good are the ones that recover fully. You need to be able to spend supported time in *fine* in order to consolidate what is going well, what has been learned. You need time to experience yourself as solid, to be able to think clearly and make decisions from a place of *fine* and not survival.

So what does time in *fine* look like? It looks mostly like most other people's lives and other days. It looks like you doing what you need to be doing, but really living in the present experience of it. When you are making a batch of brownies, you are making the brownies. When you are washing your car, you are washing your car. You talk about the mundane things and the dreams you haven't talked about in a while. You are able to talk about the *other* things in your life—outside of your healing and outside of the trauma. And you aren't ignoring it or holding it back; it's just out of your view. That's the thing about the Consolidation phase—you aren't working at it, you are letting it happen. You are riding the current of it. You are staying out of its way so it can work its powerful healing magic on you.

Staying out of its way. This sounds so simple, and yet because *fine* is the new learning, it seems a more complicated dance step than the tango with trauma that you are used to. And maybe dancing is a good metaphor. *Fine* is leading; it is your job to relax into it and follow. Learning to follow isn't easy. You have to trust, to breathe, to actively relax. Sometimes closing your eyes can help—remind yourself that you are following, that you aren't in charge of the direction for now. Staying out of its way. I learned about staying out of the way as a rower. After you take a stroke, there is a period called recovery in which your blades are off the water and the boat glides. You need to be quiet with your body and your hands, and you need to stay out of the way of the work that the boat is doing on its own from the momentum you gave it during the drive. You need to stay out of the way so you can recover to take another strong stroke so the boat can glide ahead.

Going Through the Cycle
of Healing Again

The safety of Camp One didn't supply much peace of mind, however: I couldn't stop thinking about the ominously tilted slab a short distance below, and the fact that I would have to pass beneath its faltering bulk at least seven more times if I was going to make it to the summit of Everest.

JON KRAKAUER, *Into Thin Air*[1]

Books are linear. They have a beginning, a middle, and an end. They go from one end to the other. It is difficult to truly capture the nature of a cycle in the form of a book. When I first had the idea for this book I actually wanted each part of the cycle to be its own separate book, the way trail guides of mountain ranges are often broken into shorter manuals by mountain. If each phase had its own book, no one would feel pressured to move to the next phase of the cycle until they felt ready. There is something about a book describing a cycle that makes you feel like you *should* move on to the next phase—as if this process could be done quickly or in a straight line. The problem with my vision of separate books is, of course, that it is not practical to publish six different books as a lovely boxed set. So we are stuck with the standard format of a book and the linear quality that it brings.

So here in the Consolidation phase, before we start back up in the Preparation phase, it seems important to spend some time talking about the cycle—you will go around again. You will keep cycling back around. Coming to the end of this book is not an ending but a time to reflect and shift back to the beginning again—to take in what you need to. This is the very nature of healing and of growth—even healthy growth. Cycling means that the healing process is going well. You don't generally have to do anything about this. If you are engaged in healing, you will move through the cycles. In this chapter I want to talk about the shift from one phase to another and how the phases might differ a bit from the beginning of your healing journey to the end.

PREPARATION

As you spend time now in the Consolidation phase, you may notice that your mind begins to cast about for the next piece of work. You don't have to hurry it along. Your unconscious has a superb sense of knowing when it's ready to start climbing again. After resting at Base Camp for a while, you can prepare for the next climb. You will head back through the Preparation phase. In the early part of treatment, the Preparation phase may be a really long phase as you go through it each time. It is the phase where you are getting to know yourself and your guide or your group and really learning to trust yourself and them. I encourage you to spend as much time as you can in this phase, shoring up or strengthening whatever you need to. Time spent here is time well spent. The other parts of your healing journey will be smoother. As time goes by, you will spend less time in the Preparation phase—you will use it more as a check in time: How is everything going? What do we need to attend to? What is working well with treatment? What is interfering in treatment? What would strengthen the healing relationships? What would provide me with more support outside of treatment?

You may notice that you spend more time in the Preparation phase after separation from your group or your guide. Or you may spend more time in the Preparation phase after a crisis or a setback. In fact, I recommend that after any crisis or setback (loss, relapse, self-abuse, illness), you intentionally take some time in the Preparation phase, no matter where you are in your healing expedition, to figure out what would support your healing—what may have contributed to the setback or relapse. It is always supportive to your healing to descend and get some rest, get some perspective, and strengthen your relationship to your guide or your support team. Remember that the Preparation phase is about strengthening all of your resources—including your physical self. There may be parts of your journey where you focus more on the physical aspects of recovery or reconnecting with your body. There may be parts of your journey where you focus more on your work life, your home life, or your spiritual beliefs.

It can be useful as you head back into the Preparation phase to re-read the Preparation section of this book. There may be parts that were important to you before that become unimportant. Or parts you don't even remember that suddenly seem relevant. Use the section to remind you of the things you need to attend to in order to support your work and patience during this phase. Both the Preparation phase and the

Consolidation phase can be good reflective times. It may be useful to choose one of these phases for extra journaling or writing as a way to check in with where you are for each cycle through. What has changed since the last time you went around? What can you do differently? What do you understand more of? Where do you feel more open, less defended? What new experiences have you allowed yourself?

UNINTEGRATION

The work in the Preparation phase creates the experience of trust and safety that allows for the work of unintegration. Remember that unintegration depends on your ability to let go, to lean, to trust. When your system feels sufficiently supported, it will venture toward the edge of your inner diving board and leap. You will not need to force it. And the plunge into the Unintegration phase usually comes as a surprise.

The biggest piece of advice I can give you about the Unintegration phase, no matter when you go through it from the beginning of treatment until the end, is this: it always catches you off guard, and therefore it is always uncomfortable. It defies the logic of a learning curve. You will swear that because you have been through this before, it should get easier. But it doesn't. It is the necessary shifting of inner tectonic plates that allows the pieces to come out, the pieces to get named, to come in contact with each other and heal. But inner earthquakes always rock the system. The more that you can be kind to yourself and remind yourself that this part always feels bad, the more tolerant you will be of the process and the more solid the healing process will be.

When you are still early in treatment, I recommend that you head back into the Preparation phase when treatment feels too overwhelming or if you are unsure of your footing. You don't have to worry about stopping the forward momentum of the work of healing, because as soon as you feel solid and safe again your inner explorer will run off the high dive again—*splash*. And you will be back in the Unintegration phase. This is the beauty of healing: your system wants to heal, and it will move forward with healing when given the right support. The bad news is that it doesn't always feel good to heal. That's what this book is for—to help you understand and hang on to what is going on inside you when it can feel choppy and rough.

In the middle phases of your treatment, you will spend more time going back and forth between unintegration and identification: finding pieces, sorting them, and talking about them. This middle phase of treatment is a tough stretch of work. This is a good time to review the sections on unintegration and identification. It is a good time to remind yourself that you need to have two tracks running during this healing process. That it is okay to feel bad on the inside and still engage in your daily life and enjoy those moments when you are able. That both the experience of the past and the experience of the present are true. Both are true and live inside you. In fact, during this middle phase of treatment, it is important to balance the work of the past with an appreciation of what you are doing in the present. You need to have a strong anchor or rope hold in the present to belay into the past.

IDENTIFICATION

The shift from unintegration to identification is one of degrees. You thrash around in the Unintegration phase, and the Identification phase is the phase of making sense of it—finding the words, finding the other pieces. This phase highlights the power of naming and the power of speaking your truth. Early on it may be that one word, one statement, one truth out loud is enough to send you all the way through the cycle. You will name it, feel it, and then need to take a break. This is actually typical—not problematic. You are lifting the emotional weight you can, building emotional muscles. The beauty of the Identification phase is that it helps you know what to do when you feel undone with the feelings in the Unintegration phase—bring language to them and see what they are connected to.

Remember that repeated trauma can come with a sort of mandate of silence. The very nature of trauma is that it is unspeakable. The act of finding words and language for your experience is actually a radical act—and it is the result, often, of very hard work. Remember that when you put your experience into language, it becomes understandable—first and foremost to you. You actually take in, sometimes for the first time, what you experienced.

Also remember that the Identification phase has a lot of elements of trial and error. You sort and name through practice rather than certainty. This is a phase of repetition and practice. You go over and over the same story, experience, or feeling. You keep trying to sort it, name it, or map the territory. In this phase you will have a lot more patience with yourself and your healing if you think like an explorer rather than an expert. Curiosity is the needed stance: curiosity about the process, about what you find, about the impact.

My recommendation to you about the Identification phase is simple. Whenever you feel stuck, just state exactly where you are. Give an internal compass reading. "I am stuck." "I feel frustrated." The magic of putting words to your current experience helps remind your unconscious that all of your experiences can be connected to words. Giving your emotional GPS coordinates helps your guide or your group find you so that you aren't so lost. By giving them coordinates, you are throwing them a rope to get to you—to help you stop feeling so stuck. If it feels like it's moving too fast, then they can use the rope to pull on you and slow you down.

As you progress through the Identification phase, you will have more and more of the pieces. Like putting together a jigsaw puzzle, the more identified pieces you have, the more the picture becomes clear. This clarity of the picture, the story, your past nudges you into the Integration phase.

INTEGRATION

As the pieces come together—thoughts, feelings, experience—you begin to take in the trauma you experienced, the ways you protected yourself from the trauma, and the things that you missed as a result of the trauma. You begin to take in the whole picture. Integration is the goal of treatment for repeated trauma. Often when you take in your history you are hit with big waves of mourning. Early in treatment these waves of mourning may feel really big and destabilizing. You may feel it for a flash and head right back to the Preparation phase. Or right back to naming and sorting. Once again—trust your timing. Trust what you can hold, when you can hold it. What is being mourned in repeated trauma is big. It needs to be done in pieces over time. It is really different for everyone who has experienced trauma, so there isn't a perfect map for this section of the journey. Each of you is creating the map for yourselves, and in the process you will offer your trail guides as possibilities for others. Your healing and your capacity to mourn your losses will give others the courage to do the same. The ripple effects of healing go well beyond you.

Each person needs something different during mourning. As I mentioned earlier, in the Integration phase I encourage you to find time to live life more slowly if possible. It is similar in function to mourning a death—and we know that we don't expect much of people who are in the throes of mourning a loved one. We know that they need more time and space. The same is true of the Integration phase—regardless of where in your treatment journey you are meeting it. Because of the cyclical nature of the healing journey, you just need to trust that when you move out of this phase you will be in consolidation and then preparation again—and you will get some of your energy back to make up some lost ground.

The other important part of the Integration phase is to let others help you and support you. The process of mourning in the Integration phase can really erode the hope that helped you survive the trauma. This loss of hope is one of the casualties of integration—and it can feel really frightening. This can range from feeling completely hopeless to feeling suicidal. Hope functions like a north star, like gravity. Without the old hope, you can feel like there's no point. This is an expectable feeling, but it is important that others know how you are feeling and where you are. The loss of the old hope is really the birth of the new hope—in a real future that is possible. The mourning you are doing is tilling the soil of the new hope, and your experience of new beginnings, which also are a part of the Integration phase, allow you to live for moments, and then minutes, and then hours into this new future. Live without the old protections; live experiencing the relationships you are in.

Integration, like Unintegration, requires you to remember that no matter where in the healing journey you are, it often hits you harder than you think it should. Mourning almost always feels like hard work, and the Integration phase is no exception. I recommend that you and your therapist and your support system have a way of communicating about your experience of mourning and what you need to feel safe and supported on your climb. This is the experience of high altitude—where even short pieces of work can feel tiring and where you need others to know where you are. More contact, more connection, more communication—not less—is the rule. Remember that you already know how to survive difficult things without support—you already did that. You survived your trauma. In the healing of repeated trauma you are bringing your story forward now not to simply relive it, but to be able to hold it while having a different experience in the present. You take in your story in small enough pieces that you can carry, and you do it with the support and safety that didn't exist when you were living through the trauma. You wire your brain to hold the past and help it experience that it is truly over—you are safe now.

And as the past becomes the past, as you no longer protect yourself in the old ways, you have moments that are new—moments of experiences that were missed during your personal war years. Taking time to appreciate these moments and celebrate them will help you solidify the healing and growth. The new moments help you see how far you have come.

CONSOLIDATION

As you move through the Integration phase, you will shift into a quiet phase again. You will be back in the Consolidation phase. At first this phase will be so short you may miss it entirely—and it will often blend back into preparation. But the longer your healing journey goes on, the more you will notice the stretches of calm water that mark this phase. At first you may mistrust them as I did—Am I just numb? Where did the work go?

If you are uncertain, ask your guide or your group. Take time to talk about where you are and what is top of mind for you. Remember that the middle phases of the cycle—Unintegration, Identification, and Integration—can take so much time and energy that your present life can lose some of your focus. Often in the Consolidation phase you have some energy and time to talk about what is happening now and what you need in your life outside of healing. Use the Consolidation phase to understand and appreciate the journey. These are the rare moments in a long hike when you take off your heavy pack, get your water bottle out, and enjoy the view. Look back to where you started your hike. Be grateful to your strength for bringing you this far. Breathe in the fresh air and let it sink into your being. Look ahead to where you want to go and what you will feel like when you get there.

Helpful Practice for Consolidation

Practices that support the work in the Consolidation phase are things that give you a break from the intentional work of healing, allow you to take in your story and the healing that you have done to make it happen, and allow you to practice or teach new learning you have acquired. Consolidation is both a time away from the steep climbing of the journey, which allows the growth and learning you have done through your healing to be absorbed and become more solid, and active measures that help you solidify your learning through practice or conversation.

So one obvious practice is taking a break from the steep climbing of healing from trauma; you can take a literal break from treatment, which can happen because of a vacation or a planned break to focus on a project or other life event. Or you can remain with your schedule in treatment and instead decide to focus your energy on consolidation. To use the hiking metaphor, think of it as settling into a campground for a while on a lovely plateau or valley, where you stop climbing and simply enjoy where you are with no pressure to move forward. You take a deep breath and look around, and your only job is to be right where you are. In this space you can take time out to review the work you have done and talk about what it means for you. You can talk about and reflect on what has changed for you, what has really helped you, what you still feel like you are missing. You will be surprised how much healing and work can get done when, paradoxically, you stop climbing for a bit and just stay still.

Because you are not trying to climb or move forward in the same way, you may actually get to see things more clearly. Here in consolidation you can have conversations about the conversations—you can talk about what it felt like to be brave enough to talk. You can talk about what it felt like to understand your children differently because you suddenly understood how children really develop and what they need. You can talk about what allowed you to trust someone enough to share your story. Consolidation allows you to walk around the entirety of your healing, wherever you are in your healing journey, and have a more comprehensive view.

It's probably most helpful if consolidation best supports the work that preceded it. When you are in the Consolidation phase after a very steep climb or difficult piece of work, it is best if consolidation can be more restful—a chance to rejuvenate and recover from the hard work. And if the work is less strenuous, then consolidation can be a time of reflection and review or active practice of new skills. The reflection and review can be verbal—simply conversations—or you can also play with using art to draw or paint aspects of your story or your healing or create a timeline of your experience. You can make collages that speak to the work you have been doing or find music, poetry, or art that helps you communicate where you are and where you have traveled from. You can play with conversations between aspects of yourself: the self who has come to this place in consolidation and the self who didn't believe that healing was possible—what are the different beliefs you now hold?

If you are someone who is high energy or highly achievement oriented, you may find it difficult to do the work of consolidation because you don't like to sit still or feel like you are not making active forward progress, and so you may need some active practices to stay here on the plateau or valley. Some of these practices we have talked about before, but here their purpose will be to help you slow down, recover, and solidify your learning. You can use mindfulness, meditation, or yoga to slow down and physically feel that you have stopped climbing—physically feel yourself at rest. And you can use journaling in a travel writing sort of function: Where have you been? What have you seen or felt? Whereas the Integration phase is more about integrating your story of trauma and aspects of your identity, the Consolidation phase allows you to see that work in the context of the larger picture of your current life, and not just what you understand about your history but how you came to understand it. Consolidation allows you to learn about how you learned—and this makes it possible to bring your capacity to learn to new challenges in the future.

Because the healing journey can be so difficult and there can be so many times when you feel frustrated, it's important in the Consolidation phase to have conversations about what you are proud of. When were you particularly brave or hardworking? When did you behave in a way that was new? When did you have a conversation with your family or co-worker that was entirely different than it was before? When did you do something you didn't think you could do? When did you listen to someone instead of assume what they were going to say? When did you manage your emotions entirely differently? These are huge milestones to celebrate and spend time appreciating. These moments of success and pride will support you when you begin climbing again, and they will support you in solidifying all that you have learned through your hard work. They help you see yourself not just as someone who has survived, but also as someone who is confident and capable—and in the process of growing and changing.

The work of consolidation naturally lends itself to the work of preparation. As you reflect and talk about what has been helpful to you in your work of healing, you will also naturally talk about what some of the roadblocks were. As you talk about what you were able to do well, you will also naturally talk about what aspects of healing or conversation were particularly challenging and difficult for you. As you reflect on what you have learned during your journey of healing, you will also naturally talk about what you are still curious about and what you might work on next. And so these conversations will gradually become preparation conversations—conversations about what you need, what else might support your healing, and what may be getting in the way. You can look at what other muscles you need to strengthen or stretch before you start climbing again, what other equipment or communication strategies you may need, and how long you need to rest before you start climbing again. And so the work of consolidation will gradually give way to the work of preparation, and when you feel ready, you will prepare to climb again or shift out of your healing journey altogether and into your life after healing.

Epilogue

The end of a healing journey looks different for everyone. Some of you may finish this chapter and head right back onto the trail, much like some of the through-hikers on the Appalachian trail who, when they reach the peak of Mt. Katahdin in Maine, decide that they are not done with their journey and instead turn right around and head back on the trail toward Georgia. Some of you may look out at the view you now have and decide that you aren't done with your healing journey yet; you will rest as long as you need to and then start again. As we have said all the way along, healing from trauma isn't a linear path; it's a spiral, so this end may just be a pause until you start again at the Preparation phase and cycle back around. Some of you may rest here at the trail's end for weeks or months or years—taking time away from the arduous climbing on the trail for a while, or even forever.

All along this journey you have been living your daily life in the outside world, but through your trauma and your healing you know that you have juggled many worlds simultaneously. In the traditional hero journey the hero returns home, master of two worlds[1]—the world of the adventure and the world at home. And in the hero journey of trauma, I would say that you come home a master of three worlds—the world of your trauma, the world of your healing, and the world of your present daily life that you now get to inhabit fully. You get to inhabit your life and your relationships more fully because you have worked hard to inhabit yourself and your history more fully. And you get to inhabit it more fully because all of the energy you have been devoting first to survival and then to healing can now be used toward your life in the present and your work toward the future.

It can be a relief to be done with the difficult journey, but it can also be disorienting. Being on the journey of healing can give you a focus, a sense of purpose—it can be grounding. And sometimes when it ends, it can feel like you are not sure what to focus on or what is holding you steady. It can also be hard to describe the journey you have been through. There is a loneliness in healing that is both necessary and true. The people who live with you and the people who love you may never fully understand the worlds you visited on this journey—the world of your trauma and the world of your healing. These are experiences you worked to integrate and consolidate, to weave into yourself, to make yourself whole. You may have a way of communicating these worlds to the people in your life, or you may not. But either way, the experience belongs to you in a way that few will understand. Your job isn't to get those around you to understand your other worlds. Your job is to bring your hard-won wisdom and compassion from those worlds into your present world. Your job is to bring the gift of your healing into your life, your relationships, and your work. Your job is to bring your hope about healing to others who need it.

I don't think misery just loves company—I think it loves understanding, it loves being understood and known. For those of us who have experienced trauma, there may have been a time when we only felt at home with people who had experienced what we had experienced; we sought out people who had been through the same hurt as we had. There can be bonding over the hurt. And there is a time and place for that. But misery needs more than understanding, it needs healing—and all of us who have worked hard to heal can be more than a voice that says, "Yes, that happened to me too." We can also reach out a hand and be the voice that says, "But it can get better. Healing is possible."

You may be wondering after all your work on this journey whether you can still be triggered by your old trauma. And the answer is, "Yes, you can." There may be times when you are reminded of your trauma; the reminder can be as big as an anniversary of one of the bigger events, or a holiday, or when your children become the same age that you were when your trauma started. And it can be as small or fleeting as a piece of music playing on the radio or the smell of something baking. There will be times when you feel a sore spot where you healed, or your emotions feel raw, or your heart feels bruised. Having your trauma reappear now and again isn't a sign that you failed in your healing or that you have to start all over again. It's simply a normal aftereffect of an old wound, in much the same way that physical injuries can show up again when you strain something or when you are run down. The good news is that your hard work on your healing journey has helped you build muscles that help you through the times when you may feel the soreness of your trauma again—and you now have many more ways of working with any old hurts that may arise. Your trauma, if and when it reappears, now sits inside a bigger story, your story, where you hold it differently—where you have an understanding of the trauma and yourself that allows you to ride out the times when it may resurface.

Are you ever completely healed? The answer is both yes and no. I say yes because you can come through your healing and into your life in such a way that your trauma is just a part of your story and life, and not the biggest part. The trauma and your healing from it becomes woven into both your strengths and your challenges, and your life becomes devoted to the people, the work, and the things that are most important to you. Your trauma recedes into the background, and the trauma and your protections from it are no longer the operating system that is organizing your thinking, your emotions, and your behavior. But because we keep growing and learning, there may also be times, especially times of great transition or loss, when the trauma seems to come back full force. I have had so many people sit in my office and say, "But I thought I was completely done with that! I already went to therapy for that! Why is it coming up again?" First, the good news. It's a different kind of work with the trauma when it shows up again. It's a shorter hike, and you know what the hiking entails. It's not a sign that you didn't do the work of healing, but rather that you are in the process of growing. Think of books you read as a high school student and then read again as an adult—and how differently you were able to understand and think about the dilemmas of the characters. There is something similar at play as we grow as adults, go through transitions or loss, and understand the world a bit differently. It seems at these times that we also go back and make meaning of and come to understand our own trauma differently, and this requires a bit of healing. Normal, healthy development is about integration—so when we go through these stages of adult development, we find ourselves reintegrating some of our trauma.

The end of a healing journey is a lot like the commencement ceremony for a college graduate—it marks the end of one type of journey and the beginning of another. And while there may be a formal ending—the end of your therapy or your group, or a decision to take a break from the work of healing—the work that you completed during the journey gets richer and deeper over time. Think of it like planting a tree—the roots continue to grow deeper, and the branches continue to reach toward the sky. I graduated in 2002 from my doctoral program in psychology, ready to head out into the workforce, but the learning that I did during my years as a student and a trainee have taken me nearly two decades to fully absorb and use. And I still read and reread texts that help me understand how people learn and grow—and I get something new from them as I reread them. And I still reflect on the lessons I learned from my teachers, supervisors, and patients during that time— and take in those lessons once again. Your healing journey from trauma is similar. A lot of healing continues after your formal journey of healing is over—and it will be absorbed and enriched as you continue to live your life and grow. You will come to understand your trauma and your healing from it with a richer and more grounded perspective than you even hold now.

And so like any good commencement ceremony, it is important not just to reflect on the work done, but also to turn your eyes and your heart toward the future. Your healing is not just for you. Your healing impacts your relationships, your families, your communities, and the places you work. As you bring your full, integrated selves into the world, so much more is available to everyone. Your journey was a generous contribution and your hard work is felt way beyond you. As you are able, tell your story of healing to others. Let others know that there is a road back. If each person who lived through repeated trauma reached back and helped another person who experienced trauma, the healing of our communities would be exponential. This is true of everyone, but it is especially true for men. I believe that the suicide rate of veterans would decrease if men would make it socially acceptable for other men to get help. But all genders and all communities need to do a better job of encouraging people to get help and accept help. We need to honor healing and growth, the way we honor getting physically strong. We need to see psychological strengthening as being just as cool as we see physical strengthening.

And the next thing I would tell you is that you have particular gifts from healing from trauma that one can only get from living through trauma and healing from it. I'm not saying that it was good to live through trauma; I am saying that because you did live through it and were brave enough to do the work of healing from it, you possess gifts that others don't. Among these gifts are compassion for yourself and for others; you possess an empathy and understanding of others' struggle and courage, and this shows in the way you meet people, work with them, and help them. You also have the gift of hope and possibility for the broken parts of your communities and the world; you have faced despair and survived it, and this gives you the capacity to sit with others' despair and hold the hope for them. But this empathy and hope that you have isn't just an idea; it is what I would call *empathy in action* or *active hope*, because your journey of healing through trauma has given you the confidence in your own ability to roll up your sleeves and do something about any problem that may cross your path. The helplessness of trauma is gone, and in its place is a sense of purpose and passion that you can put into action.

So yes, healing gives you gifts that you worked hard for. But the last thing I want to say is that the most important thing that you can do after your journey of healing is to bring not just the gifts that are a result of your healing, but *your* gifts, the ones that make *you* uniquely *you.* The ones that the world needs from *you.* Through all the years of surviving trauma and healing from trauma, you may not have had a chance to really explore or use *your* strengths, *your* passion, and *your* love in the way you can now; I am excited for you, and I challenge you to bring yourself fully into your relationships, your work, and your communities. Bring your love to your families and your loved ones in a way you might not have been able to before—and take in their love. Bring your purpose and your passion to your work in a way you might not have been able to before—and let your light shine and inspire others. Now all of your gifts—the ones you came to the world with and the ones you fought and worked so bravely for—they all belong to you, and I believe that you have both the possibility and, dare I say, the responsibility to use it all. And more than anything I want to thank you for your brave and courageous work of healing. You have not only brought healing to yourself, you have brought more healing into the world—and so I thank you and wish you all the love and life you can grab hold of.

Acknowledgments

For all the years I knew her, my grandmother Martha Cadle had a yellowed piece of paper on her refrigerator with the following quote from Margaret Mead: "Never doubt that a small group of thoughtful, committed citizens can change the world; indeed, it's the only thing that ever has." This book was powered by that ethic—that any one of us can make a difference and that groups have the power to change the world. Groups certainly changed my life and made this book possible. This book is a product of thirty years of study, training, and work—in clinical, organizational, and international settings, and it would not have been possible without the many, many groups of thoughtful, committed teachers, colleagues, friends, family, students, clients, and patients.

Over the course of my writing a group of people offered to be part of "Team Gretchen"—I sent them updates and they sent both encouragement and wisdom. Thank you for getting me through two challenging years of writing: Laura Morgon, Susan Reisbord, Holly Noel Wagner, Heather Wood, Makenzie Newman, Vic Gulas, Laurie Carrick, Bob McDowell,

Acknowledgments

Judy Issokson, Barry Lydgate, Eddy Rayden, Lee Chalmers, Kristin Von Donop, Lindsey Bingaman, Ann Begler, Jenn Moyer, Lizza Robb, Jennifer Milwee, Jessica Reviere, Sarah Medary, and Letizia Amadini Lane.

Having a place to write may be one of the biggest gifts a writer can get, and I was so very fortunate for amazing gifts of beautiful and loving places to write. I want to thank Donna Parssinen for generously allowing me and my dog, Davey, to spend the winter of 2013 in her house in Rhode Island, where the first manuscript was completed. Beth Gaudet generously gave me two different and important weeks in Florida for new writing to emerge—complete with mojitos and grilled oysters. And all of the Peck-Eysenbach extended family gave me space and time in Maine to write and rejuvenate—thank you for boat rides, island picnics, and cozy fires, and all of the love and support of this long journey: Lucy and John Eysenbach, Laura Peck and Fran Johnston, Jamie and Liz Peck, Abby Peck and Chris Gardner, Hans Eysenbach and Jesse Hayward Eysenbach, Jamie Eysenbach, Jesse Eysenbach, Laurel and Brian Smith, James Peck, and Lucas and Miguel Johnston-Peck.

There were many readers along the way who helped me shape the book. I want to thank Billie Fitzpatrick for her early comments about organization and help with learning to write a proposal. I want to thank Suzanne Rotondo and Laura Clark for their belief that it could be published and Page Lindroth who took a lot of time and care on an early draft. I want to thank Molly Watson for her wisdom about connecting my ideas to a speech. I want to thank the later readers: Ray Fisher, Cory Bryant, Elsie Boudreau, Eddy Mwelwa, Cheryl Rosenthal, Jane Clarke, Laura Parker Reorden, Heather Wood, and Aunt Suzy Waterman for your comments and helping me see how they could be useful. And I want to thank my dear friend Melanie Morgon, who edited my dissertation and taught me how to write in the process. I am grateful for your help with the final edits and feedback on my manuscript and for all of the wonderful walks.

Acknowledgments

Psychology is really an apprenticeship of learning, and I am deeply appreciative that I got to learn with great teachers and in institutions, clinics, and hospitals that took training seriously. I want to thank Barbara Okun for being with me on my journey, from my first interview at Northeastern through my dissertation to putting on my hood at graduation and the many weekends since. I want to thank Lise Motherwell for teaching me how to "hear" the language of play and for our continued work and play together. Camille DiBenedetto helped me to find my voice in writing reports about clients, and her compassionate view of clients became an early North Star. Thank you to Sharon Greenfield for an unsolicited recommendation letter that gave me hope for my future at a dark time and which I still reread when I am having a bad day. And thanks to Barbara Gortych, Pat Harney, Elizabeth Wheeler, David Dinklage, Karlen Lyons-Ruth, Ann Munson, Arnie Cohen, Mary Ballou, Judy Van Raalte, and Rick Paar—supervisors and teachers who helped me integrate my learning and become a better clinician and writer. I want to acknowledge the supervisors, colleagues, and patients at some of the many institutions I trained in or worked at over the years: Northeastern University Counseling Psychology Department, Behavioral Medicine Department at UMASS Memorial Medical Center, Center for Mindfulness, Somerville Hospital Adolescent Inpatient Unit at Cambridge Hospital, Boston Regional Medical Center, Somerville Mental Health Clinic, Massachusetts Department of Youth Services, Beaverbrook Counseling Center, Parents and Children's Services, Germaine Lawrence, Patriots Trail Girl Scout Council, and the Northampton Center for Families and Children. I want to thank Linda Watt for her support of the meditation groups and I want to especially thank Shelly Hirschberg, one of the best child psychologists I have ever worked with, and Katrina Schuman, whose bravery, optimism, and persistence is inspirational.

It's not just the teachers I was privileged to work with, but the teachings I was privileged to read. As a psychologist I am indebted to the wise teachings and keen observations of those whose work I have read and re-read and who have shaped how I work and understand growth, development, and healing: Michael Balint, D. W. Winnicott, Robert Kegan, Jean Baker Miller, Dan Siegel, Dan Goleman, Leston Havens, Martha Stark, Judith Herman, and Bessel van der Kolk.

This book would never have taken on the scope that it did without the Leadership Development Program for the UNDP that I got to be a part of with Teleos Leadership Institute. Thank you to my colleague and soul sister Fran Johnston, who spirited me away from child psychology and into the world of leadership development and inspired me to understand growth and change from a broader perspective in large and complicated systems—I would not be the person I am without you, and I am eternally grateful for your belief in me and for being my continual learning and adventure partner. And to Eddy Mwelwa, whose wisdom and heart heals any group he is a part of. And to the Cambodia LDP Faculty/Facilitators: Dr. Tia Phalla, Madame Chou Bun Eng, Dr. Seng Suth Wantha, San Vandin, Huot Totem, Va Sopheak, Kong Udom, Dr. Ngin Lina, Dr. Hy Someth, Dr. Tan Sokhey, Ith Sokum, Nith Sopha, Sia Phearum, Ven Muny Vansaveth, Dr. Veung Yanath, Sim Kheng Kham, Hen Sokunkolroth, Chun Bora, Poan Phoun Bopha, and Dr. Bun Chhem and the Alaska Native LDP Facilitators, Elsie Boudreau, Paula Cinero, Cory Bryant, Debbie Demientieff, Tiffany Simmons, Teisha Simmons, Roxanne Frank, Cesa Sam, and Tim Boudreau—all of whom bravely helped the people in their communities work with and heal trauma all the while building their leadership and creating solutions for their communities. To my fellow TCDP faculty: Shirley McAlpine, Ray Fisher, Kristin von Donop, Michael McElhenie, Marco Bertola, and all of the participants of TCDP since 2009 who were part of the journey of this project as I used "I want to write a book" in the Resistance to Change exercise—and some of the rest of the Teleos gang over the years—Bobbie

Nash, Sarah Renio, Lindsey Bingaman, Annie McKee, Felice Tilin, Dave Smith, Makenzie Newman, Laura Peck, Greg Yerkes, Christina Yerkes, Delores Mason, Laurie Carrick, Kristin von Donop, and Eric Vandersluis—I learned so much from all of you.

Over the course of this book, I was lucky to be a part of three groups that helped me stay on track through love, encouragement, mutual coaching, and of course, really good meals. Thank you to the Ingerdinner Group: Inger Nielsen, Melanie Morgon, Maud Chaplin, Bonnie Leonard, Jeannie Benton, and Anne Gothro; and my Salon Sisters: Cheryl Rosenthal, Alison Streit Baron, Sara Quay, Laura Parker Roerden, and Jane Clarke; and my Philly Group: Fran Johnston, Janet Gilease, and Ray Fisher. And to my peer coaches Shirley McAlpine, Carolyn Murphy, Una O'Connell, and Paula Boyle, who kept me on track to submit my manuscript and who kept me hopeful and working hard in the years it took to get it published.

I want to thank Guy Macpherson from The Trauma Therapist Project and Carol Anna McBride from The Trauma Project for supporting the blog and writings about trauma. And all of the readers of my blog, *The Trail Guide*, at gretchenschmelzer.com, who made "The Letter Your Teenage Can't Write You" go viral on Facebook—thank you to Kathie Pories, who saw the Facebook post and helped me find an agent.

Thank you to my father, who taught me to work hard and never give up; and my mother, who gave me the gift of creativity.

I am grateful to my brother, Matt, for being the other half of memory and a fellow companion throughout our lives and this work. I am grateful for your love and your sense of humor.

Thank you to Helga and Ulli Schmoecker for taking me in as a teenager and sharing your home and family.

To my best friend, Jane Clarke—who has been on this journey from the Zeacliff Trail in college through every up and down along the way. Your love and support have made my healing possible—and your wonderful children, Nate and Jack, helped me have hope and compassion for my own growth. Your kindness inspires me, and hearing your voice nearly every day is one of the great joys of my life.

I was so very lucky to land in the hands of my agent, Ellen Geiger, who believed in my big idea and worked as a real partner with me to bring the pieces into a sturdy and beautiful offering. Caroline Sutton, my editor at Penguin Random House, has shown me how wonderful it is to have someone with a keen mind and a good heart take your work under their wing. She has been such a gift to me and this project. She had the amazing capacity to hold the whole arc of the book and the journey of healing and help me see where I needed to rework and rethink the connections and distinctions between the phases. The book is stronger and will serve more people because of her. I am deeply grateful.

Last, I want to thank Gail Donaldson. This book would not exist without our work together. They may be my words, but it is your deeply compassionate, respectful, and hopeful view of healing that is woven into the very fabric of this book. May it help others heal as much as you helped me.

Notes

PART 1: THE TRAIL GUIDE

1 **Exploration is still the epic journey:** Priit J. Vesilind, "Why Explore?" *National Geographic* 193, no. 2 (February 1998): 41.

UNDERSTANDING TRAUMA

1 **PTSD is defined by a set of symptoms:** American Psychiatric Association, *Diagnostic and Statistical Manual of Mental Disorders*, 5th ed. (Arlington, VA: American Psychiatric Association, 2013), 271–280.

THE HERO JOURNEY

1 **There is what I would call the hero journey:** Joseph Campbell, *The Hero with a Thousand Faces* (Princeton, NJ: Bolingen, 2004).
2 **hero journey:** Campbell, *The Hero with a Thousand Faces.*
3 **Beowulf:** Christopher Booker, *The Seven Basic Plots: Why We Tell Stories* (New York: Continuum, 2005), 245.

THE TRAIL GUIDE

1 **It is my contention:** Robert Louis Stevenson, "My First Book: 'Treasure Island,'" in *Essays in the Art of Writing* (London: Chatto & Windus, 1905), https://en.wikisource.org/wiki/Essays_in_the_Art_of_Writing/My_First_Book:_%27Treasure_Island%27.

2 **Shackleton's voyage:** Alfred Lansing, *Endurance: Shackleton's Incredible Voyage* (New York: McGraw-Hill, 1959).
3 **Maurice Herzog's team:** Maurice Herzog, *Annapurna* (New York: Popular Library, 1960).

THE WHOLE TRAUMA STORY

1 **restorying:** John Lederach, *The Moral Imagination: The Art and Soul of Building Peace* (New York: Oxford, 2005), 147. "Restorying as imaginative narrative looks for the deeper social story and meaning, not just of what happened, but how stories are connected to a far more profound journey of discovering what these events mean for who we are as both local and global communities."
2 **a mosaic is a conversation between what is broken:** Terry Tempest Williams, *Finding Beauty in a Broken World* (New York: Vintage), 20.
3 **definition of coherence:** Bessel van der Kolk and Onno van der Hart, "The Intrusive Past: The Flexibility of Memory and the Engraving of Trauma," in *Trauma: Explorations in Memory*, ed. Cathy Caruth (Baltimore: Johns Hopkins University Press, 1995), 177.
4 **psychology researchers can identify:** Mary Main, "Meta-Cognitive Knowledge, Metacognitive Monitoring, and Singular (Coherent) vs Multiple (Incoherent) Model of Attachment," in *Attachment across the Life Cycle*, ed. Colin Murray Parkes, Joan Stevenson-Hinde, and Peter Marris (London: Tavistock/Routledge, 1991), 127–159. "They exhibited logical and factual contradictions; inability to stay with the interview topic; contradictions between general descriptors of their relationships with their parents and actual autobiographical episodes offered; apparent inability to express early memories; anomalous changing in wording or intrusions into topics; slips of the tongue, metaphor or rhetoric inappropriate to the discourse context; inability to focus upon the interviews" (p. 143).
5 **Trauma is processed in your brain differently:** Bessel van der Kolk and Rita Fisler, "Dissociation and the Fragmentary Nature of Traumatic Memories: Overview," *British Journal of Psychotherapy* 12 (1996): 352–361.
6 **memory and language:** Scott Rauch et al., "A Symptom Provocation Study of Posttraumatic Stress Disorder Using Positron Emission Tomography and Script-Driven Imagery," *Archives of General Psychiatry* 53 (1996): 380–387.
7 **full trauma story:** Richard Mollica, *Healing Invisible Wounds: Paths to Hope and Recovery in a Violent World* (New York: Harcourt, 2006), 246.
8 **working the narrative aspects of our lives:** Dan McAdams, "Personal Narratives and the Life Story," in *Handbook of Personality: Theory and Research*, 3rd ed., ed. Oliver P. John, Richard W. Robins, and Lawrence A. Pervin (New York: Guilford, 2008), 242–262.
9 **The first principle is that life is storied:** McAdams, "Personal Narratives and the Life Story," 244.

10 **veteran who did three tours in Vietnam:** Jonathan Shay, *Achilles in Vietnam: Combat Trauma and the Undoing of Character* (New York: Scribner, 1994), 33.

11 **The second principle is that stories integrate lives:** McAdams, "Personal Narratives and the Life Story," 244.

12 **The third principle is that stories are told in social relationships:** McAdams, "Personal Narratives and the Life Story," 245.

13 **Sharing the trauma:** Jeremy Holmes, *The Search for the Secure Base: Attachment Theory and Psychotherapy* (Philadelphia: Brunner-Routledge, 2001), 91.

14 **We need people to listen:** Susan J. Brison, "Trauma Narratives and the Remaking of the Self," in *Acts of Memory: Cultural Recall in the Present* (Hanover, NH: University Press of New England, 1999), 46.

15 **The fourth principle is that stories are located in time and change over time:** McAdams, "Personal Narratives and the Life Story," 246.

16 **an inner survival skill:** Shay, *Achilles in Vietnam*, 176; Brison, "Trauma Narratives and the Remaking of the Self," 43.

THE FIVE-PHASE CYCLE OF HEALING REPEATED TRAUMA

1 **I am a pilgrim:** Wendell Berry, *Jayber Crow* (Berkeley, CA: Counterpoint, 2000), 133.

HOW TO GET HELP

1 **A mountain this size:** Alex Lowe, quoted in Jon Krakauer, "On the Edge of Antarctica: Queen Maud Land," *National Geographic* 193, no. 2 (February 1998): 46–49.

PART 2: PREPARATION

1 **Our bodies need time to adjust:** Jim Haberl, *Risking Adventure: Mountaineering Journeys around the World* (Richmond, BC: Raincoast Books, 1997), 54.

PREPARATION

1 **When we're guiding here on Everest:** "Nova Online Adventure: Ed Viesturs," http://www.pbs.org/wgbh/nova/everest/exposure/viesturs.html, accessed July 10, 2013.

2 **significantly improves safety:** In research on the use of checklists in medicine before surgery, there have been reductions between 67 percent and 47 percent in relative mortality. Axel Fudickar et al., "The Effect of the WHO Surgical Safety Checklist on Complication Rate and Communication," *Deutsches Aertztblatt International* 109 (2012), 695–701.

Notes

BASE CAMP

1 **Despite the many trappings of civilization:** Jon Krakauer, *Into Thin Air* (New York: Anchor, 1997), 72.
2 **Lewis and Clark:** Lewis spent the months prior to the trip learning astronomy, botany, anatomy, navigation, biology, and medicine. "To Equip an Expedition," http://www.pbs.org/lewisandclark/inside/idx_equ.html, accessed June 30, 2017.

AWARENESS

1 **Awareness:** John Kabat Zinn, *Wherever You Go, There You Are: Mindfulness Meditation in Everyday Life* (New York: Hyperion, 1994), 4–5; Daniel Goleman, Richard Boyatzis, and Annie McKee, *Primal Leadership: Realizing the Power of Emotional Intelligence* (Boston: Harvard Business School Press, 2002), 40.
2 **Mindfulness is the practice of paying attention:** Zinn, *Wherever You Go, There You Are*, 5.
3 **my dissertation:** Gretchen Schmelzer, "The Effectiveness of a Meditation Group on the Self-Control of Adolescent Boys in a Secure Juvenile Detention Center," doctoral dissertation, Northeastern University, 2002.

TRUST AND ROPES

1 **in every real and important way:** Anne Lamott, *Traveling Mercies: Some Thoughts on Faith* (New York: Anchor, 2000), 202.

RESOURCES—THE THINGS WE NEED AND THE THINGS WE CARRY

1 **They carried all the emotional baggage:** Tim O'Brien, *The Things They Carried* (New York: Houghton Mifflin, 1990), 86.
2 **Emmons and McCullough studied gratitude:** Robert Emmons and Michael McCullough, "Counting Blessings versus Burdens: An Experimental Investigation of Gratitude and Subjective Well-Being in Daily Life," *Journal of Personality and Social Psychology* 84 (2003): 377–389.

SAFE PLACES

1 **the establishment of safety:** Judith Herman, *Trauma and Recovery* (New York: Basic Books, 1997), 155.
2 **Reconstruction of trust:** Mary R. Fabri, "Reconstructing Safety: Adjustments to the Therapeutic Frame in the Treatment of Survivors of Political Torture," *Professional Psychology: Research and Practice* 32 (2001), 452–457. As Fabri notes, "The torture survivor learns from experiencing extreme harm at the hand of another human being that danger is inherent in all human relationships. The resulting

mistrust of others nags at the survivors, even after they have been able to come to terms with the fears they live with after torture" (p. 452).

HELPFUL PRACTICES FOR PREPARATION

1 **the rest of the day:** Albert Trieschman, James Whittaker, and Larry Brendtro, *The Other 23 Hours: Child Care Work with Emotionally Disturbed Children in a Therapeutic Milieu* (Piscataway, NJ: Aldine, 1969).
2 **dialectical behavior therapy:** Marsha Linehan, *Cognitive Behavioral Treatment of Borderline Personality Disorder* (New York: Guilford, 1993), 19–22.
3 **how to soothe with the five senses:** Marsha Linehan, *Skills Training Manual for Treating Borderline Personality Disorder* (New York: Guilford, 1993), 167.

PART 3: UNINTEGRATION

1 **We think that the point:** Pema Chödrön, *When Things Fall Apart: Heart Advice for Difficult Times* (Boulder, CO: Shambhala, 1997), 115.

UNINTEGRATION

1 **fissures in the sandstone:** Lennart Berg, "The Salvation of Abu Simbel Temples," *Monumentum* 27 (1978), 36.
2 **integrity of the temple:** VBB Valtenbyggnadsbyran, "The Salvage of the Abu Simbel Temples," *Concluding Report* submitted to the Arab Republic of Egypt, Ministry of Culture, sponsored by UNESCO. (1976); Georg Gerstner, "Abu Simbel's Ancient Temples Reborn," *National Geographic Magazine* (May 1969) 724–744.
3 **The sculpted faces:** Anne Michaels, *The Winter Vault* (New York: Knopf, 2009), 27.
4 **unintegration:** D. W. Winnicott, "Ego Integration in Child Development," in *The International Psycho-Analytical Library* (London: Hogarth Press and the Institute of Psycho-Analysis, 1962/1965), 60.
5 **the child could experience himself as whole:** Donald W. Winnicott, *Playing and Reality* (New York: Routledge, 1971), 55.
6 **compares this resting state to meditation:** Mark Epstein, *Going to Pieces without Falling Apart: A Buddhist Perspective on Wholeness* (New York: Broadway Books, 1998), 36–39.

UNDERSTANDING ATTACHMENT

1 **children who had been placed in care:** John Bowlby, *Attachment and Loss, Vol. 2: Separation* (New York: Basic Books, 1973).
2 **system of self-regulation:** Judith Schore and Allan Schore, "Modern Attachment Theory: The Central Role in Affect Regulation in Development and Treatment," *Clinical Social Work Journal* 36 (2008): 9–20.

3 **The attachment system:** Kenneth Levy et al., "An Attachment Theoretical Framework for Personality Disorders," *Canadian Psychology* 56 (2015): 197–207.

4 **we cannot describe the baby without describing the environment:** Donald Winnicott, "The Mother-Infant Experience of Mutuality," in *D. W. Winnicott: Psycho-Analytic Explorations*, ed. Clare Winnicott, Ray Shepherd, and Madeleine Davis (Cambridge, MA: Harvard University Press, 1969/1989), 251–260.

5 **safe haven:** Bowlby, *Attachment and Loss, Vol. 2: Separation.*

6 **good enough:** Donald Winnicott, "Clinical Regression Compared with Defense Organization," in *D. W. Winnicott: Psycho-Analytic Explorations*, ed. Clare Winnicott, Ray Shepherd, and Madeleine Davis (Cambridge, MA: Harvard University Press, 1969/1989), 193–199. "For me, a good enough mother and good enough parents and a good enough home do in fact give most babies and small children *the experience of not having ever been significantly let down.* In this way average children have the chance to build up a capacity to believe in themselves and the world—they build a structure on the accumulation of introjected reliability" (p. 196).

7 **repair:** Beatrice Beebe and Frank Lachmann, *Infant Research and Adult Treatment: Co-constructing Interactions* (Hillsdale, NJ: Analytic Press, 2002); Edward Tronick, "Emotions and Emotional Communication in Infants," *American Psychologist* 44 (1989): 112–119; Daniel Stern, *The Interpersonal World of the Infant: A View from Psychoanalysis and Developmental Psychology* (New York: Basic Books, 1985).

8 **insecure attachment:** Mary Ainsworth and Barbara Wittig, "Attachment and the Exploratory Behaviour of One-Year-Olds in a Strange Situation," in *Determinants of Infant Behaviour, Vol. 4*, ed. B. M. Foss (London: Methuen, 1969), 113–136; Amir Levine and Rachel Heller, *Attached: The New Science of Attachment and How It Can Help You Find—and Keep—Love* (New York: Penguin, 2011).

9 **disorganized attachment:** Mary Main and Judith Solomon, "Procedures for Identifying Infants as Disorganised/Disoriented during the Ainsworth Strange Situation," in *Attachment in the Preschool Years*, ed. Mark T. Greenberg, Dante Cicchetti, and E. Mark Cummings (Chicago: University of Chicago Press, 1990): 121–160; Karlen Lyons-Ruth, "Attachment Relationships among Children with Aggressive Behavior Problems: The Role of Disorganized Early Attachment Patterns," *Journal of Consulting and Clinical Psychology* 64 (1996): 64–73; Karlen Lyons-Ruth, Lisbeth Alpern, and Betty Repacholi, "Disorganized Infant Attachment Classification and Maternal Psychosocial Problems as Predictors of Hostile-Aggressive Behavior in the Preschool Classroom," *Child Development* 64 (1993): 572–585.

10 **closeness-distance:** Andrew Bush MD, Psychology Fellow Family Therapy Case Conference Seminar, Cambridge Hospital, 1998.

11 **brain is organized into different parts:** Daniel J. Siegel, *Mindsight: The New Science of Personal Transformation* (New York: Bantam, 2011), 15–22.

12 **The limbic brain goes through massive growth:** Rebecca Knickmeyer et al., "A Structured MRI Study of Human Brain Development from Birth to 2 Years,"

Journal of Neuroscience 28 (2008): 12176–12182; Hannah Kinney et al., "Sequence of Central Nervous System Myelination in Human Infancy: Patterns of Myelination in Autopsied Infants," *Journal of Neuropathology and Experimental Neurology* 47 (1988): 217–234.

13 **the developing right brain:** Louis J. Cozolino, *The Neuroscience of Psychotherapy: Building and Rebuilding the Human Brain* (New York: Norton, 2002); Allan Schore, *Affect Regulation and the Origin of the Self* (Mahwah, NJ: Lawrence Erlbaum, 1994).

14 **attachment as buffer:** Megan Gunnar et al., "Dampening of Adrenocortical Responses during Infancy: Normative Changes and Individual Differences," *Child Development* 67 (1996): 877–889; Megan Gunnar and Karina Quevedo, "The Neurobiology of Stress and Development," *Annual Review of Psychology* 58 (2007): 145–173.

15 **soldiers who were securely attached:** Sandra M. Escolas et al., "The Impact of Attachment Style on Posttraumatic Stress Disorder Symptoms in Postdeployed Military Members," *U.S. Army Medical Department Journal* (July–September 2012): 54–61.

16 **window of tolerance:** Daniel Siegel, *The Developing Mind*, 2nd ed. (New York: Guilford, 2015): 281–286.

17 **selves-in-relation:** Jean Baker Miller, *Toward a New Psychology of Women* (Boston: Beacon Press, 1976); Judith Jordan et al., *Women's Growth in Connection: Writings from the Stone Center* (New York: Guilford Press, 1991).

CONTAINER: MANAGING THE EMOTIONS OF UNINTEGRATION

1 **touchpoints:** T. Berry Brazelton and Joshua D. Sparrow, *Touchpoints: Birth to Three*, 2nd ed. (Cambridge, MA: Da Capo Press, 2006): xix–xxi.

2 **creating a container:** The notion of a container comes from the conversation that trauma therapists have about the work of containment. Jody M. Davies and Mary G. Frawley, *Treating the Adult Survivor of Childhood Sexual Abuse: A Psychoanalytic Perspective* (New York: Basic Books, 1994), 202–208.

3 **window of tolerance:** Siegel, *The Developing Mind*, 281–286.

4 **inner speech:** Lev Vygotsky stated, "We could say that the relations between higher mental function were at one time real relations between people. . . . I relate to myself in the same way people related to me." Lev Vygotsky, in *The Collected Works of L. S. Vygotsky, Vol. 4: The History of the Development of Higher Mental Functions*, ed. Robert W. Rieber (New York: Plenum Press, 1997), 103.

DISMANTLING DEFENSES

1 **resistance:** Emmanuel Ghent, "Masochism, Submission, Surrender: Masochism as a Perversion of Surrender," in *Relational Psychoanalysis: The Emergence of a Tradition*, ed. Stephen Mitchell and Lewis Aron (Hillsdale, NJ; Analytic Press, 1999), 215.

2 **tension between "yes" and "no":** Martha Stark, *Working with Resistance* (Northvale, NJ: Jason Aronson, 1994), 2.

HELPFUL PRACTICES FOR UNINTEGRATION
1 **amygdala hijack:** Goleman, Boyatzis, and McKee, *Primal Leadership*, 28–29.
2 **flipping your lid:** Siegel, *Mindsight*, 22.

PART 4: IDENTIFICATION
1 **I had less and less control over my history each day:** Kevin Powers, *The Yellow Birds* (Boston: Back Bay Books, 2012), 172.

IDENTIFICATION
1 **The Dead Sea Scrolls:** "Learn about the Scrolls: Conservation," The Leon Levy Dead Sea Scrolls Digital Library, http://www.deadseascrolls.org.il/learn-about -the-scrolls/conservation?locale=en_US, accessed May 22, 2017; Edmund Wilson, "The Scrolls from the Dead Sea," *New Yorker*, May 14, 1955, http://www .newyorker.com/magazine/1955/05/14/the-scrolls-from-the-dead-sea; Naomi Pfefferman, "The Art, Science and History of the Dead Sea Scrolls," *Jewish Journal*, March 4, 2015, http://jewishjournal.com/news/los_angeles/164075 /; "Dead Sea Scrolls Come to Boston," *Sparks: A Newsletter for Members and Friends of the Museum of Science*, April–May 2013, https://www.mos.org/sites /dev-elvis.mos.org/files/docs/membership/mos_sparks_aprmay-2013.pdf.
2 **a twelfth cave was discovered in 2017:** Kevin Loria, "A New Dead Sea Scrolls Cave Has Been Discovered—and It Might Not Be the Last," *Business Insider*, February 9, 2017, http://www.businessinsider.com/new-dead-sea-scrolls-cave -discovered-2017-2.
3 **Researchers in Israel:** Rivka Tuval-Mashiach et al., "Coping with Trauma: Narrative and Cognitive Perspectives," *Psychiatry* 67 (2004): 280–293.
4 **this survivor described himself:** Tuval-Mashiach et al., "Coping with Trauma," 287.
5 **what we saw or what we imagined seeing:** Lenore Terr, *Too Scared to Cry* (New York: Basic Books, 1990), 133.

MEMORY
1 **declarative memory:** Eric R. Kandel, *In Search of Memory: The Emergence of a New Science of Mind* (New York: Norton, 2006), 132–133.
2 **amygdala:** Kandel, *In Search of Memory*, 132–133.
3 **implicit relational memory:** Karlen Lyons-Ruth et al., "Implicit Relational Knowing and Its Role in Development and Psychoanalytic Treatment," *Infant Mental Health Journal* 19 (1998): 282–289.

4 **It is your memory that guides your behavior:** Karsten Baumgartel et al., "Control of the Establishment of Aversive Memory by Calcineurin and Zif268," *Nature Neuroscience* 11 (2008): 572–578.

5 **activation of the amygdala:** Release of norepinephrine heightens activation of amygdala and intensifies memories of trauma. James L. McGaugh, "Significance and Remembrance: The Role of Neuromodulatory Systems," *Psychological Science* 1 (1990): 15–25.

6 **stress hormones shut down the neural networks:** Louis Cozolino, *The Neuroscience of Psychotherapy: Building and Rebuilding the Human Brain* (New York: Norton, 2002).

7 **reduced blood flow to the parts of the brain:** Rauch et al., "A Symptom Provocation Study of Posttraumatic Stress Disorder."

FINDING YOUR PATH

1 **If its interest in truth is linked:** Antjie Krog, *Country of My Skull: Guilt, Sorrow, and the Limits of Forgiveness in the New South Africa* (New York: Broadway Books, 1998), 16.

2 **Do you like sentences?:** Annie Dillard, *A Writing Life* (New York: Harper, 1989), 70.

3 **courage:** Bessel van der Kolk, *The Body Keeps Score: Brain, Mind, and Body in the Healing of Trauma* (New York: Penguin, 2014), 235.

4 **every trail:** Robert Moor, *On Trails* (New York: Simon and Schuster, 2016), 91.

5 **trails extend backward:** Moor, *On Trails*, 61.

6 **the struggle of memory against forgetting:** Milan Kundera, *The Book of Laughter and Forgetting*, trans. Michael Henry Heim (New York: Knopf, 1981), 3.

HELPFUL PRACTICES FOR IDENTIFICATION

1 **shitty first drafts:** Anne Lamott, *Bird by Bird: Some Instructions on Writing and Life* (New York: Anchor, 1995), 21–27.

2 **traumatic play is grim:** Terr, *Too Scared to Cry*, 238.

3 **There is this thing that happens with children:** M. R. Montgomery, *Saying Goodbye: A Memoir for Two Fathers* (New York: Knopf, 1989), 143.

4 **Anger and tenderness:** Adrienne Rich, "Integrity," in *A Wild Patience Has Taken Me This Far: Poems 1978–1981* (New York: Norton, 1993), 8.

5 **Imagine a ruin:** Barbara Kingsolver, *The Poisonwood Bible* (New York: Harper and Row, 1998).

PART 5: INTEGRATION

1 **Once again I had found myself in the presence:** Antoine de Saint-Exupéry, *Wind, Sand and Stars* (New York: Harcourt, 2002), 198.

INTEGRATION

1 **The last 300 feet:** "Nova Online Adventure: Ed Viesturs," http://www.pbs.org /wgbh/nova/everest/exposure/viesturs.html.

2 **transitional space:** Donald W. Winnicott, "The Fate of the Transitional Object," in *D. W. Winnicott: Psycho-Analytic Explorations*, ed. Clare Winnicott, Ray Shepherd, and Madeleine Davis (Cambridge, MA: Harvard University Press, 1959/1989), 53–58.

3 **mourning:** Herman, *Trauma and Recovery*, 175–195.

4 **new beginning:** Michael Balint, *The Basic Fault*, 3rd ed. (Chicago: Northwestern University Press, 1992), 143.

5 *The Miracle Worker*: William Gibson, *The Miracle Worker: A Play* (New York: Scribner, 2008).

MOURNING

1 *Year of Magical Thinking*: Joan Didion, *The Year of Magical Thinking* (New York: Knopf, 2005).

2 **The child's mother talked about using a strategy:** Eli Saslow, "After Newtown Shooting, Mourning Parents Enter into the Lonely Quiet," *Washington Post*, June 8, 2013, https://www.washingtonpost.com/national/after-newtown-shooting -mourning-parents-enter-into-the-lonely-quiet/2013/06/08/0235a882-cd32-11e2 -9f1a-1a7cdee20287_story.html?utm_term=.802692b83952.

NEW BEGINNINGS

1 *Room*: Emma Donahue, *Room*, dir. Lenny Abrahamson, 2015, Element Pictures.

2 **Balint recognized that people who had been very hurt:** Balint, *The Basic Fault*.

3 **As Kegan writes:** Robert Kegan, *The Evolving Self: Problem and Process in Human Development* (Cambridge, MA: Harvard University Press, 1982), 31.

4 **Good parents:** Kegan, *The Evolving Self*, 147–148.

HOLDING BOTH

1 **War is hell:** O'Brien, *The Things They Carried*, 235.

2 **polarities:** Barry Johnson, *Polarity Management: Identifying and Managing Unsolvable Problems* (Amherst, MA: HRD Press, 2014).

3 **wise mind:** Linehan, *Cognitive Behavioral Treatment of Borderline Personality Disorder*, 214–216.

4 **the trauma of war:** Sebastian Junger, "How PTSD Became a Problem Far from the Battlefield," *Vanity Fair*, May 7, 2015, http://www.vanityfair.com/news/2015/05 /ptsd-war-home-sebastian-junger.

5 **Take your well-disciplined strengths:** Rainer Maria Rilke, "Just as the Winged Energy of Delight," in *The Winged Energy of Delight: Selected Translations by Robert Bly* (New York: HarperCollins, 2004), 177.

IDENTITY

1 **Will I lose myself entirely if I lose my limp?:** Kingsolver, *The Poisonwood Bible*, 493.

2 **The rate of suicide for returning Iraq and Afghanistan vets:** "VA Suicide Prevention Program: Facts about Veteran Suicide," July 2016, https://www.va.gov /opa/publications/factsheets/Suicide_Prevention_FactSheet_New_VA_Stats_070616 _1400.pdf.

3 **appearances can be misinterpreted:** Gay A. Bradshaw, *Elephants on the Edge: What Animals Teach Us about Humanity* (New Haven, CT: Yale University Press, 2009), 119.

4 **peace accords:** Lederach, *The Moral Imagination*, 47.

5 **Last night:** Edward Tick, *War and the Soul: Healing Our Nation's Veterans from Post-Traumatic Stress Disorder* (Wheaton, IL: Quest Books, 2005), 99.

PART 6: CONSOLIDATION

1 **The difficulties of attaining a durable peace:** Lederach, *The Moral Imagination*, 41.

CONSOLIDATION

1 *periodization:* Christopher Frankel and Len Kravitz, "Periodization: Latest Studies and Practical Applications," *IDEA Personal Trainer* 11 (2000): 15–16.

2 **rest is a big contributor to moving information:** Jan Born and Ines Wilhelm, "System Consolidation of Memory during Sleep," *Psychological Research* 76 (2012): 192–203; Michaela Dewar et al., "Brief Wakeful Resting Boosts New Memories over the Long Term," *Psychological Science* 23 (2012): 955–960.

GOING THROUGH THE CYCLE OF HEALING AGAIN

1 **The safety of Camp One:** Krakauer, *Into Thin Air*, 84.

EPILOGUE

1 **master of two worlds:** Campbell, *The Hero with a Thousand Faces*, 229.

Index

Index

C

cages, 170–76, 174
cairns, 208–10
calling for help, 89
camaraderie, 255–56
Campbell, Joseph, 19
causal coherence, 34, 37
cause and effect, 37
childhood
  abuse and neglect in, 136–37, 141, 143
  happy, 6
  learning trust in, 102–3
  shattered milestones of, 257
childhood development
  attachment in, 138, 144
  regression in, 156
  study of, 133–34
  trauma interfering with, 257
  unintegration in, 125
children
  holding environment of, 126
  intermittent grieving and, 238
  need to find a self, 260–61
  parental intervention with, 147–48
  play and practice of, 216–17
  safe relationships and, 109
Chödrön, Pema, 121
climbing. *See* mountaineering
closeness-distance problem, 143
code of silence, 118
cognitive-behavioral interventions, 253
coherence, 34, 37–38, 245
collages, 263–64, 289
commencement ceremony, 295–97
communication and communication skills
  with belayer (guide), 87–88
  in distress, 178–79
  of feelings, 172–73, 289–90
  reenactment as, 173–74, 176
community-as-self, 50
connection and connectedness
  attachment and, 139–40
  belaying as, 85
  of brain to outer world, 197
  humans as hardwired for, 108–9
  in meaningful activity, 97
  weaving, 86
conscious memory, 199–200
Consolidation (solidifying and
    stabilizing)
  during breaks in therapy, 47
  fine (feeling) in, 274–77

helpful practices for, 288–91
phase in Cycle of Healing Repeated
    Trauma, 39, 269–91
rest in, 270–73
contact (of pieces), 231–32, 254
container, 156–63
control, 151, 158–59, 190–91
conversations
  about conversations, 289, 291
  in healing relationship, 157–58
  needed for trust, 91–92
  perseverance in, 105
cortex, 146, 197
cortisol, 146–47
Country of My Skull (Krog), 207
couples therapy, 53–54
courage
  needed to show up for treatment, 72–74
  in surviving repeated trauma, 20
crisis, 65, 127, 280
current daily life, 160–63, 292–93
Cycle of Healing Repeated Trauma
  Consolidation phase in, 47, 269–91
  as five-phase process, 39–47
  Identification phase in, 39, 43–45, 183–223,
    282–84
  Integration phase in, 45–46, 227–65,
    284–86
  macrocycles and microcycles in, 40
  middle phases of, 42, 194, 246, 282, 287
  Preparation phase in, 40–42, 61–119,
    279–81
  as repeating spiral
    8, 227, 278–87, 292
  time of phases in, 59
  Unintegration phase in, 42–43, 123–80,
    227–29, 281–82
  use of book in, 58–60, 228, 278–87

D

danger, 12
date rape, 68
Dead Sea Scrolls, 184–85, 189–90
decentration, 245
defenses. *See also* protection(s)
  dismantling, 164–69
  in repeated trauma, 13–15, 204
  types of, 165–66, 167
  unlearning, 178
defensive state, 14
defensive trait, 14
denial, 239